Ask Me No More

Ask Me No More

· An Autobiography ·

JENIFER HART

PETER HALBAN
LONDON

FIRST PUBLISHED IN GREAT BRITAIN BY
PETER HALBAN PUBLISHERS LTD
42 South Molton Street
London W1Y 1HB
1998

British Library Cataloguing in Publication Data

A catalogue record for this book is available from the British Library.

ISBN 1 870015 66 5

Typeset by Computape (Pickering) Ltd, North Yorkshire
Printed in Great Britain by
WBC Print, Bridgend

Ask me no more, for fear I should reply;
Others have held their tongues, and so can I;
Hundreds have died, and told no tale before:
Ask me no more, for fear I should reply –

A.E. Housman
Additional Poems VI

Contents

Acknowledgements

I AM EXTREMELY grateful to the many people who have helped me with the writing of this book. The whole typescript was read by Gabriele Taylor, Marianne Fillenz, Heather Milne, Anthony Grayling, Gunnar Beck, and Alan Ryan, and certain parts were read by Anne Ridler, Robyn Marsack, Roger Crisp, Philip Allen (Lord Allen of Abbeydale), Heather Pritchard, Catherine Paxton, Carol Graham-Harrison, and my children Joanna, Adam and Charles. I have benefited greatly from their comments, criticisms, advice, and judicious encouragement.

Others have kindly supplied me with information. These include relations – my sisters Judith Hubback and Mariella Fischer-Williams, my nephew Hubert Montagu-Pollock, my niece Fidelity Dean, and my cousin Michael Wheeler-Booth – and many friends and colleagues, among whom were: Mark Bostridge, Sally Chilver, Valerie Cromwell, Sheila Dickinson, the late Elaine Griffiths, Stuart Hampshire, Henry Hardy, Brian Harrison, Bridget and Christopher Hill, the late Douglas Jay, the late Henry Lintott, Marion Milner, Edward Playfair, Barbara Proctor, Marjorie Reeves, Wendy Rintoul, the late Stephanie Robinson, Hazel Rossotti, Ruth Runciman, Betty Rutson, Hugh Trevor-Roper, and Richard Wilberforce.

I also wish to thank the officers of various institutions who have answered my enquiries. These include Jeremy Brown of Jardine Matheson, Arthur Packham of the Civil Service Commission, John Hall of the Warneford Hospital, Eddie Earl of the National Trust, Charles Martineau of Volunteer Reading Help, and the archivists and librarians of Oxfordshire County Council, King's College (Cambridge), Balliol, New College, Somerville, and St Hugh's at Oxford.

Finally I must pay tribute to my friend Anthony Grayling, not so much for persuading me to embark on an autobiography, but for his unflagging interest and help at many levels during the last years.

I was lucky in having such friendly and efficient publishers as Martine and Peter Halban.

Oxford
November 1997

Foreword

ISAIAH BERLIN

Jenifer Hart's autobiography is a clear and fascinating account of a very varied and interesting life. Not only is it a beautifully written description of the incidents in the life of a distinguished and remarkable woman and her altering opinions, but it is a vivid expression of the outlook and experience characteristic of a large social group in England – something far beyond the author's own family and friends – in fact a valuable contribution, at once most readable and important, to the social and political life of a considerable section of the English nation of the day. At my very advanced age I find it difficult to get through the whole of any new book, but I can truthfully say that this one bound its spell on me from start to finish, and not, I believe, only because it is by one of my oldest and best friends, of whose life and doings I have always known a good deal.

The book begins by setting the stage: the affluent, well-connected, professional upper middle class of the turn of the century – her father an outstanding lawyer and public servant, educated at Harrow and Oxford, respected for his ability, integrity, great learning and devotion to the liberal ideals of his day (and ours). Her mother was artistically-inclined, of Scottish aristocratic descent, typical of the strongly conventional view of life and people of her social milieu.

Since her father worked for the British Government, on the Reparations Commission in Paris after the First World War, Jenifer was largely brought up in that city – she gives a very vivid, sharply written account of her French school; no one, I believe, has given a better description of the methods, somewhat nationalistically inclined, sternly disciplined, of a unique institution as it was, and may still be. In due course Sir John Fischer Williams took his family back to England, and his daughter's English life begins.

She goes to the famous school, Downe House – Shakespeare, fresh air, games, Church of England – and the new life of the emotions (not encouraged in Paris) – schoolgirl passions, the friendships and informal life of a modern school. Then holidays in Cornwall in a house deliberately built to be open to all the winds, with a view on stormy seas; visits from eminent scholars – the historian G.M. Trevelyan, the historian and politician H.A.L. Fisher (Warden of New College), the influential, once-famous, now (I believe justly) forgotten philosopher H.W.B. Joseph, who is the godfather of one of Jenifer's sisters, the famous head of Morley College, Eva Hubback, full of modern ideas on education, and in particular of musical life in her establishment, Ka Cox (Rupert Brooke's lover); a house of five attractive sisters – some thought Jenifer the most attractive one – and high-minded talk. Then, inevitably, Oxford. The entire family moves to Oxford. Jenifer becomes a student at Somerville College. Before Oxford life could have its indelible impact, a greater liberation in her took place.

Among her parents' friends was one Elliott Felkin, an official of the then new League of Nations, who had been a Scholar at King's College, Cambridge, before the First World War, and then, like so many before and after him, fell under the influence of Goldsworthy Lowes Dickinson, who, virtually single-handed, seems to have invented the morality of the writers and painters of Bloomsbury. Dickinson was a gentle, somewhat recessive homosexual, who preached that the great values of life are love, friendship, personal relations, beauty, a peaceful civilised world. At King's Felkin became a friend not only of his tutor but of his followers, J.M. Keynes, E.M. Forster, Arthur Waley, Francis Birrell, David Garnett, Lytton Strachey, who all believed in love, friendship, avoidance of worldly life, opposition to conventional morality, respectability, 'bourgeois values'. Felkin invited Jenifer to Geneva, where he worked, and there he and his friend Raisley Moorsom changed her personal outlook for good. To love, to be loved, provided no hurt was done to others – that was the ideal; conventions were rooted in baseless prejudice and hypocrisy. Jenifer was introduced not only to free love but to a wider horizon of literature – German, French – the free life of the intelligentsia and of bohemianism. She returned to Oxford a changed person. Wide liberties, left-wing views, were natural concomitants of this humanistic hedonism, and above all the supreme values of free personal life. She felt exhilarated and liberated. These views clashed with those of her parents' liberal disapproval of socialism, and so she was not allowed to accompany the notoriously leftish R.H.S. Crossman (by then an Oxford don), who in 1934 was to pay a visit to Germany, to talk to so-called liberal Germans. But the die was cast.

Jenifer Hart's distaste for conventional morality, 'bourgeois values' and so on, derived in large measure from her conversion to Bloomsbury freedoms, gradually took a social form. Like many of her Oxford contemporaries, she was upset by the social condition of England – unemployment, hunger marchers, social injustice of every kind, to which the Conservative government appeared indifferent. Many students, deeply affected by this, came to believe that only the Communist Party could put an end to such things. Such people as a rule knew little or nothing about the facts of Soviet communism – the horror of fascism was in the forefront of their imagination; Mussolini was bad enough, but Hitler, Franco, the dictators in the Balkans and the Baltic States, Japanese militarism – only communism seemed a powerful enough movement to oppose these abominable regimes. The West showed no signs of resistance, not even New Deal America appeared deeply enough committed to resist the political monsters who dominated central and Eastern Europe. It is astonishing how little of the real events in the Soviet Union had penetrated the consciousness of the West – whether left or right wing. Certainly those who supported the Republic in Spain (myself, for example) had no notion then of the sinister part played in that war by Soviet agents and Spanish communists. If I had not myself spent some years of my childhood in the Soviet Union, I think I too might have drifted in that direction – that was the world I was surrounded by. But those few years, even at the age of eight or nine, had completely inoculated me against illusions about Soviet reality – I remained passionately anti-Stalinist, and indeed, anti-Leninist, for the rest of my life; but my words fell on deaf ears: my contemporaries thought that there was something curiously perverse in my failure to understand who were the sheep and who the goats in the political world. There is no doubt that Soviet propaganda remains the most successful hoax ever perpetrated on the human race. The Soviet trials made some impact, and the Soviet-Nazi treaty of 1939 opened a good many eyes – and yet, not enough. My liberal friends – the world in which Jenifer moved – at that time believed that although no doubt mistakes, even crimes, might have been perpetrated in the Soviet Union, yet despite that they were moving in the right direction – they were in some sense on 'our', the decent, social-justice-seeking, side – and much could be forgiven to so backward and impoverished a land. It took a great deal of revealed monstrosities to lift this particular veil. At any rate, Jenifer was much taken in by what I have described, and that is what made her drift towards the Communist Party; a great many friends had done the same, and in peaceful, civilised England communism must have seemed mainly a strong remedy against illiteracy and injustice, an illusion which persisted in the West for a very long time.

Jenifer was always opposed to irrationality and injustice – the huge wave of sympathy for the Spanish Republic only strengthened this feeling, and her sympathy with the unemployed caused her to go to a camp where she fell in love with an unemployed worker, which drew her further and further in the communist direction. She joined the Communist Party in 1935, vaguely agreed to act as one of its secret agents, but in the meanwhile had to think of her career and sat for the Civil Service examination. She came third from the top – the first woman to rise so high, and this in itself caused a minor sensation. For some reason never clear to me she wanted to go to the Department of Agriculture, but her performance in the examination was too good and she was persuaded to go to the Home Office, where after a time she became the Private Secretary to the Permanent Under Secretary of State. The Party was probably pleased to have an agent in so sensitive a place, but in fact Jenifer never did anything for the benefit of the Party – gave no secret information – this has never been refuted in all the examinations of Soviet penetration that took place in later years. She gradually became disillusioned by the behaviour of the Party; she drifted away from it before the Russo–German Pact – she doubtless remained on friendly terms with some communists, but when later, after the war, she was interrogated by MI5 she had nothing to tell and they discovered no sins in her conduct.

In 1937 her life changed again. She fell in love with a lawyer, Herbert Hart, who had been an outstanding undergraduate philosopher at Oxford, had kept up his interest in the subject and by this time was a very successful and greatly admired barrister. In due course he became a very distinguished and original philosopher of law, of deserved world-wide fame and authority. But at this time – by the beginning of the war – he had been recruited by MI5 (Counter-Intelligence), and Jenifer continued at her post in the Civil Service. At that time there was a rule that female civil servants could not marry – nevertheless, her connections were such that she persuaded the authorities to let her marry Herbert Hart in 1941 (this was regarded as very exceptional at the time). They lived in Well Walk in Hampstead, among a great many charming, amusing, sharp-witted and interesting friends – Douglas Jay, who became a Labour Cabinet Minister and remained a life-long socialist (Jenifer owed something to him in the formation of her views), Christopher Cox, a New College don who taught ancient history – an eccentric, delightful, clever, sensitive, very lovable man, who by this time was working in the Colonial Office. The celebrated Oliver Franks was there too; so was Francis Graham-Harrison, who remained, like the others, her (and my) lifelong friends. Bombs fell on Well Walk, but life in the house (which belonged to Douglas Jay) continued to be blissfully happy. I remember staying there myself during the war; bombs duly fell but better, more exhilarating company one could not ask for.

When the war was over, Herbert was elected to a Fellowship in Philosophy at New College, Oxford, where I too was teaching. Although a very successful barrister, the life of the mind appealed more to him, and as a result the entire family moved to Oxford. Jenifer did so a trifle reluctantly – her parents lived in Oxford, and everything reminded her of her bickerings with her mother and the world which she had, in her view mercifully, left. But come to Oxford she did, and became a Fellow teaching Modern History at St Anne's (women's) College. Again a new world opened, that of her husband's academic and intellectual friends, which she found stimulating, and indeed fascinating, despite never having studied philosophy herself. Herbert Hart was and remained one of my greatest and most admired friends, an extraordinary combination of moral virtue, sensitiveness and humour – a man I was glad to be able to love and respect all my life. At times Jenifer wondered if she was looked upon merely as the wife of a great man, but these moods passed; her independence and strength of character made it easy to make her own friends and to some degree to continue to live her own life.

Once she decided on academic life, she bent all her great energies towards it. Like her husband, she began with a nervous fear that after all the years spent on another pursuit she might not be equal to academic duties. But, as in his case, she recovered her confidence, and plunged into teaching, research, administration, organisation, with all her customary vigour and conviction. She became a much admired history and politics tutor, a firm if reasonably moderate champion of the women's cause in Oxford, and an academic figure of note. Nuffield College also elected her to one of their fellowships, and there she became a member of a small but distinguished cultural élite, which saved her from the somewhat narrow and arid atmosphere of the rest of the establishment (in effect, an institute confined to the study of economics and politics). But her main work remained at St Anne's. Under the benevolent and wise rule of two remarkable Principals she blossomed. She was a kind but exacting teacher; sometimes she began by scaring, but in the end inevitably inspired her pupils. Nor was her emotional life inhibited by total immersion in her academic work. She tells us that she fell in love with the well-known political theorist Michael Oakeshott, whose conservative views of history and politics she abhorred but whose charm and intellectual subtleties fascinated her. In due course he left Oxford and her feeling evidently evaporated. Nor was he her only lover. In short, Jenifer led a full life of her own, in spite of her devotion to family life – her children (one daughter and three sons) and her immensely distinguished husband. She grew to be a personality of note in the university, and a prominent member of the City Council. She tells us how surprised and disappointed she was never to be considered as a possible head of her own college when a vacancy occurred. But there is a sense in which she never fully understood herself. She did not realise that her qualities, her unswerving pursuit of knowledge, truth, social justice, her incorruptible integrity and inability to deviate from what she knew to be right, simply terrified some of her more conventional and traditionalist colleagues. Her intolerance of what she believed to be wrong or weak or confused or disreputable obviously made some of her colleagues nervous. Arrangements in colleges, as in many other places, sometimes call for closing one's eyes to deviousness or intrigue, or some degree of moral flexibility, at least silence, in order 'not to rock the boat', to let things drift into shallows for a while. Jenifer could never accept this. Before her unyielding integrity, her acute moral sense, even the cynical or complacent or indolent or wheeler-dealers, were bound to quail, or at least feel pretty uncomfortable. She was, and still is, thought of, I feel sure, as 'difficult', not circumnavigable – more credit to her. Such people are not chosen to preside over a self-conscious, somewhat insecure body, as women's colleges to some degree then were. Her surprise at not being considered for a headship showed her very genuine unworldliness, her innocence of the realities of political practice, no matter how acute an analyst of the theory of it she may be. So, an officer without a Field-Marshal's baton she remained.

The first of two of the best and most sensitive and moving chapters in this book is that devoted to Jenifer's life with her husband, Herbert Hart, its ups and downs, their love and devotion and deep respect for each other, and the effect of this deep relationship on their differing, often incompatible, tastes and forms of life. This account is precise and full and records sympathetically and often with deep affection their life together, especially at Oxford. It is a very remarkable story of harmonies and disharmonies in this closely interwoven life of parents and children, the educational problems and solutions of the three older children and the relations of the children to the parents.

The next, even more wonderful, and surely original, is the story of the birth, disabilities, difficulties, of their last child, Jacob, born with a brain injury which made him autistic and at times epileptic. The problems this created were obvious and painful: yet love, care, devotion, continuous efforts at understanding a socially abnormal mentality, led to an astonishing degree of success. I do not believe there is anywhere to be found so patient, detailed, unselfish, understanding and intelligent a description, step by step, incident by incident, crisis by crisis, of the life of a damaged child, boy, adolescent, youth, as this history of Jenifer and Jacob. It goes without saying that it is a deeply moving story of a noble mother and her arrested child; but it is also immensely instructive – it could do much to help other parents in a similar predicament. No one who is not dead of heart can fail to respond to this deeply affecting part of this scrupulously truthful, brave and fascinating book. It is followed by a final chapter summarising the author's view of her ambitions and failures, her ideals and sense of social duty, her character, her full self-awareness – in short, a summary of a life. But the substance of the book is in the previous chapters. I read them, so far as I could, as an ordinary reader, but I cannot deny that my friendship with the author made it more deeply affecting than it might otherwise have been.

Oxford
May 1997

Introduction

PUBLISHING AN AUTOBIOGRAPHY requires some excuse, explicit or implicit. My excuse is not Gibbon's who said 'My own amusement is my motive, and will be my reward'.[1] On the contrary I have found this enterprise taxing and at times painful: taxing because of the perennial difficulty of deciding what to include and exclude, and painful because, like an offender on probation, I had to confront my often nasty nature. So why did I, in my eightieth year, embark on this work? The answer is that I succumbed to the pressure of friends who think (rightly) that I have had an interesting life and that an account of it would inform and even at times amuse others as well as them. For, as V.S. Pritchett wrote in his seventieth year, 'time has turned us into curiosities in some secondhand shop'.[2]

Before starting I looked at some of the extensive literature about the art of autobiography. This was often intimidating: for instance that it needs daring to be truthful but that candour often shocks; that it is easy to deteriorate into vanity, complacency and self-indulgence, talking at inordinate length about the ordinary details of life; and that the events to be related in an autobiography are of a kind which most seriously unsettles the author's judgement. But I was encouraged by some of the observations I read: that it is impossible for an autobiography to be dull, the nearest approach to dullness being caused by volubility; that the best specimens are generally the shorter ones written late in life; that the distortions of the truth belong to the values of autobiography and are as revealing as the truth.

[1] *Autobiography of Edward Gibbon*, World's Classics edition, p. 1.
[2] V.S. Pritchett, *Midnight Oil*, 1971, p. 9.

In writing this book I do not intend to be rigidly chronological, though it will delineate the development of my personality in response to the world I lived in. I hope I have not been too egomaniacal, writing about things which are not important to others. I have tried to build it round a theme or subjects, for, as Pritchett has said, 'autobiography fails when it has no attitude, when it has no special subject which rescues the self from the cliché of having lived. There is no credit in living; the credit is in being able to specify experience.'[3] My main theme is that I have been lucky. It would be ludicrous to couple my modest *oeuvre* with Gibbon's exquisite autobiography, but it is not presumptuous to suggest that the famous passage where he describes his lot applies substantially to mine. 'My lot [he writes] might have been that of a slave, a savage or a peasant; nor can I reflect without pleasure on the bounty of Nature, which cast my birth in a free and civilised country, in an age of science and philosophy, in a family of honourable rank, and decently endowed with the gifts of fortune.'[4] 'An age of science and philosophy' fits the twentieth century as well as it did the eighteenth, and in addition I have had the advantage of living amongst philosophers.

'Family of honourable rank' fits in a limited way, for my mother, Eleanor Marjorie Hay Murray, born in 1880, was descended from John Murray, the third Duke of Atholl (1729–74). She was proud of her aristocratic and Scottish connections, revering in particular, though rather curiously, the Duke's father, Lord George Murray, the Jacobite general who in 1745 joined the army of Prince Charles Edward, the Young Pretender, in his futile invasion of England aimed at restoring the Stuarts to the throne. She would even when she visited Holland put a sprig of juniper, the family emblem, tied with a Murray tartan ribbon, on Lord George's grave at Medemblik where he died after being expelled from England. I fear all this ancestor worship made me feel I had blue blood in my veins and that I was in some way superior to people who were not members of the upper crust, and in particular of a clan, the chief symbol of which was our right to wear Murray tartan kilts. As a child I was

[3] V.S. Pritchett, 'All about ourselves'; *The New Statesman*, 26 May 1956.
[4] Op. cit. p. 18–19.

proud of this garment and of my sporran, but rather regretted that, being so expensive, it precluded the purchase of other clothes.

More important and certainly more useful than the qualities attributed to blue blood was the fact that my mother's family spawned large numbers of relations – Murrays, Strutts, Trittons and others. We benefited from getting to know our aunts, uncles and cousins, some of whom conveniently owned quite grand country houses in which my sisters and I went to stay. Others were minor country gentry, colonial servants, tea planters, or army officers.

My mother's parents were not well off, as her father, a country gentleman with five daughters, was rather improvident. So she brought no dowry when she married my father, John Fischer Williams, in 1911. However he was, in Gibbon's phrase, 'decently endowed with the gifts of fortune', for his father and grandfather were members of the prosperous China-trading firm Jardine Matheson, as was also my grandfather's father-in-law, Maximilian Fischer. The fact that the firm had made most of its fortune from the opium trade in the mid-nineteenth century was never mentioned at home, and it may be that my grandfather was more involved in tea tasting than in importing opium to China. I don't know how much my father inherited, but it must have been a sizeable amount, for it enabled him to buy in 1910 a considerable piece of land, to build a substantial second home in Cornwall, and in due course to pay for the education of his five daughters. My father also earned a modest income from his practice at the Chancery Bar for twenty years before the First World War, and then as a civil servant. From 1920 to 1930 when he worked on the Reparations Commission, his salary was I believe in the region of £3,000 a year, and his income from investments, which he managed very carefully, amounted to about the same. After 1930 he was much less well off, but nevertheless his offspring have all been helped by the sums they inherited from his estate. My father did not, like my mother, claim to be of noble birth, but he was very proud of his Swiss ancestry, his mother being one quarter Swiss, which accounts for his second name, Fischer.

Apart from rank and fortune, I was lucky in my parenthood: my father and mother did not quarrel; indeed their marriage was a great success. This may have been partly due to the fact that it contrasted so favourably with my father's previous experience of marriage, the tragic circumstances of which are of interest as they illustrate why things can go wrong. His childhood was bleak: his mother died very soon after his birth in 1870. His only sibling, a sister twelve years older, paid him little attention. It is clear from her diary that she was not interested in him as a small boy, except to complain that he was tiresome. Occasionally she took him out for a walk in a London park or had a meal with him, but, it seems, only when he requested this. There is no mention of her playing with him. His relations with his father too were distant. He was unhappy at the boarding school (Elstree) to which he was sent at the young age of seven. He was happy at Harrow and Oxford, at both of which he did brilliantly, but neither provided experience of female company. So in his mid-twenties he succumbed precipitately to the charms of probably the first girl he met, Florence Keown-Boyd. The story was that he married her in 1896 after six weeks' acquaintance because he was pressed to do so by her godmother, Lady Phillimore, who wanted her settled before she died. As early as his honeymoon he felt the marriage was a mistake. Florence's 'inside' did not function normally. This was my mother's way of describing the fact that Florence had not menstruated before marriage. The first child, a boy, was stillborn, and the next, a daughter, was premature, tiny and delicate. My father, whose own constitution was excellent, found it difficult to cope with physical weaknesses. Florence, fun-loving and high spirited, was no doubt bored by a serious husband who spent much of his time working. This miserable state of affairs lasted for about ten years and only ended when Florence fell in love with another man and decamped. After a time and much agonising my father divorced her on the ground of adultery. He described the last three years of his first marriage as 'mutilated, hopeless, almost tragic'.

Although all this of course happened before I was born (in 1914), it had repercussions on me and on our family life, for the relations between my half-sister Barbara and my mother were never easy. As a child Barbara, born in 1902, had had a hard time, first of all living with unhappy parents, then alone with her father. She was not allowed to see her mother for many years after her disappearance. Barbara alleged that she was told by a maid or a nurse that her mother was a wicked woman and that she was not to talk about her. Inevitably my mother found it difficult to cope with a rather disturbed step-daughter whose nature she found antagonistic, and who even after she came of age lived an unsettled life, requiring endless financial subsidies from my father. She had an unsuccessful year at Oxford and then tried different careers including cosmetics, the stage and journalism. Though attractive, she never married. In the end she moved to the USA where she was happier, working quite successfully as a journalist and in the United Nations. Her appearances at home tended to cause tension as my mother disliked her flashy clothes and considered her dissipated. I was never close to Barbara, partly because I was disconcerted by the effects on her manner of her training as an actress, but I realised she was warm, amusing and compassionate.

My parents' life together was, I feel sure, strengthened by the traumatic circumstances surrounding their marriage. For my mother's mother opposed it on religious grounds: her daughter was not to marry a man who had been involved in a divorce, although he was not the guilty party. My mother was sent off to be counselled by the Bishop of Birmingham and other clerics. She found these consultations deeply disturbing, being torn between respect for her church, affection for her mother, and passionate love for my father. After much heart-searching she decided it would not be wicked to marry him, though distressed that the wedding could not take place in a church. But her mother remained implacably hostile to my father and as a gesture of disapproval left the country at the time of the wedding, taking her youngest daughter with her so that she should not be contaminated. My father was understandably so mortified by this whole business that he concealed much of it from me and my sisters. For many years we were given to understand that his first wife had died, and when, at the age of seventeen I learnt the truth from him, I was deeply shocked, not by the divorce but at having been deceived.

This incident did not damage my relations with my father which had always been good. From an early age I instinctively preferred him to my mother because he was more rational and logical. She was deeply emotional and, I felt, embarrassingly anxious to have intimate relations with her four daughters. Her hunger for heart-to-heart talks made me clam up and, as an adult, treat her really badly. Ever since her death, thirty seven years ago, I have felt terrible guilt at my unkind and inhuman behaviour, and at my unwillingness to appreciate her considerable artistic gifts. I suspect the seeds of these difficulties lay to some extent in the fact that when we were young she tended to prefer my elder sister Prue, her first born, to me. Prue was lively and charming; she shone when visitors came to the house, my mother reported in 1925, whereas 'Jen is a bit rough and tomboyish and inclined to be rude. I am leaping on her ruthlessly.' Although I allegedly improved after moral castigation, nothing could breach the gap between our temperaments. It is sad that my tomboyish behaviour did not in my mother's mind make up for her great disappointment at never having a son. So desperate was she for a boy that when pregnant she referred to the unborn baby by a boy's name.

My father too no doubt wanted a son, but he never allowed any regrets he may have felt at the lack of one to affect his attitude to his daughters. This was partly due to the fact that he did not think men as a sex stood above women intellectually. He worked with many women on various committees – for the suffrage, peace, equality regarding divorce, proportional representation – and found some of them marvellously capable. It was wrong to think of a flighty and garrulous mind as being a typical feminine failing, he told my mother, and reading Olive Schreiner's book, *Women and Labour*, in 1911, he agreed with her views that women should not be parasites, dependent on men.[5] My mother, by contrast, basically felt men were superior to women. Being herself one of five daughters who never went to school, she revered my father's immense learning and powerful brain, and did not realise that much of the male competence she saw around her was due to the vastly superior education given to boys. There was in fact no justification for much of her modesty, as even before she met my father she had acquired a considerable knowledge of literature both English and foreign, and many cultural interests and skills; but it was difficult to eradicate her stereotypes and to change her deep-seated beliefs. One of these, to which I was particularly antagonistic, was that women had a duty to take trouble about their personal appearance whereas there was no parallel obligation on men. The archetype offender against this canon of womanly behaviour was Naomi Mitchison who came

[5] Olive Schreiner (1855–1920) was South African. Her most famous book was *The Story of an African Farm*, 1883.

to our house from time to time in the 1920s, once without wearing stockings. My mother would not even allow that Mrs Mitchison, already acknowledged as a gifted author, was clever, artistic or original.

Some aspects of this family story figure in the novel *The Sea Has Many Voices* by my sister Judith Hubback. The book, which won a prize, is partly grounded on established fact, but it also explores the unconscious thoughts, hopes and fears of the characters who appear in it.

My book as it unfolds will portray other facets of my parents and of their relations with me where these seem relevant or of wider interest. It will also describe both those aspects of my life which were atypical and those which were more usual. As examples of the atypical, I would cite being educated as a child in France, living in League of Nations circles in Geneva, changing career, as did my husband, in mid-life, and my particular solution to the classic problem of how to combine a professional life with marriage and children. In other ways I conformed to a type by being in the 1930s passionately anti-fascist, distressed by unemployment and inequalities, in revolt against bourgeois values, and attracted to communist ideals. Though I have lived more than half my life in Oxford, the canvas which I paint will be more varied than this fact might suggest. Moreover I shall intersperse the narrative with some general reflections, using my experiences and acquaintances as a peg on which unashamedly to hang what I consider important ideas and key values. But throughout I will bear in mind the opening words of David Hume's autobiography: 'It is difficult for a man to speak long of himself without vanity; therefore, I shall be short.'[6]

[6] *The Life of David Hume*, 1777.

I

Paris and Downe House 1920–31

In 1920 when I was aged six my family moved to Paris where my father was to work on the Reparations Commission. This was a body set up by the Treaty of Versailles to administer its contentious provisions requiring Germany to compensate the victors for the damage done to them during the war. Before then we had lived in London, where my father had worked as a barrister and in the Home Office since 1914.

For the first two years in Paris we rented a furnished flat which, being small and liable to spawn bed bugs, contrasted unfavourably with our spacious five-floor house in Chelsea. When it seemed clear that my father's job was going to continue, some of our London furniture was brought over and installed in another flat (in Passy) into which were crowded the whole household of parents, four children, nanny and servants.

My elder sister Prue and I were at once sent to school at the Lycée Molière situated nearby. Before then I had had no formal education, but had, it seems, learnt at home the rudiments of reading and writing in English. I say 'it seems' because I have no recollection of my education at that time. We knew no French, but picked it up quickly, assisted by the fortunate fact that about half the lessons were on French grammar. After a year or so we were doing well in most subjects even though the classes were large, often numbering 35 to 40, sometimes more. I remember one teacher whose method of coping with a class of about 50 was one day to ask a question of pupils whose names started with the letters A to M, and the next day to interrogate the N to Z lot. Disaster ensued when she reversed the order of procedure.

The post-war years no doubt posed many problems for the

French, and it is only right to remember this when writing perhaps a little critically about public education in France at that time. Certainly anything we learnt we learnt thoroughly, particularly grammar, multiplication tables, French geography and some important dates. The curriculum also included '*Leçon de Choses*' in which I learnt the only anatomy I know. But we were not encouraged to think for ourselves. For instance history was taught by making us learn paragraphs of a book by heart. Moreover the tone of the history lessons was distinctly chauvinistic. For several years we studied mainly Joan of Arc and the iniquities of the English, and the Great War of 1914–18 highlighting France's sufferings and the iniquities of '*les Boches*'. Indeed when a pupil did well, the reward was a picture of Germans perpetrating barbarous acts such as shooting Boy Scouts or nurses. My father was naturally horrified when we showed him these trophies. The curriculum included no physical education apart from occasionally some feeble gymnastic exercises which we performed in our ordinary clothes and footwear – in my case boots, as my parents thought (wrongly) that firm leather boots would strengthen our ankles.

Pupils had to wear overalls which wholly covered their clothes. For most of us these were white, but for a few children they were black. These were the poorer pupils whose parents paid no fees. On Saturdays we were expected to bring contributions towards their cost. This was known as the '*Sou du Samedi*'. On discovering that some of the Jewish children were not allowed to handle money on their Sabbath, I suggested, no doubt unsuccessfully, that they could entrust me with their donations on Fridays. There were quite a lot of Jews at the school, and my father who was very pro-Semitic used to ask us to tell him the names of the pupils who did well in the exams. If they sounded Jewish, this demonstrated, he said, that Jews were usually clever. His admiration for Jews did not fortunately foster anti-Semitism in his children, at least if their choice of partners in later life is significant, for four of his five daughters married or linked up with Jews.

In 1925 I was taken away from the Lycée Molière and sent to a private school, the Cours Fénelon. This was I think partly because my parents thought it would, with smaller classes, offer a better education, but also because, realising that my father's job in Paris would not last for ever, they had it in mind to send Prue and me in a few years' time to school in England. If the family moved back to London we were to try for St Paul's; if not we were to go to a boarding school. In any case we needed to study a wider curriculum. One attended the Cours only two mornings a week to be examined in the work one had prepared at home, assisted in our case by a French governess. We also studied Latin and extra maths with an English male tutor. The sessions at school were little less than extraordinary. The class of about twenty girls sat round a long table covered in green baize, with a teacher at the top. Parents and governesses could also attend, sitting along the side of the room, to watch their children's performances. This naturally added to the child's anxiety, though she may have taken some comfort from knowing that parents could complain if they thought the teacher had been unfair. Our parents luckily did not attend. The teacher would ask one girl a question, which required a short factual answer. If the girl got it right, she was thrown a *jeton* (a tiddlywink). If she got the answer wrong, the teacher called out in stentorian tones *La suivante* (the next girl). This procedure was sometimes repeated several times. Finally in exasperation the teacher would scream out *Ecrivez Mesdemoiselles*. We then all had a shot at writing the answer down, taking care to try to prevent our neighbours from seeing what we wrote. The teacher walked round and threw a *jeton* at those with correct answers. This procedure was then repeated. At the end of the session, every pupil's *jetons* were counted up. The system naturally created great tension and anxiety. My youngest sister was sometimes sick on Cours days on the way to school.

The curriculum at the Cours Fénelon included, as had the Lycée's, a thorough grounding in French grammar and syntax which was excellent. We also acquired a meticulous knowledge of French geography as we had to know and place on a map not only every one of the 83 *départements*, but also the *chef-lieu* (capital) of each *département* and its *sous-préfectures* (minor towns) which could number up to five. We learnt pieces of Racine and Corneille by heart, and great emphasis was put on the need for essays to be carefully planned according to the standard framework of *Introduction*, *Développement*, *Dénouement*, *Conclusion*, but we were not expected to have our own ideas on anything we studied or wrote about.

Besides our school work, our education included music, dancing, tennis and riding lessons, all arranged by our parents. We were taught the piano by a fierce lady for an hour a week each, and had to practise every day for an hour – first scales, then five finger exercises by Hanon, more exercises by Czerny and a piece which we had to get perfect. Dancing consisted of many different skills. The worst was Dalcroze Eurhythmics, my main memory of which is that it involved walking round the room dressed in a bathing dress beating three time with one arm and two with the other. Much more pleasant were the ballet classes and those where we learnt the Charleston, which stood me in good stead in my later dancing days. We were taught how to ride very thoroughly in a *manège* on large horses, and in due course were taken riding in the Bois de Boulogne. These expeditions terrified me: they involved going through streets with tram lines on which the horses could slip, and then going much faster than I liked on horse tracks in the Bois. These were crossed at intervals by roads, at which point it was necessary to try to bring one's horse to a halt.

Our education did not include the domestic arts. We had always at least three servants, plus a nanny and a nursemaid. I did know how to make a bed, but complained if I ever had to, e.g. in a crisis. We were not allowed into the kitchen, as it was thought we would get in the cook's way, so I never when young learnt the rudiments of cooking, as fortunately my children have. Later as a Girl Guide I was taught how to clean a house systematically, but my culinary experiences were confined to frying sausages over a camp fire, a fact subsequently bemoaned by my husband. My mother was entirely undomesticated, not knowing, I believe, even how to boil an egg until the Second World War. Her interests were predominantly artistic and she spent much of her time drawing, painting, etching and creating remarkable, beautiful embroideries. Her involvement in household duties was limited to settling the menu every day with the cook who then went out shopping. Being easy-going, my mother did not, like many French housewives, vet and even weigh the food on the cook's return, checking how the money had been spent. We ate very well, but no doubt not economically. The children had most of their meals in the nursery, though two of us were detailed off to lunch with our parents in the dining room if they were alone, in order to teach us good manners. Indeed at times we attended even when there were guests, my main recollection of whom is that if they were American they were very rich and left half their food.

Religion was included in our home curriculum. The English (Anglican) church in Paris was rather far from where we lived, so we only went there on special occasions like Christmas. Instead there were family Bible-reading sessions on Sundays. I found these an ordeal as my father's interrogations revealed how little I had understood about Christian theology and those complicated Old Testament stories. When in Cornwall we all went to church every Sunday. My parents were both believers, but my father would not go to Holy Communion as a protest against the attitude of the church to his divorce. We had to say our prayers every evening kneeling in front of a parent.

All this meant a high-pressured life. Prue and I usually started work in bed at 6.30 a.m. We also worked in the evenings, six or even seven days a week. I began to keep a diary in May 1927. In this I recorded that 'I live a life in which I do nothing but work from morn to night.' This was not quite true as we went out every day for a walk, always accompanied of course by an adult, and on Sundays often on expeditions with our parents outside Paris or to a theatre. Moreover there were three months of *Grandes Vacances* from 30 June to 1 October which we spent in England. We also went on delightful family holidays at Easter to the Pyrenees or the Italian Lakes. These expeditions gave us a good grounding in the techniques of hill-walking, and inspired me with a life-long love of mountains. It would be wrong to suggest that I was unhappy. I enjoyed a lot of our work and activities which I saw (priggishly) as aids to my chief desire in life – to be intelligent; but I longed for a more out-of-doors existence. The rooms in our second floor flat were small, and its outlook onto a closed-in courtyard seven or eight floors high was uninspiring. Nor do I wish to reproach my parents for the rather intense regime to which we were submitted. They rightly wished to make the most of the great opportunities offered to us by life in France, opportunities to imbibe French culture and history by visits to palaces, chateaux, cathedrals and churches. But sometimes I would have preferred to be walking in the country on a Sunday afternoon rather than sitting through interminable soliliquies in the plays of Racine or Corneille at the Comédie Française. Moreover looking back at my time in France, I slightly regret that our regime did not enable me to make more friends among my French contemporaries. Our social life outside the home consisted mainly of children's parties given by the families of my father's British colleagues: McFadyeans, Armitage-Smiths, Goodchilds, Bradburies, Eric Phippses, Knatchbull-Hugessens, and by Lord and Lady Crewe at the British Embassy. However these events were highly enjoyable.

The pressure increased during 1927 as the time to do an entrance exam for an English school drew nearer. My knowledge of English literature was virtually nil. This was revealed when my father questioned me on various plays of Shakespeare. The climax of this ordeal came when he asked me what I knew about Richard III, meaning the play. I did not know one existed, presumed he meant Richard II and tried to get by by discoursing on the Peasants' Revolt. My diary records that 'my parent's anger, wrath and astonishment of my ignorance was inexpressible'. I was told to read the works of Scott and Dickens. I once opened a Scott novel and found it incomprehensible, though Prue annoyingly said she enjoyed it. My reading was limited to the monthly magazine *Little Folks* and stories about schoolgirls, particularly those by Angela Brazil. I enjoyed these intensely, though they made me long to go to a proper school where one played games, won matches, and had midnight feasts. Some of these dreams were to be realised during the next four years, which I spent at an English boarding school, Downe House. Indeed these years were also the source of undreamt-of pleasures.

I don't know what made my parents choose Downe House, but they may have acted on the advice of their friends Kit and Violet Bradby whose daughter Anne was a pupil there. I doubt whether my parents were fully aware of the philosophy on which the school was based, but they would have known and approved of the fact that religion (Anglicanism) played an important part in its life. The only other school they considered was rejected by them because, being somewhere on the east coast, my father thought it was likely to subside into the sea.

Downe, as it was always known by *cognoscenti*, was a unique institution, wholly the brainchild of its creator, Olive Willis. She was born in 1877 into a cultured middle-class family. Her father had taken a first in Classics at Cambridge, and after a time at the

Bar, became an Inspector of Education. Her mother was musical and religious. Both parents considered freedom of thought and speech vitally important, and encouraged their children to have their own opinions. Olive Willis' aim in founding a school was to create a place which would avoid the defects of the educational establishments with which she was familiar either as a pupil or teacher. There were many of these: girls' boarding schools such as Roedean and Queen Anne's, Caversham, and various state schools where she had done supply teaching. Her school, whilst having good academic standards, was to be different from the typical high schools for girls and the boarding schools modelled on boys' public schools in the second half of the nineteenth century. They had, she felt, been wrong in distrusting the emotions. She was also influenced by some of the theories of the 'progressive' educationalists of the time, such as J.H. Badley, the founder of Bedales, and the American philosopher John Dewey. She wanted to break down the prevalent autocratic relationship between older and younger people. Teachers should not be on pedestals, remote from their pupils. They should share activities out of school hours and become real friends. Life should be normal and relations between people easy. So at Downe there were to be no petty rules, no school exams, no prizes. Nor were pupils to be divided up into separate houses, as this encouraged rivalry and group loyalty. The school was to be run on democratic lines in that the equivalent of prefects (known as Seniors) were to be elected from the sixth form by the whole school. They were to some extent responsible for discipline, but, unlike prefects in boys' schools, could not back up their authority by punishment. There was no Head Girl.

The school started in 1907 in Charles Darwin's former home at Downe in Kent; hence its name. It moved in 1922 to Cold Ash, near Newbury on the Berkshire Downs, to premises which had been built in 1913 for a slightly cranky American religious order. These included cloisters with cell-like rooms for meditation, which made excellent places for music practice. The property, which included several other buildings, extended over a hundred acres of woodland and open hillside. It had tremendous character. The site and the surrounding country were stunningly romantic and beautiful. This was part of Miss Willis' design for education: the young should be exposed to the beauties of nature, though left to discover them for themselves. Many new buildings had to be added, and were still being added when I went there in 1927.

When first approached by our parents, Miss Willis said the school was full with 160 girls, but she agreed to see my sister and me. We were taken there by an aunt, interviewed and made to do an exam. This included having to write an essay on a poem by Shelley. I was completely flummoxed as I could not understand it, and moreover had not been accustomed to thinking out my own ideas on works of literature. However, Miss Willis said, 'We will remedy that,' and decided to accept us, perhaps thinking that we might be interesting pupils because of our French background. I later came to realise that she could never say 'No' to a parent or child she liked, even if their fees had to be reduced or waived; hence her problem in keeping numbers down to manageable proportions.

After summer holidays in Cornwall we were packed off by a tearful mother with huge trunks, bicycles and our pet guinea pigs in the back coach of a train to London which was to be 'slipped', i.e. dropped off, at Newbury. Most of the girls went on the school train from Paddington, but my father, being always in favour of travelling by the shortest route, had typically discovered the existence of this slip coach. Unfortunately it was slipped before Newbury, leaving us marooned on the line. We were in due course rescued by another engine, but the teacher sent to meet us at the station was not too pleased at being kept waiting in the late evening, and obviously thought it would have saved trouble if we had come by the afternoon school train.

Another embarrassment was to follow. For on our arrival at the school we found that Miss Willis' misgivings about overflowing numbers had been justified: the only beds available for us were in the sanatorium, situated five minutes away in the woods. We could stay there provided our room was not needed for the sick, which indeed later it was. This did not upset me, but I was disappointed that it meant sharing the room with my sister, with whom my relations were not very amicable. I had thought that one of the benefits of going away to school would be fewer contacts with her. As we were close in age, we had in the past been thrown together for all activities. We were very different from each other, not only physically but mentally. She had a neat attractive figure; I was fatter and less graceful. She was extremely feminine in her attitudes; I longed to be a boy and aped masculinity wherever I could. I thought her silly, irrational and illogical; she thought me over-serious, unimaginative and devoid of literary and artistic sensitivities.

My first reactions to life at Downe were mixed. I felt the content of the lessons was too vague: they did not contain enough solid facts. I had to write essays about history and literature, but did not seem to be learning anything thoroughly. I hated my piano lessons, as the teacher was not impressed by my technique of which I was rather proud, and concentrated on the need to 'phrase' (a concept I did not understand) and to play more musically. My other main worry was how to cope with the complexities of personal relationships which had not arisen in French schools. But many of my new experiences were exciting and delightful. I loved wearing the school uniform, even the strange djibbahs, garments copied from Roedean, based on the dress of North African tribesmen. The uniform's rather unusual colours of purple and green had been chosen to represent Scottish heather and the colours of the suffragettes, though Miss Willis had not herself been a militant. Indeed I regretted that we changed into our own clothes every day after games, as my dresses with short sleeves were more suited to a centrally-heated Paris flat than to the austerities of Downe. In the summer term we could wear what coloured tunics we liked. This was a great pleasure, especially if one managed to inherit a tunic from one's favourite senior girl who was leaving: and it produced a beautifully varied scene, particularly at the massed gym displays which took place every year on the great lawn. Another delight in the summer term was sleeping out of doors or in the cloisters which we were allowed, indeed encouraged, to do if we provided our own camp beds.

I enjoyed our daily gym or dancing classes and games of lacrosse, netball or cricket. The school did not set such a high premium on prowess at sport as did many girls' boarding schools, but physical education in the broadest sense was an important part of the curriculum, and for this I have been in later life very grateful. This is not to deny that at the time I was often deeply miserable and envious because I lacked certain skills possessed by many other girls, for instance to climb a rope or to do a handstand, and I longed passionately to get into lacrosse and cricket teams. When I did occasionally scrape into some lowly team, I was downcast at my poor performance in the ensuing match.

I soon got to like the central role which religion played in our daily lives. We had to attend brief chapel services twice a day and longer ones on Sundays, and though I sometimes wished Miss Willis' sermons had been shorter and less rambling, I found the experience emotionally satisfying, at least for a time. It is difficult to know quite what religion meant to me. I found parts of the Church of England liturgy, especially the Litany, beautiful and deeply moving, but there was a great deal in Christian theology and doctrine which, I regret to say, I never understood in spite of listening to many sermons, going to Sunday School and being prepared for confirmation. I think Christianity's main message for me focused in some confused way round 'the sins of the world' for which Christ had come to save us. In my diary I constantly reproach myself for being 'stuck up', jealous and corrupt; so I go to church, take the sacrament, repent, pray and feel better. I did not find it taxing to 'love my neighbour as myself', for I did not love myself. On the contrary I frequently despised myself, feeling I had a debased character. But I certainly found it difficult to love my neighbour, since my natural instinct was, as it has remained, to be ultra-critical and disparaging.

I did not lose my faith completely until the age of 18, but even at 15 I began to doubt whether Christianity was superior to other religions. At school we often had sermons or lectures about missionary work, both in this country and abroad. In 1929 I recorded in my diary:

> These sermons always upset me. I suppose we all ought to be missionaries, seek the good of others and not our own etc . . . But this is a very stupid argument: if everybody sought their own good, we should all be happy, as it is much more fun seeking one's own and not somebody else's. It seems to me that the negroes of Africa are quite happy as they are and are good in the eyes of God. Why then disturb them? Their religion appears to them just as much the right religion as ours appears to us. Miss Willis said once that God cared for Blacks as much as us; what then is the use of being a Christian? Have I no faith? Yes, I have in every religion.

I was clearly not so sure, as I had been a year earlier, that if I were a man, I would like to be a bishop.

Looking back on my four years at Downe I realise how lucky I was to be sent to such an unusual and stimulating school. One of its strangest features was the presence and role of a Polish woman, Miss Nickel, who not only did all the maintenance work, but also the actual construction of the many buildings which were from time to time added to the complex – classrooms, gymnasium, library, laboratory, chapel. Their planning was somewhat haphazard, and they tended to remain unfinished, but they did not actually fall down, though the roofs were liable to leak. Miss Nickel's appearance was extraordinary. She wore a long belted serge overall reaching to her ankles, rubber boots, and a felt broad-brimmed man's hat. Her life style too was strange. She slept in Miss Willis' bathroom, originally on the floor, later on a slab of wood over the bath. Rumour had it that she had vowed not to sleep in a bed until she had found her lost parents, but in fact the practice was due to her belief that wood was good for rheumatism, and to her wish not to take up valuable space by having a room of her own. She kept her few personal possessions in various sheds in the grounds. To the girls she was, with her deep voice and strong foreign accent, a rather alarming phenomenon, and we were nervous about approaching her to report defects in the plumbing, water supply, or heating system; but we knew she was devoted to the school and to Miss Willis, and we appreciated her manifold skills and great funds of idiosyncratic knowledge. She had lived in Russia and France, had studied forestry and medicine, and had taught geography, science and cookery at Downe before 1914.

The education on the arts side was excellent. I came to enjoy the Romantics, especially the Lake poets, Browning, Tennyson and Matthew Arnold. Some people complain that 'doing' the plays of Shakespeare at school ruins the enjoyment of them in later life. I have never felt this, and am grateful that we studied and acted in many of them. Inadequate though my knowledge of English literature has remained, it would have been infinitely worse if I had not been introduced to some of it by the combined efforts of Miss Willis, who was very widely read, and the attractive English mistress, Mamie Poore. One of the strengths of her teaching was an insistence that we should focus on the works themselves and not read the literary critics. Love of poetry was also fostered in me and others by the lectures and passionate recitations given from time to time by the poet and author Charles Williams, a friend of Miss Willis' who had influenced her profoundly. My knowledge of French literature was extended by our frequent performances of French plays – not only those of Molière, but more ambitiously in my time, Rostand's *Cyrano de Bergerac* and *L'Aiglon*. The history teaching of Evangeline Evans and Jean Rowntree was so good that it enabled me to get a place at Oxford when aged just 17. Another remarkable teacher was Jean Smith, a classical scholar and poet who later worked with Professor Gilbert Murray and edited his autobiography. Classes were small; indeed sometimes I was taught individually. School societies, literary, historical and philosophical, flourished and went a little way, I felt, to satisfy my desire for unbounded knowledge and my absurd ambition, confided to my diary, to read every book in the least worth reading and to be the wisest person in the world.

The school provided great scope for the development of our emotions – not just by the very important parts played there by music and religion, but by the many opportunities it offered for friendships between girls, and between girls and teachers. Pupils shared bedrooms usually in twos, and we had to change our room-mates every term. We went for frequent walks and bicycle rides in groups of three, exploring the superb countryside which surrounded the school. Groups of eight to ten for meals were built up by a sixth-former to include girls of all ages. The group moved regularly from one table to the next, each table being presided over by a member of staff. Emphasis was placed on the duty to converse with your neighbours, and particularly to keep the staff interested and entertained. Certainly several of the teachers fulfilled one of Miss Willis' aims when founding the school, for they related to us out of school hours, took us on expeditions, sometimes invited us to meals in their lodgings, even wrote to us in the holidays. Some people ridicule the tendency of schoolgirls to develop strong attachments to other girls or teachers, and think this creates an undesirable, unhealthy emotional hothouse. But I would like to suggest that far from being harmful, such attachments are positively good in that they develop a capacity in the young to admire and even to love.

Miss Willis put this well when she said at a staff meeting that she was glad to know that a certain girl, 'such a selfish little toad', was capable of caring for anyone besides herself.[7] People who have never fallen in love in their lives seem to me to lack a whole dimension, and I am glad that at Downe I began to learn how to cope with the pleasures and pains of passionate feelings. Apart from anything else, these helped us to develop the art of letter writing, an activity in which I and my friends engaged on what seems now an extraordinary scale. Some of us were also inspired to compose poetry. My friend Barbara Clapham in particular translated our emotions into reams of fluent and even amusing verse, known as 'Raves'.

Downe also taught us to be tough in all sorts of ways. Physical conditions were distinctly spartan. On the top of a high hill, the site was open to the winds. Moving from one part of the school to another usually involved going out of doors. From time to time the heating system, such as it was, would break down. During a cold winter there would be ice on the water jug in one's bedroom. A hot bath was not guaranteed, as the water supply, which came from our own wells, was temperamental. None of this worried Miss Willis. She had a liking for fresh air and thought cold forced one to generate energy; so we had to run every forty minutes from one classroom to another. Indeed she rather welcomed an emergency such as the absence of light or water, because she did not want either the staff or the children to get into grooves. She herself had extraordinary physical stamina and was apt to expect the same in others. Illness should be treated in a bracing way. Her moral teaching too was bracing, and designed to strengthen the will. If things were going well, now was the time to look about one for ways of improvement. Miss Willis valued highly independence of mind, so although she would make suggestions about behaviour, we were to decide whether to take them up or not as we thought fit. I am sure she would have been scornful of the present simplistic exhortations constantly emanating from politicians, churchmen and moralists that parents should teach their children 'the difference between right and wrong', and 'instil' virtue in them.

[7] Anne Ridler, *Olive Willis and Downe House*, 1967, p. 98, an excellent book on which I have drawn extensively.

I did not mind the cold and the material austerities – at least not much – but I found it difficult to cope with the rather intense regime of self-analysis to which we were subjected. Each girl was given a private interview with Miss Willis at the end of every term. Sometimes I found these painful and embarrassing – painful because the conversation focused on my shortcomings such as intolerance and a desperate desire to be popular, and embarrassing because I did not wish to confide in her. 'She always wants one's soul outpoured at her,' I wrote in my diary. 'She thinks one is reserved if one doesn't approve of this way of controlling one's thoughts.' Nor did I appreciate her practice of coming round almost every evening to each girl's bedroom to say goodnight. I became labelled as 'the girl who does not want to be kissed'. I realised she was good and I admired her deep religious beliefs, but I was not attuned to her techniques. Maybe they were ultimately to my advantage, but at the time I found them unhelpful, even profoundly upsetting. I must however make it clear for the sake of her reputation that my ambivalence about Miss Willis was exceptional and that the school as a whole was a brilliant creation. Above all, life there was never dull. This was partly the result of a deliberate policy: Miss Willis believed in the value of unexpectedness. She wanted to prepare her pupils for what lay ahead of them: they must be accustomed to dealing with surprises. Thus the school was saved from institutional formality by its traditions of improvisation. When we played matches against other schools we realised Downe's great virtues, and no doubt irritated some of their pupils by perhaps excessive pride in our claims to uniqueness and even eccentricity.

For me one of Downe's assets was that in spite of its modest size it attracted a remarkable number of interesting pupils with varied talents. I was too young of course to be there with the school's most famous old girls, the novelist Elisabeth Bowen and the anthropologist Audrey Richards, who is described by Edmund Leach in his interesting article about her in the *Dictionary of National Biography* as a member of what has been called 'the intellectual aristocracy'. But my contemporaries included the great oboeist Evelyn Rothwell (later Lady Barbirolli), the writers Alethea Hayter and Anne Ridler, the archaeologist Rachel Maxwell-Hyslop, Rosemary Murray who became the first head of New Hall, Cambridge, other academics such as Edith Whetham (economic historian) and

Celia Westropp (physiologist), Bridget Richmond (Lady Plowden) and Lena Westropp (Lady Townsend) who both had distinguished public careers, and members of the great Downe dynasties of Verneys, Stewarts, Nowell-Smiths, Milfords, Norman-Butlers, Stainers, Buxtons and Lubbocks.

My life during this period illustrates the value of 'connections', some due to my family and some to school. Thus my sister and I stayed on several occasions with my mother's relations on their estates. The most enjoyable of these visits were those to Dudmaston, a beautiful late seventeenth-century house in Shropshire, near Bridgnorth, owned by my uncle Geoffrey Wolryche-Whitmore whose family had lived there for six centuries. In spite of the size and grandeur of the place, life there was informal, amusing and not at all alarming. It was also very interesting. I realised even then that my uncle and aunt were examples of archetypal English paternalistic squirearchy at its best. They joined in local life, even (though both deaf) acting in the Christmas village play. They were obviously much appreciated, even loved, by the villagers who often named their children after them. Walking round the 3,000 acre estate with my uncle, I learnt a bit about the problems of agriculture at that time, and I admired his compassionate attitude to his tenants' difficulties. Visits to Dudmaston widened my horizons, as my uncle and aunt were so very different from my parents whom they regarded with a certain awe and curiosity. They saw themselves as simple English country people, steeped in rural activities, lacking my father's brains, my mother's artistic gifts, and their international interests. I was fascinated by this contrast in life-styles. Dudmaston is now owned by the National Trust and inhabited by Sir George Labouchere whose late wife was my uncle's niece.

The experience of staying with a great aunt, Augusta Hannay, in her grand house, Coldhayes, near Liss in Hampshire, was also stimulating, but in a different way. She was something of a martinet and rather intimidating, but her niece, Audrey Murray, who usually lived there as a companion having apparently no home of her own, softened the atmosphere. She was witty, amusing and easy to relate to in spite of being one of the world's saints. I came to admire the way she acted on her deeply held Christian beliefs. My great aunt had a curious but harmless desire that as many things as possible should be black and white. She dressed accordingly; her dogs had to be dalmatians, and the paddock was adorned by black and white ponies on which she could gaze from her room. She moved in circles where everyone had a 'place', meaning a family estate. I decided she was 'a bad thing', a snob, which my relations at Dudmaston, though privileged, were not. However in spite of the strain of gracious living, my sister and I managed to enjoy ourselves riding her ponies and playing in the large garden. Looking back at those times at Coldhayes, I feel guilt that I do not write with more warmth and gratitude for the opportunity to be there.

Perhaps the most remarkable of the establishments I stayed in as a girl was the home of my school friend Katherine Pass: Wootton Fitzpaine Manor in Dorset. Her father, a scientist and rich businessman, was a great power in local government. A strong conservative, he naturally disapproved of my political views though at that time I was only a lefty liberal, but it was rather ungracious and tactless of me to criticise his standpoint. His recreations listed in *Who's Who* were fishing, hunting, shooting and stalking. The family owned a large number of magnificent horses on one of which I was immediately mounted. A few days later we went hunting. I was terrified and did my best, when no one was noticing, to slink away in order to avoid having to jump over some fence. On another occasion we went on a vast cross-country ride to have breakfast with their friends the Pinneys. This was in fact marvellously romantic for me as they lived at Racedown, the house occupied by Wordsworth for two years in the 1790s and visited by Coleridge. I was also initiated into beagling. This entailed running over very rough ground for some purpose which I never quite fathomed. I was usually left stranded the wrong side of a valley. In spite of these rather curious experiences, Katherine and I remained good friends. She had many interests besides horses, and I appreciated her disinterested keenness for me to take part in the activities which gave her pleasure. She felt she was privileged and wanted me to share in her good fortune. At the same time I enjoyed our lively discussions in which I rather self-righteously peddled my system of values, particulary on political and social issues.

I was sad when my time at Downe came to an end, but buoyed up by the prospect of a delightful holiday in Cornwall.

2

Cornwall

No account of my childhood or indeed of the whole of my life would be complete without describing the important part played in them by our family's Cornish home and the numerous experiences it has offered. The story of the creation and development of this unique place also illustrates the imaginative genius of my parents, especially of my father who was justified in referring to it as his 'inspiration'.

The idea of building a holiday house in Cornwall probably occurred to my father when he was proposing to marry my mother. He had known and loved Cornwall for many years, having stayed quite often with Professor and Mrs Westlake in their house, Tregerthen, near Zennor between St Ives and Land's End. John Westlake (1828–1913) was a Cornishman who became Professor of International Law at Cambridge in 1888. His wife was one of the daughters of Thomas Hare, the initiator of the campaign for Proportional Representation in this country, and it seems probable that it was the Westlakes who sparked off my father's life-long commitment to this cause. Tregerthen, later renamed Eagle's Nest and now owned by the artist Patrick Heron, is situated in a romantic position on the moors 600 feet above sea level. This gave my father the idea that one could build a house in an exposed position, but my parents wanted to make their home in less forbidding surroundings, with sea and beaches more suitable for children, so they opted for the south coast of the county. My father bicycled about looking for a suitable site, and ended up buying for £3,000 in 1910 nearly one hundred acres of land near Gorran Haven, including Lamledra Farm and a headland. He planned to place the house two hundred feet above the sea, with a magnificent view looking out towards Dodman Point. Local people advised against building in such an exposed position – it was then very unusual to do so – but my father was undeterred by their warnings and went ahead with this bold project, describing himself at the time as 'reckless'. 'It is a beautiful place,' he wrote to my mother, 'very, very beautiful, and not like other places – it is to places what you are to other women- just so fresh and life-giving – it sweeps all the rest of the world away.' The house was extremely well built and has on the whole stood up well to the onslaughts of wind and rain. The original structure of 1911 was enlarged in 1914 and again in 1926, with the result that it could easily accommodate about fifteen people.

Lamledra provided idyllic holidays for me and my sisters throughout our childhood and thereafter, with all the amenities resulting from its position by the sea. But it did far more than this. It made us aware of environmental and ecological problems; introduced us to the rights and duties of landowners and tenants and to the economic base of the fishing community; taught us to respect the villagers' life-style and to understand some of their problems. These may sound exaggerated, pretentious claims, so I will lay out some of the evidence on which they are based. For instance our water supply came partly from a small well, but mainly from rain caught on the roof and stored in underground tanks from which it was pumped up for many years by hand. The level in the tanks was measured by putting a long marked rod down the manholes. In spite of having a large roof area, deliberately constructed to catch as much rain as possible, we always had to be extremely careful. It was a sin to wash under a running tap, and undrunk water was collected from glasses after meals to be put to some use. Thus we learnt to appreciate the value of this scarce commodity. We had no bathroom until the late 1920s. If anyone had to have a bath, they had a small tin one in their bedroom, but in the summer everyone was expected to bathe in the sea and not to take a bath. Indeed we, as children, were made to bathe every day unless it was pouring with rain. My father, the servants and the gardener all had earth closets in the garden. Those using indoor lavatories were encouraged not to waste water. The house was not connected to the mains until 1962, after the supply came to the village. Our extensive kitchen garden was ingeniously watered from the cesspit, which acted as good manure. There was no electricity in the house until the mid-1920s, so we had to make do with candles and oil lamps.

We were not expected to do any gardening, but we inevitably learnt a good deal about plants as my father had botanical interests, knowing even how to identify them in the famous complex manual, always known as *Bentham and Hooker.*[8] Moreover we were encouraged to dig up weeds on the tennis court, to scythe bracken when it encroached on agricultural land, and as we walked through the fields to pick the fluff off the tops of thistles to prevent them seeding. The fluff was then used to stuff cushions, which were inevitably very lumpy. The need for windbreaks in the garden and the importance of planting trees became ingrained in us.

Nor were we expected to help on the farm which was let to a tenant, but we became familiar with the habits and needs of the many animals which surrounded us: cart horses, cattle, sheep, pigs, geese. We owned a pony, and so learnt how to catch and harness it for riding or to pull the trap. I used to accompany my father on his annual tour of the property with the farmer and a handyman to see what repairs were needed to buildings, gates and fences. I became interested in the economy of the farm and developed romantic ideas about becoming a farmer.

On Sundays we all walked to church, a mile and a half away, uncomfortably dressed in our best clothes. We considered with no justification that the family had a right to a certain pew, and if any unsuspecting visitors occupied it, we tried to edge them out. My sister and I used to help ring the church bells, having learnt the art from the village blacksmith. We also sang in the choir and had organ lessons, but were never accomplished enough to play for a service.

The great advantage of having a fairly large house was that, although conditions there were far from luxurious, we could have many people to stay, such as relations of all ages and our school and college friends. This had been one of my father's aims from the start. 'I want to pack Lamledra tight with the jolly children of our friends,' he wrote to my mother in June 1911. There were also more august guests such as the historians G.M. Trevelyan and

[8] George Bentham and J.D. Hooker, *Handbook of the British Flora*, 1887.

H.A.L. Fisher, Sir Claud Schuster and Sir Arthur Salter, both important civil servants, and the philosopher H.W.B. Joseph who picked us up at once on any loose use of words or defective logic. Even though as children we were relegated to the nursery quarters for most meals, we mixed freely with our parents' friends who were, like us, as was common in middle class households, looked after by numerous servants, some recruited locally, others brought from Paris or Oxford. Besides the company provided by those who stayed in the house, other family acquaintances such as the Bradbys and (Edmund) Phippses with their many children, lodged in the village and spent much of their time with us. Anne Bradby (now Anne Ridler) and Nicholas Phipps, the later actor and script writer, even started a house magazine. I greatly enjoyed the rather extraordinary, strenuous, old-fashioned beach games such as 'French and English' and 'Finkenstein' which were played by our large merry party of 20 or 30 people.

Our parents took a great interest in the locality. My father was what is now known as a 'New Liberal', that is a post Gladstonian Liberal advocating progressive social reforms. He was dissatisfied with his work at the Bar which he described as 'dull guinea grubbing' (it did not even bring in many guineas), and in the years before the war he spent much of his time working for various quite radical causes e.g. education for all children up to age 18, the municipalisation of much land, and the reform of industrial life insurance companies who exploited the poor quite scandalously. He thought seriously about leaving the Bar and going into politics. Indeed he stood as a Liberal candidate for Oxford City in the December 1910 general election. He did not expect to win, as Oxford had returned a Tory since 1885, but he did quite well getting 42% of the vote. He was a little alarmed when he realised that Gorran Haven generally looked to him as 'an earthly Providence', but he soon saw that, though he would be a poor substitute for providence, there were things he could do for the community, thus giving him a chance, even in a small way, to put some of his ideals into practice.

My father's most important achievement locally was to persuade the fishermen to start a Co-operative Society, for he saw that they were in the hands of buyers who gave them poor prices. The Gorran Haven Co-op, with two or three dozen members, was a great success. It owned a lorry which drove the fish daily to St Austell for direct despatch by train to retailers in the Midlands or London, and it secured with his help a Treasury grant to build an engine to winch the boats up and down. He also arranged for a watch hut to be built on his land to provide shelter for the coast guards, planted a field of willows out of which the fishermen could make their crabpots, and sold local people plots of land for modest sums to build themselves better accommodation than their existing cramped quarters. His only stipulation was that the roofs of the houses should be green, not red.

Right from the start my parents provided books for the villagers, in spite of disapproval from the Plymouth Brethren who thought one should not read anything except the Bible. The Cornish were in my father's view a whole generation behind the rest of England in education. Later my mother collected money to build an Institute to house a library and to be a centre for other activities. The library opened in the summer of 1918. She was clearly the main driving force behind this successful project, securing gifts of books from her friends, though sometimes she felt their offerings were unsuitable, as when Janet Trevelyan sent not as hoped for the novels of Mrs Humphrey Ward (Janet's mother), but a book on German socialism and a report on the drink traffic.

My mother regularly went visiting in the village and often took us with her. The villagers did not seem to regard these social calls as patronising or intrusive; on the contrary they appeared to enjoy them and to be interested in our growth and progress. This kind of deferential, almost feudal relationship sounds curious today, but there were for many years people in the village who spoke of my parents with genuine affection and gratitude for what they had done for the community. Life there for the 'natives' was hard economically, and socially restricted. There was no pub in the Haven. Some local people had never been 'up in England', as they put it, and most of them had at some time been 'down on their nerves', the cure for which was to go 'up to Bodmin', that is to the Mental Hospital/Poor Law Institution. Little income was derived from tourists, as they were scarce until after the Second World War, and indeed were not welcomed by some of the villagers whose strict Methodist morals made them disapprove of the life-style of those outsiders who walked down the street in their bathing suits and swam on Sundays. My father too was not keen on 'trippers', and indeed was reluctant to bathe if he espied one even at the other end of the long beach beneath our house, and this in spite of the fact that he had a large tent in which to undress, with my mother in another. There was a right of way over our land, so visitors were rather quaintly requested on a notice board, after admonitions not to leave litter or to light fires, 'So to enjoy this place that others may have the same pleasure.'

During the First World War my mother stayed at Lamledra with the children for long periods each year, and in the 1920s she was usually there for at least three months every year. The rather novel experience of living in this community with the new relationships which it involved had the effect of developing and solidifying her feelings about the social classes. She admired and got on easily with the village people. They were not aspiring to rise, and so were not threatening. But she could not stand those she called 'the coms', that is people who were in her view 'common' – not what social historians call 'the common people'. 'Common' people were, though she did not use the phrase, the lower middle class. A few of these had apparently built bungalows and settled in the locality. My mother desperately wanted a different sort to settle in Gorran Haven, in order that her children could have neighbours of our class as companions. In this she was not successful. The only middle class new arrivals were a rather well off family who had made money in trade. They were dubbed 'nouveaux riches' and not favoured as our playmates.

My parents did not move much in 'county' society, though after we had a car in the 1930s there was some tennis party life which I enjoyed when it was not too posh. More significant from my point of view were the opportunies Cornwall offered to get to know two remarkable women, Eva Hubback and Ka Arnold Forster, both of whom I liked and greatly admired. Eva had a holiday home on the north coast, and Ka lived with her husband at Eagle's Nest near Zennor. This is not the place to give a proper account of Eva Hubback. The labels 'feminist' and 'social reformer', though she was both, leave out so much. Her life and work have been brilliantly described by her daughter, Diana Hopkinson, in her book *Family Inheritance* (1954) and she has at last found her way into the *Dictionary of National Biography*. For me she was an inspiration –

what is now called a 'role model' – because her life demonstrated that a woman, even a widow, could both have a family and engage in outside employment. She encouraged me to aim at a career in the Civil Service. Besides her voluntary work, she was Principal of Morley College for non-vocational adult education. In my youth when I first met her I contrasted her favourably with my mother (who did not take to her) because of her clear mind and concentration on her public work for all sorts of causes – such as family allowances, birth control and education in citizenship – rather than on what I saw as less important matters such as domestic and sartorial issues. Later on when I saw a lot of her in London before her tragically premature death in 1949, I was particularly struck by her unflagging interest in new ideas and her unusual capacity to make real friends with younger people.

Ka Arnold Forster fascinated me because I knew that, as Ka Cox, she had had a love affair with Rupert Brooke and that in her youth she had been a close friend of Virginia Woolf, who had stayed several times at Eagle's Nest. But I did not find, as I now know Virginia did, that Ka lived in the past. She was a magistrate, much involved with a range of local affairs, and – as a great admirer of Kurt Hahn, the founder of Salem and Gordonstoun – very interested in educational theories. Observing Ka's life-style, I began to realise how desirable it was to have a great variety and number of friends. She took an encouraging interest in my life and tried to lessen the tension between me and my mother, a laudable goal which might have been more successful if she had not died in 1938 at the early age of 51. She is described most interestingly in Christopher Hassall's biography of Rupert Brooke (1969), and figures frequently in Virginia Woolf's *Diaries* and *Letters*, where like so many others she is the butt of much, often unfair, malice.

My parents were at Lamledra when the Second World War broke out and decided to stay there for the duration. After the war ended they returned to their Oxford house where my father died in 1947. Most of our land in Cornwall was sold but with restrictive covenants ensuring that it could never be built on or developed. The house was for a time let to a school on condition that our family could go there in the holidays. But there were problems: the water supply was inadequate and people in the locality were alienated by the alleged ringing of bells for Compline. We then installed a caretaker, but this too was unsatisfactory. He was an ex-army man and made the garden look like a barrack square. Worse still he took to thieving in the neighbourhood; so he had to leave. For some years the house and gardens deteriorated badly as my mother could not cope with the many problems they posed. When she died in 1961, I was reluctant to take Lamledra as my share of the total estate left by my parents to be divided amongst the five of us. My husband was even less keen on this. He liked the place, but felt it would be a white elephant and prevent us going on foreign holidays. However our children were adamant that we should have it. Only one of my sisters, Mariella, was anxious to take it on; so she and I became co-owners. Since then we have tackled the damage done by the long years of neglect, and have made a number of improvements without altering the delightfully Edwardian character of the house. We let it to holiday tenants and to University reading parties when we are not occupying it ourselves.

It may well be asked how I reconciled inheriting this property – a house and about twenty acres of land, together with some capital – with my socialist principles. I had long accepted as correct the powerful case against inheritance put forward by many socialists, particularly Douglas Jay in his book *The Socialist Case* (1937). He argued that inherited income was the main factor in perpetuating inequality of wealth and that the case against it was the core of the case for socialism. As far as Lamledra was concerned, the answer is that unless it was sold, which from our extended family's point of view was unthinkable, it would not for many years be a source of income, except in so far as it provided us with rent free holidays. On the contrary unless it was allowed to deteriorate further, it would be a drain on our finances. The realisation that on inheriting it I would be liable to death duties also helped me to square my conscience.

Some years later I had to go through the arguments again. I had given my half share of the property to my daughter to avoid the payment of further taxes on my death, though we agreed that I should, while *compos mentis*, manage it on her behalf. She became more and more radical and, feeling unable to justify her ownership, wanted to give the place to the local authority to run for some good cause, such as turning it into a home for the mentally handicapped. I was appalled, as by then I had become deeply attached to it and had put much effort into improving the house and gardens. Worst of all was the fact that she won her father over to her side, though he was moved less by ideological than practical considerations. I defended retention by arguing that my policy of letting the house at well below market rents, and sometimes for none, to low or middle income families or groups increased the sum of human happiness and was socially justifiable. I also argued that when my family occupied it they were able with our 21 beds to have as guests many friends and relations of all ages, some of whom might not otherwise have had a holiday in such a magnificent place. Some of these justifications of inheritance and ownership may have been specious, but I won the day and prevented the alienation of Lamledra. I must confess that I have derived pleasure from owning it and from the sense it has given me of belonging, albeit only peripherally, to the local community, though I cannot claim to have contributed to its welfare as my parents did, apart from keeping intact the natural beauties of the environment.

Inheriting stocks and shares, as I did, required a different defence. This was that, as I had by then a mentally handicapped child for whose future maintenance it was desirable to make financial provision, it would have been unnecessarily scrupulous to refuse to accept this assistance on the ground that it was not morally justified. However I have to admit that my socialist principles as regards inheritance have evaporated, as I have not cut my other three children and their offspring out of my will. I do not propose to try here to justify my position by either specious or more plausible arguments.

3

Geneva, Munich, Home 1932

EVER SINCE THE age of thirteen when I read my father's diary of his student days, I was determined to go to Oxford. I had of course little idea of what the women's colleges were like or of how easy or difficult it was to get in, but I was encouraged when at Downe to discover that Miss Willis and several of my teachers who had been there did not think my ambition ludicrous. So I sat the exam in January 1931 and was offered a place at Somerville for 1932, eighteen months later, being thought too young to come up before then. At the same time the college suggested that I should do the exam again in the autumn to try for a scholarship. This plan turned out a disaster. I left school in the summer of 1931 and worked on my own at home. The atmosphere there was gloomy. When the Reparations Commission was wound up in 1930 my father was aged sixty. He had had an extraordinarily interesting and successful time in Paris and was still at the height of his powers. But on returning to England he in effect retired from stable employment. Various offers were made to him: a county court judgeship which he thought too lowly a post, and the professorship of International Relations at Oxford which he declined on the ground that he was an international lawyer and not a 'relations' expert. The post was given to Alfred Zimmern. This combination of pride and modesty had unfortunate results, not the least of which were financial. He presumably received some sort of occupational pension, but this would have been much smaller than his previous salary. At the same time his private income was severely hit by the effects of the world economic depression. Later on he did various jobs such as international arbitrations and the chairmanship of a Royal Commission (on Tithe), but he was never fully occupied and much given to melancholy.

My parents decided to settle in Oxford. For a year we lived in a rented house in the pleasant residential area of north Oxford. After our cramped Paris flat my sisters and I thought this large rambling Edwardian pile was seventh heaven. But as my mother suffered from rheumatism, it was considered desirable to avoid the mists and damp of low lying land and to live on a hill. So we bought a plot at Headington on the outskirts of the city and built a house, moving there in the autumn of 1931. The site had some attractions, particularly the beautiful view of the 'dreaming spires', but for me there were disadvantages. The neighbours were mostly staid middle-class retired couples. There was no village. I felt the surroundings to be lifeless and a great comedown after the delights of my last year at Downe. I missed my school friends and had not yet made any new ones.

I describe all this to explain why I found it so difficult to work for the scholarship exam. Apart from doing some Latin with my father, which was not a good idea, I had no tutorial assistance. I read without taking things in, partly because I was depressed. My mother complained that I was unsociable, shutting myself away in my room. Our relations deteriorated. I was not awarded a scholarship, and an exhibition only after other better candidates had withdrawn. I was bitterly disappointed as I had had inflated views of my abilities.

However plans for the next nine months looked good and turned out well to start with, for I was to go and stay in Geneva with Elliott and Joyce Felkin. My parents had got to know them as a young couple when Elliott worked on the Reparations Commission in the early twenties. Our families became close friends. We went on holidays together – to the Vosges and to Italy – and continued to meet even after the Felkins moved to Geneva in 1923 when Elliott joined the League of Nations Secretariat. As he became a key figure in my life, I must explain why. The most important influence on Elliott was King's College, Cambridge, where he was an undergraduate from 1911–1914. There he became a close friend and great admirer of his tutor, Goldsworthy Lowes Dickinson. He also got to know Dickinson's friend E.M. Forster, and through them some of the people who became known as the 'Bloomsbury set'. 'Goldie', as Dickinson was called, put the love of friends above all other values (as did Elliott), but he was also deeply concerned with public affairs. During the war which had filled him with black despair he devoted himself to propaganda for a League of Nations, and did as much as any man in England to promote both the idea and the machinery necessary for its implementation. Elliott was unfit for military service, but being a good linguist worked as interpreter in prison camps in Dorset where he met and became a friend of Thomas and Florence Hardy. He had already developed a deep feeling for poetry and literature, and had started to keep a journal which he did until the end of his life. He clearly thought it was a work of literary and personal interest – and it no doubt is – because he bequeathed it to King's College with a view to eventual publication, though not before the year 2007. Through Elliott I came to admire Lowes Dickinson and his *Weltanschauung*. I was particularly fascinated by his book *The Magic Flute*, which Elliott gave me in 1930. Forster considered *The Magic Flute*, written in 1920, 'the most original of all his books if not the most perfect'. In it Dickinson tried to express all he owed to Mozart.[9]

As a child I adored Elliott. He was an unabashed hedonist and also believed that the young should be indulged. In his presence the atmosphere became relaxed, contrasting favourably with the high-powered tone of my family life. This is not to suggest that my father, who was the dominant figure at home, was other than an excellent parent. He was devoted to his children, writing to them regularly when he or they were away from home. He enjoyed our company, read aloud to us, especially from J.C. Harris' famous *Uncle Remus* series which he loved, and on walks told us riveting stories such as *Ali Baba and the Forty Thieves*, the adventures of Ulysses, *Europa and the Bull*. But he was formidable and not very tolerant of stupidity or ignorance. For instance he was upset when my sister and I failed to realise that the clues for a Latin crossword he had devised were in Latin *verse*. Elliott admired my father, his brain, his learning, his integrity, his conversation; so my enjoyment of Elliott's company did not disturb my feelings of reverence and indeed affection for my parent. The fact that they both abhorred war and were working in international organisations created bonds between them and with me.

My stay in Geneva turned out to be exciting and idyllic: exciting

[9] See E.M. Forster, *Goldsworthy Lowes Dickinson*, 1934, p. 177–8.

because I was living in a circle of international civil servants deeply committed to the purposes of the League, often leading unconventional personal lives, and idyllic because of my relationship with Elliott. Members of the League Secretariat drawn from over 30 countries had been carefully, indeed brilliantly, hand-picked by Sir Eric Drummond, Secretary General from 1920–33. From the start it had been made clear to them that they were not responsible to their respective national governments, but collectively to the governments of League members when meeting in the Assembly or Council. In his authoritative book *A History of the League of Nations* (1950), F.P. Walters says that taken as a whole the members of the Secretariat 'developed a corporate sense, a pride in the record and reputation of their service, not inferior to any that can be found in the best of national institutions'. My contacts with the League, which were not confined to my time at Geneva, dispose me to endorse Walters' description of the Secretariat.[10] It certainly fits people such as the masterful British civil servant Sir Arthur Salter who became head of the Economic and Financial Section in which Elliott worked, and Frank Walters himself, but it is also true of more colourful characters such as Konni Zilliacus and St George Saunders. Zilliacus' origins alone made him interesting, for he was the offspring of a Finnish/Swedish father and a Scottish/American mother and had been educated at Bedales and Yale. Politically on the left, he published from 1923 onwards many books and articles about the League and international relations under various pseudonyms including 'Vigilantes'. They were hard-hitting and powerfully argued. It is not strange that later in his career in 1949, when an MP in England, he was expelled from the Labour party for criticising the British Government's foreign policy.

Saunders in contrast was a boisterous *bon viveur*, who wrote numerous novels and detective stories under the pen name Francis Beeding. His main work for the League was as private secretary to the man who has been described as the noblest citizen of post-war Europe, Frijthof Nansen, the High Commissioner for Refugees – the creator of the Nansen passport for stateless persons. Saunders and

[10] Walters was a tutor at University College, Oxford, before the war and a member of the Secretariat from its start, rising to be Deputy Secretary General.

his wife, Helen Foley, also a member of the Secretariat, made a strange pair as she was a subtle, complex personality, steeped in great literature. Elliott was devoted to her and after her sad death in 1937 published her poems.

Many interesting people came to Geneva at this time. For me the most charismatic was Philip Noel-Baker who was assistant to Arthur Henderson, the president of the Disarmament Conference which opened in February 1932.[11] Phil, an Olympic runner, was a brilliant dancer and I was, like many women, flattered by his attentions. I was also impressed, though in a different way, by the orientalist Arthur Waley, with whose translations from the Chinese I was already a little familiar through my mother's admiration for his work. He was passing through Geneva on his way to the mountains, accompanied by his friend the anthropologist Beryl de Zoete; but meeting her was rather embarrassing, because at school I had not appreciated her efforts to teach us Eastern dance forms. At week-ends we would all often go on skiing parties staying in a modest hotel at Sallanches, beneath Mégève. I enjoyed the mountains, the sun and the company, but I was never much good on skis. Anxious not to go too fast, I learnt a useful device. This was not to remove for the descent the skins we used then to put on our skis to prevent slipping backwards as we walked up. My friends by contrast waxed their skis in order to go faster.

A few days after I arrived in Geneva, Joyce Felkin was suddenly summoned back to England because her schoolboy son, Hugh, was seriously ill. She was pleased that I would be living in her house whilst she was away, providing company for Elliott and their four-year-old daughter, Penelope. Joyce did not return during my visit. Penelope was a charming child, but I was not a success in handling her. Brought up on libertarian principles, she did not welcome my efforts to discipline her. I was, I hope, not positively unkind, but I am ashamed when I now reflect on my intolerant authoritarian attitudes. By contrast 'providing company' for Elliott proved no problem, for very soon he and I grew more and more attached to each other. I find it genuinely difficult to know why he loved me, apart from the attraction of youth (I was twenty years younger

[11] Henderson had been Foreign Secretary in the Labour Government of 1929–31, Noel-Baker a Labour MP.

than him), but it is easy to explain why I found his whole persona so enthralling. On almost my first evening, as we sat up late talking about 'life', he questioned the value of Christian virtues such as humility and self-sacrifice. My religious faith, already waning a little, disappeared rather rapidly in the presence of his agnosticism. It would be absolutely wrong to suggest that he tried to 'convert' me aggressively to his philosophy of life. I simply changed because he opened my eyes to different value systems which can, I think, best be described as broadly those of Bloomsbury, in particular absolute candour in personal relationships and a passionate dislike of hypocrisy. Moreover, like the Bloomsbury set, Elliott and his friends did not subscribe to conventional morality in connection with sexual relations. They were not indiscriminately promiscuous, but they saw no harm in the natural consummation of loving relationships. Indeed they went further and positively advocated this kind of behaviour unless it would cause pain to others. They themselves seem not to have felt sexual jealousy. Their attitude is brilliantly expressed in Shelley's famous lines from *Epipsychidion*:

> I never was attached to that great sect,
> Whose doctrine is, that each one should select
> Out of the crowd a mistress or a friend,
> And all the rest, though fair and wise, commend
> To cold oblivion, though it is the code
> Of modern morals, and the beaten road
> Which those poor slaves with weary footsteps tread
> Who travel to their home among the dead
> By the broad highway of the world, and so
> With one chained friend, perhaps a jealous foe,
> The dreariest and the longest journey go.
> True love in this differs from gold and clay,
> That to divide is not to take away.
> Love is like understanding, that grows bright
> Gazing on many truths.
>
> Lines 149–163

To me these were at first shocking attitudes, but I gradually accepted them, as I came to see that the people who held these beliefs and acted on them added to the richness of life and fostered pleasure rather than pain.

Before this time I had had no experience of physical love-making. Indeed I was largely ignorant of 'the facts of life', having received no sex education at home or in school. So although I was soon deeply in love with Elliott, I tolerated rather than enjoyed the physical side of our affair, though it was by modern standards fairly restrained, and indeed later I even felt a certain revulsion towards this kind of activity. But at the time I was distraught when I had to leave him, returning home to do, of all tiresome things, a Latin test for Somerville. How true, I felt, was the saying quoted to me by Elliott , '*Partir, c'est mourir un peu.*'

My stay in Geneva had been emancipating and exhilarating in many different ways. I had acquired some self-knowledge and got rid of feelings of unwarranted guilt. I realised for the first time that I could be attractive to men, even though I was no beauty and my clothes were dowdy. My intellectual horizons had been extended, as Elliott had introduced me to a dazzling variety of literature, ranging from the works of Goethe and Heine to those of Samuel Butler, Norman Douglas and Aldous Huxley. I had seen the League of Nations in action – particularly over Manchuria which the Japanese had invaded, and disarmament – at a time when a degree of optimism about international affairs did not seem wholly unwarranted. My only disappointment was that I had little success in getting to know my Swiss relations, the de Plantas. I got the impression that they, like many of the Swiss, did not move in League circles and indeed wished to keep their distance. The de Plantas considered themselves to be the oldest Swiss family, claiming, according to local wits, that they, and not the de Sales, were present at the Crucifixion. Back at home I desperately wanted to tell someone about my important emotional experiences. I even, with incredible naivety, thought of sharing them with my father. When I told this to Elliott he panicked understandably and sent me a beautiful pig-skin case in which to lock up his love letters.

After a month at home, in May 1932 I went to live with a family in Munich mainly in order to learn German. The family, the Obrists, had been recommended by someone in Geneva as being internationally minded and generally suitable. This turned out to be wholly misleading. The household consisted only of Frau Obrist, the widow of a minor artist, and her grown-up daughter. They lived in a fairly substantial house, but were badly off as they had been hit by the terrible inflation of 1923. Judging by the meals provided, they found it necessary to economise on food; and I was made to turn out my light at 10 p.m. to save electricity. But more important than these material conditions was their ideological stance: they were in favour of the National Socialists. Hitler had not yet come to power as Chancellor, but his party had considerable and growing support. Since September 1930 the Nazis had, with 19% of the national vote, been the second strongest party in Germany, and they more than doubled their vote in July 1932, soon after the end of my stay. Frau Obrist was attracted to their anti-communism, particularly because the unsightly block of flats opposite which obscured their light had, she alleged, been built by communists. I was not a communist, but decidedly anti-Nazi. On my first evening we argued about the Treaty of Versailles which Frau Obrist denounced. As I had been brought up on Keynes' *Economic Consequences of the Peace*, I did not wish to defend the treaty, but I pointed out that its reparations clauses were by then a dead letter.

After this bad start to our relationship, we never discussed politics or international affairs, and as these were of great interest to me, life at the Obrists' house was boring. I got on well at a certain level with the daughter e.g. playing table tennis, but found conversation on walks with her mother limited and unrewarding. I met virtually no other German people as few visitors came to their house, and I did not know how to establish social contacts in other circles. My German improved a little, but alas only a little. I should have worked at it more than I did instead of reading Maitland's *Constitutional History of England* as required by Somerville. I visited art galleries and took myself off on sight-seeing expeditions. I even went to Salzburg for a few days, but this was not a success as I felt lonely and neurotically nervous of being pestered by strange men. This was partly due to the unpleasant experience I had in the train when travelling to Munich from England. Sleeping alone in a second class compartment, I woke up to find a man molesting me. I managed to kick him off and resolved thereafter to travel only in third class crowded carriages, but the incident shook me badly and inhibited me from sitting in places such as cafés or public parks.

I was naturally depressed and disappointed as I had imagined my time in Munich would be interesting and fruitful, instead of which it contrasted lamentably with my stay in Geneva. I was therefore not unduly disconcerted when after a month in Germany my parents summoned me home because my father had had an operation which shattered him psychologically and financially. Endowed up to then with excellent health, he tended to see illness as a sign of moral weakness and he was panicked by the huge bill which the surgeon thoughtlessly sent him the day after the operation. In a way I was relieved that I would not have to spend another month in Munich, but at the same time I felt a sense of failure and regretted that I was denied the chance of making the experience more successful. Moreover I was sad that returning home at once meant that I could not, as previously planned, stay with the Felkins in Geneva on my way back.

An important offshoot of my time in Geneva was the relationship it generated between me and Elliott's great friend Raisley Moorsom who came to stay while I was there. He was called Raisley after Raisley Calvert, a friend of Wordsworth's. I had met him before on some of the family holidays we took with the Felkins, but I did not know him well. A contemporary of Elliott's at King's College, he too was deeply influenced by Lowes Dickinson who was later in love with him for a short time. Raisley revered and loved Dickinson but was not interested in a homosexual relationship. His other friends at King's included E.M. Forster, Arthur Waley, Francis Birrell and J.M. Keynes. He served in the army throughout the war and was profoundly affected by the horrors he experienced. Having inherited some money, Raisley had no need to work, and feeling disorientated by the war he was not drawn to any career. So he followed the advice given him by the famous controversial Fellow of King's, Oscar Browning, whose fascinating life from 1827 to 1923 is well described by Dickinson in the *Dictionary of National Biography.* Browning's advice was: 'Do whatever you want to do whatever that may be; if you have no master passion, do whatever offers first which will lead on to something else but never do what you do not really care about for the sake of money or career.' The result was that after attending a psychology course at University College, London, Raisley spent his life travelling, reading, talking and enjoying the company of his many friends. He told me once that he never met a stranger without hoping to discover a friend, adding, 'And how tenaciously I cling when I have found one.' Sometimes he felt it difficult to know how to get through the day, but on the whole he carved out for himself an interesting and happy existence. This was partly due to the fact that he had an insatiable interest in people and was skilled at drawing them out. He said he had learnt the art from Dickinson who considered that the more one disliked people, the more unpleasant they became; the only way to make them nice and to evoke their sympathetic qualities was to like them. No wonder, Raisley added, Dickinson seemed at times to have the most unlikely friends.

Raisley was naturally interested in my relations with Elliott who showed him the relevant entries in his journal. So on my return to England from Geneva in the spring of 1932, he invited me to stay at his modest but attractive house, Ramsdean near Petersfield in Hampshire, where he lived with his wife and three children. During the next four years I stayed there often, usually for a week, and we corresponded regularly. Raisley was in love with me, but I not with him, though I was very happy in his company. For during this period I became chronically neurotic about the atmosphere at home where, because I had very little money, I often had to reside. I complained to him endlessly about my parents' political and moral attitudes and their ideal of family life. My mother wished me to be 'softer' and 'more gracious', to dress better, not to abandon religious practices. They were moving to the Right politically and I to the Left. They supported the National Government and were pained at my attending Labour club meetings. They prevented my going to Germany in 1934 with Dick Crossman, then a don at New College, who was organising a party to discuss politics with University people in Marburg, for they regarded him as a dangerous socialist. They wanted me to be presented at Court as my sister Prue had been. I naturally refused just as I refused to stand up at home when the national anthem was being played on the wireless. When my mother's relations came to stay I did not find them amusing and charming as I had previously; they had for me become symbols of our wicked society, living as they did on unearned income from investments or land. They talked a lot about property and the declining fortunes of the aristocracy, to a few of whom they were proud to be related. The women did not have careers and assumed I would be living at home for good.

Raisley came to stay with us in Cornwall and got to know the whole family. He also met my father at the Athenaeum, the London club Raisley visited once a week. He was thus able to understand what I felt and helped me to be less neurotic and intolerant. He thought that nothing could probably be done to change the atmosphere at home and that some discord was implicit in the relations of children with their parents. When I told him I was rebuked for impenetrable reserve as I had resolved to be silent, he pointed out that parents want it both ways: they want to know what their child is like, but they are upset when they find out. This would certainly have been true in my case. My mother in particular was deeply apprehensive about the dangers facing her daughters. The word 'sex' was never mentioned, but she clearly had sexual and not political mores in mind, for in 1935 she wanted my sister Judy to go to Cambridge because it was in her view more moral than Oxford. And later, in 1940, my sister Mariella was not to live in Oxford because it was full of dangerous students from the Slade School of Art who had been evacuated there from London. My move to the capital when I joined the Civil Service in 1936 naturally worried my mother: she talked of the dangers besetting a young female civil servant on first going to London.

For me the amazing things about Raisley were that he was completely unshockable – one could say anything to him – and that he genuinely wanted me to have affairs with other men. Maybe he hoped that if I became less inhibited on this front, his relationship with me would be consummated. Anyway in true Bloomsbury style he would encourage me to take the initiative with anyone I was fond of. 'What had I done about X?' he would ask. 'Was it not time I wrote to him?'. 'How was I getting on with Y?' He wished to know *exactly* what had happened between me and my friends. I was usually willing to tell him, but I refused to show him letters from Philip Noel-Baker with whom I was having a mini-romance. The request was not due to vicarious inquisitiveness on Raisley's part, but to a desire to advise me on Phil's sincerity. There may have been an element of voyeurism in Raisley's inveterate interest in other people's lives – not just mine of course – but if there was it did not worry me, and in any case it was primarily due to his studies in psychology, to a genuine interest in human nature, and to a humane desire that people should learn to live happier lives.

One of the bonuses of my relationship with Raisley was that he introduced me to several interesting people. He did this partly to produce baits so that I would come to stay at Ramsdean. I did not mind his motives and was delighted to meet amongst others Francis Birrell, who with his friend David Garnett had run a famous bookshop much frequented by Bloomsbury, and Ivy Compton Burnett whose novels were little read at this time except by a small group of admirers. These included Elliott and Raisley who knew her well as they had been at King's with her brother. I became and have remained a fan of Ivy's works. I also met the psychoanalyst Marion Milner who was a particularly good person to get to know. I found her book *A Life on One's Own*, written under the pseudonym Joanna Field, very helpful as it dealt with what I felt to be a problem, namely how to harmonise the male and female sides of my character, the conflicting claims of an academic intellect with those of feminine intuition and emotions. I remember also finding illuminating the excerpts from her diary which revealed what was really in her mind when she thought she was concentrating on the book she was reading. She discovered how different her thoughts were from what she had expected.

All in all I regard my friendship with Raisley as one of my strokes of good fortune. He helped me to understand myself and to deal with some of my negative feelings. Sometimes I felt that he carried dissection too far and that emotions could evaporate if they were relentlessly analysed, but there can be no doubt that I gained a great deal from knowing him and his friends. His relationship with Elliott provided a wonderful model of a lifelong, rock solid, intimate but non-sexual friendship between two men, not marred by the fact that Raisley always regarded himself as less clever and cultured than Elliott. Such relationships are, it seems, more common among women than men. Some people felt that Raisley's unconventionality, candour in personal relations and eccentricities went too far, but these things did not upset me. For instance I did not think him selfish or mean because he struck bargains e.g. that if I carried his coat up a mountain he would pay for my tea at the top, or that if I stayed a day longer at Ramsdean I could partake of the special cream he reserved for himself, or be let off reimbursing him for a halfpenny stamp. Nor did I mind him complaining that I was intimidating and offensive. He was very generous with the time and trouble he devoted to my welfare and problems, and never demanded more affection than I was willing to give him. He was adamant that I should not do violence to my real feelings about him by trying to show more than I felt. He would, he said, accept with gratitude whatever affection came to me naturally.

I also incidentally benefited by observing how Raisley and his wife handled their three children. At first I thought they were undisciplined and allowed too much freedom. I complained that the house was a bear-garden. But I began to understand the principles lying behind the regime and the educational philosophy operating at Bedales, the school the children attended and where Raisley himself had been a pupil. In later life I brought my children up on the same lines, not only because I saw how admirably the regime had suited Raisley's gifted daughter Sasha, who married that remarkable man Michael Young, Lord Young of Dartington. She became a novelist and poet and sadly died in 1993.

Raisley was a pacifist. This may account for the family's move to South Africa in 1939 when war seemed likely. In 1940 he went to Washington to join Elliott whose League of Nations work had taken him there. Short of funds, Raisley had for the first time in his life to earn a living. He became a freelance taxi driver, conspicuous in shorts, with a newly-grown huge grey beard, and renowned for the interest he took in the lives of his passengers. I saw him seldom after his return to England, though he did not die until 1981 in his ninetieth year. I felt we had grown apart and that it was better not to try to re-create our friendship. This was probably a wise decision because I found my meetings with Elliott after the war in some ways rather dispiriting. I did not share his interest in good food or his belief in the value of idleness, and I was impatient of his concern that no one should ever get tired. But my husband, to whom I had introduced him, luckily enjoyed his company, especially his wide knowledge of literature, and could understand what Elliott and I had meant to each other. We were both sad when he died in 1968.

4
Oxford 1932–5

When seeking to go up to Oxford, I chose Somerville as the college to which to apply, partly because it was recommended by my school, and partly because I had a general idea that it stood for a tradition of free thought and progressive politics. It was a fortunate choice and I was lucky to be accepted, as competition for places was severe. Unlike the three other women's colleges, Somerville was non-denominational, that is unconnected with any church or religious sect. This was also true in a formal sense of the Society of Home Students, but it had not achieved the status of a college and its academic standing was rather poor, so I did not consider trying for it.

The Principal of Somerville when I first applied in 1931 was Margery Fry, whom I knew to be the sort of person I admired: a radical intellectual, identified with many good causes, especially penal reform. Unfortunately she was no longer there when I went up in 1932, as, finding Oxford in many ways uncongenial and obscurantist, she had resigned. Her successor, Helen Darbishire, the English tutor, was very different, though she too, I now know, did not enjoy the office of Principal, preferring the life of a scholar. She was kind and solicitous, for instance offering in her speech to freshers to lend us two shillings and sixpence if we were hard up, but I and my friends found her rather shy and embarrassing. A Somervillian who came up after me has described how at her interview Miss Darbishire beamed at her with a kind, grandmotherly air, took hold of both her hands, called her 'dear child' and gave her a chocolate.[12] We knew she was a great authority on

[12] See Nina Bawden in *My Oxford*, ed. Ann Thwaite, 1977.

Milton and Wordsworth, but this did not provide an adequate basis for conversation when we dined, as we occasionally did, in her company at the High Table. Years later I warmed to her when she and her great friend Vera Farnell welcomed me and my three obstreperous children to tea in their elegant cottage in the Lake District without turning a hair.

My first term was dominated by work for 'Pass Mods', the exam to be done after eight weeks. This was exacting, although I had prepared myself for some of it before coming up. It required knowledge of Maitland's *Constitutional History of England*, Tocqueville's *Ancient Régime et la Révolution*, some elementary economics, and *Gesta Francorum*, an account of the first Crusade. I am ashamed to say that the only thing I remember about this chronicle is that the desperate crusaders were reduced to eating the roots of thistles in Asia Minor, an economical source of sustenance I induced my family to try out, to their disgust, in Cornwall. The initiation into economic theory provided by Pass Mods made me feel I had been right to choose to read History rather than Modern Greats (Philosophy, Politics and Economics) which I had at one time contemplated taking. In later life I have regretted never having done any philosophy, but if I had studied it in Oxford in the early thirties, I would probably have been exposed only to the traditional treatment of the subject, for the new vistas which ultimately changed its scope were only beginning to emerge.

As the date for the exam approached and anxiety was setting in, I was for a moment tempted to try to postpone taking it. Such an idea only occurred to me as the result of a curious incident. At a dinner party at the house of some neighbours of my parents, the Montagu-Pollocks, I was placed next to their diplomat son William (known as Bill) whom I had never met before. He immediately asked me if I would motor to Belgrade with him two weeks hence. He was obviously an unusual, attractive character and the idea sounded wonderful though a little alarming, but after reflection I said I could not go as I had to sit an exam in Oxford. He thought poorly of my excuse for refusing, but, ever resourceful, asked if I had a sister who might be interested. I said as a matter of fact I had; she was an undergraduate but not doing an exam. A few days later I arranged for them to meet, and after understandable fluttering she agreed to go. There was a streak of impulsiveness in Prue's make-up which made her an engaging character. She never aimed to fulfil the hopes expressed by her godfather, Horace Joseph, in a telegram at the time of her birth, which ran: *Nomine decurrat dignam Prudentia vitam*, that is in effect 'May Prudence live a life worthy of her name'. *Cognoscenti* will recognise this as a line of Latin verse.

Our parents insisted that there should be some sort of chaperon on the expedition. An old school friend, Rachel Wilder, was lined up and they all set off. During an interesting and romantic month in Yugoslavia, Prue and Bill, as one could have predicted, became fond of each other and a few months later got married. Being ten years older than her, he was, I think, anxious to 'settle down'. This meant that she had to leave Oxford before completing her course. Later she bitterly regretted not getting a degree, but at the time she was rather relieved not to have to struggle any longer with philosophical problems, feeling pulverised by the trenchant brain of her tutor, who was none other than her godfather, H.W.B. Joseph.

After getting over the hurdle of Pass Mods, I embarked on the long haul of the Modern History syllabus. This included 'The continuous history of England from the beginning' – a quaint phrase which was taken to mean from the fourth century AD – until the year 1885. The study of more recent history was not favoured as this could not, it was felt, be done without bias, and because the amount of original documents on which we were encouraged to base our essays would be overwhelming. In fact I never got beyond about 1830.

Somerville being a poor college had at that time only seven tutors, but they looked after us most adequately. It is incidentally an amusing sign of the times that the subject of one of them was indicated simply as 'Science'. The main historian was Maude V. Clarke. Being relatively young she had not published much, but she was greatly venerated by other scholars and by her old pupils on whom she had made an indelible impression. I realised when in her presence that she had a most distinguished mind, but unfortunately I did not gain as much as some students did from her tutorials, partly because she was a mediaevalist and I was more interested in modern times, and more importantly because I found her intimidating. She was actually very kind and did not mean to intimidate, but I could not help feeling it was absurd for me to give my views on Richard II to someone whom I understood to be the world authority on the subject. Some of the tension I sensed when with her may have been due to the sad fact that, unknown to me then, she had been diagnosed in 1933 as suffering from cancer. When during my last year she was too ill to teach and I was sent out to a less formidable tutor, Tom Boase at Hertford, I have to confess I was relieved to be taught in a more relaxed atmosphere. The only drawback to his tutorials from my egocentric point of view was that he seemed more interested in my tutorial partner – the enigmatic, romantic, Anne Sitwell – than in me.

My other main tutor was Lucy Sutherland who took us for a wide range of subjects: Economic History, Political Theory, and several modern periods, English and foreign. She too, with her scintillating mind, was rather forbidding. After listening to my essay for twenty minutes, she would talk fast and brilliantly about the subject for another twenty minutes. I felt unable to keep the conversation going, or rather to start a dialogue, so the tutorial ended, but I learnt a lot from her as I would rush away and write down what I could remember. She was a great authority on Edmund Burke who, as the philosopher of conservatism, was anathema to me, but I was not persuaded by the case she put up in his defence. This also applied to her liking for Aristotle, whose views as expounded in his *Politics* had had, I considered, a nefarious influence for many centuries.

The tutorials I enjoyed most were those with Agnes Headlam-Morley of St Hugh's on Representative Government, a subject I had chosen to study against the advice of my tutors at Somerville. They thought it did not contain enough straight history and even that it would prevent my doing well in Finals, but I was adamant and did not regret my decision. I was not troubled by Miss Headlam-Morley's famed absent-mindedness, and benefited from our fierce arguments, especially those over Proportional Representation, the case for which I had, even as a child, imbibed from my father.

The other subject I found particularly absorbing was the eighteenth-century Enlightenment, as I was in sympathy with the doctrines of the French *Philosophes:* the replacement of superstition, divine revelation, dogmatism, authority and tradition by reason and the powers of one's own understanding. I adopted as my motto Voltaire's injunction *Ecrasez l'infame*. This ideological issue was prominent at that time in Somerville because the college, which had never had a chapel, had been offered by an anonymous donor a large sum to erect a building for religious purposes. After, it was rumoured, prolonged and heated debate in the Governing Body which was then a Council consisting not only of the Fellows but also of many prominent University figures, the offer was accepted and it was decided that the building should be called the college chapel, not just in the donor's words 'a symbol of universal brotherhood'. I was naturally opposed to the project, as were many old Somervillians who feared that the liberal and non-sectarian tradition of the college would be impaired, and who wished to maintain its complete detachment from all religions and religious practices. So, as college correspondent to the *Oxford Magazine*, I suggested that the students should, like Penelope the wife of Ulysses, stealthily pull down every night what had been built during the day, an action for which I was severely reproved by the Principal who threatened me with disciplinary measures.

In recent years the Oxford School of Modern History, as it was in my time, has been criticised on many counts. It was considered to be too much centred on England and on political and constitutional issues. The reformers recommended widening its scope with more emphasis on European and indeed on world history and on economic and social questions. The changes made have no doubt pleased many people – students and dons – but I do not wish to complain about the syllabus of the 1930s and the work I had to do. Apart from its intrinsic interest, it provided an excellent training in weighing up evidence, caution in making generalisations, and, through the simple mechanism of a weekly essay, help towards clear and close thinking about intellectual problems. Moreover its emphasis on constitutional and legal questions was of considerable use to me when I later worked in the Home Office.

Before I went up to Oxford my friends Elliott Felkin and Raisley Moorsom predicted that I would meet there many brilliant male undergraduates and that I would be fascinated by them and they by me. None of this happened. During the whole of my three years I got to know only three young men. Two of them, Norman Marsh and Alec Forrest, were nice, worthy and high-minded but stolid characters whom I met through membership of the League of Nations Union, the British voluntary body which worked to support the League. For a short time in 1934 I saw quite a lot of Forrest as we went together lecturing in Cornwall for the LNU, and I had hopes, as so often, that he might be a suitable person with whom to have some sort of affair, but I was disillusioned when he unromantically announced that he liked me more and more because I was ' as the economists say, the subject of increasing returns'. Norman Marsh had later a distingished academic and public legal career.

My introduction to the third undergraduate was different. As I was sitting in the Bodleian library one day, a note was thrown on to my desk asking me to come outside with its sender. I was terrified and refused, but later somehow we met and went for a few country walks together. He was the son of a railwayman in the Midlands, a great admirer of D.H. Lawrence and of all he stood for. Having had sexual relations with girls since the age of 15, he regretted the lack of sex at Oxford. On one of these walks, after reading me Lawrence's poems, he undressed and suggested we should make love. I had never seen a whole naked male body before and thought it revolting. After that we ceased to meet.

I went to one Commem ball, invited by my cousin Henry Whitehead, the Maths tutor at Balliol, and his wife, but I did not enjoy the experience, as the partner produced for me, Peter Pears, later to be famous as the superlative tenor singer and friend of Benjamin Britten, was not interested in dancing and I have no memory of our conversation.

I was mildly disappointed not to get to know exciting, congenial male undergraduates, and I found it galling that my sister Prue whose intellect I rather despised had friends in Balliol who seemed to enjoy her company. These included the brilliant Duncan Wilson several of whose sisters had been at Downe House with us. I supposed that the explanation of her success was that she was an attractive '*petite*' who, unlike me, dressed with style. One of my friends said she seemed rather like 'a delicately painted miniature come alive' in whose presence he felt like a country cousin. However this lack of social life had the good result of enabling me to work intensively. I was an avid attender at lectures and spent the greater part of every day in libraries. The fact that I was relatively hard up also encouraged this sober life-style. The termly fee of £50, paid by my father, covered everything, including all meals in college, so there was no incentive to spend money eating out, or to be cooking. Indeed we were not, like present day students, provided with cooking facilities. I had an annual allowance of £60 for clothes, travel, books etc . . . This no doubt compared favourably with the income of the not inconsiderable number of women students who were assisted by public funds on condition that they agreed to teach after graduating, but it was on the low side compared with that of many of my contemporaries. I did not feel hard done by, but I regretted getting nothing from my exhibition; it was means-tested and my father refused to declare his income. Undergraduates were not allowed to go into pubs, and in any case I could not have afforded alcohol. Being by nature economical, I did not even indulge in mid-morning coffee. The rules also forbade absenting oneself from Oxford during term-time, so we did not, like so many students today, go away for weekends. I did not resent these restrictions and was perfectly happy to be a law-abiding swot enjoying the company provided by college.

Vera Farnell in her reminiscences of Somerville written in 1948 says that 'Somerville for brains' was the current tag some years back and that this was sometimes translated into 'Somerville for freaks'. I would not describe my contemporaries as freaks, but they certainly included several colourful characters. The more sophisticated of these intimidated me and it is not difficult to see why. Thus the brilliant and elegant Anne Scott-James made it clear that she was disappointed in Oxford, which she later described as 'a good place for female swots with their minds concentrated on their degrees', most female undergraduates being 'ill-dressed and unattractive.'[13] She left after two years with no degree, but had a successful career as an author and journalist, working first on *Vogue*. Marghanita Laski, a niece of Harold's, was also rather formidable, and I was not astonished that she became a successful novelist and a well-known public figure. I felt more at ease with bohemian characters who had Bloomsbury connections such as Anastasia Anrep whose father, Boris, was the creator of the mosaic floor at the National Gallery and whose mother had a long association with Roger Fry, Sally Graves, a niece of the writer and poet Robert Graves, Inez Pearn who married Stephen Spender, and above all with the stylish, eccentric Audrey Beecham, a niece of the famous conductor, Sir Thomas. 'Beecham' as she was always

[13] See Anne Scott-James, *Sketches from a Life*, 1993, p. 32–3.

known, fell in love with me and extended my horizons. She remained an extremely loyal, though at times demanding friend throughout her varied and curious life. Several other contemporaries of mine had remarkable gifts and were clearly destined for distinguished careers. I have in mind particularly Barbara Ward who became an authority on developmental and environmental problems, ending up as Baroness Jackson, and Jean Taylor who as a medical scientist worked closely with her husband, Sir Peter Medawar, a Nobel Prize winner.

My closest friend was Phoebe Pool. She was an amazing phenomenon: an intellectual *par excellence* but from an entirely unintellectual background. Her father was a jolly, well-to-do meat trader in Smithfield. Her mother's interests were bridge and golf. I remember my astonishment on learning how, when they wanted to improve their home by having a picture on the wall, they hired a man from Harrods to come and paint one. Maybe the source of Phoebe's gifts was her Dutch–Jewish ancestry. Her turn of mind was in some ways similar to Virginia Woolf's, and unfortunately she too was afflicted by periodic depressions. Even at school she had slept badly. This got worse at Oxford, which she had to leave without a degree. Thereafter between nervous breakdowns she turned herself into an art historian and moved in artistic and literary circles, becoming a close friend of the painters William Coldstream and Claude Rogers. She published several scholarly works, including ominously an anthology of poems about death. She met her own, as her many friends had feared, intentionally.

Years later her name was blackened by the suggestion that she had assisted the KGB and acted as a courier for Anthony Blunt, the art historian and Soviet agent who had been her supervisor and with whom she had worked, collaborating on a brilliant study of Picasso's sources. Phoebe, I am certain, was never a member of the Communist Party or even a fellow-traveller. She was in fact little interested in politics. In this respect she was perhaps a strange friend for me to have, but I was attracted by her vast knowledge of literature and her imaginative capacity to see links and analogies between different writers, artists, thinkers and historical periods.

During several vacations Phoebe and I went with a group of friends from Somerville to stay in delightful places, such as the English Lakes and Chateau d'Oex in Switzerland, on what we rather grandly called 'reading parties'. They were different from the traditional Oxford institutions of this name, as no dons were present and the daily regime was unstructured, but we did in fact do a lot of reading, though usually unconnected with the subjects we were studying. Rather too ambitiously I tackled *Ulysses*, and Proust in French. Although we were all keen to do well in our Finals, we complied with the convention that they should not be mentioned, except that some of us, though I was not among them, maintained that they would rather be placed in the fourth than the second class. We paid little or indeed no attention to exam techniques. Nor can I remember looking at previous exam papers, much less calculating what questions were likely to occur – a deplorable practice I encountered later when teaching at Oxford, especially amongst male undergraduates. Our vacation parties were very enjoyable, though looking back I rather regret that I did not also have the chance of going on some where dons were present, for apart from the intellectual stimulus they would have provided, the experience would probably have helped me to have a more natural, relaxed relationship with my tutors. Years later I saw what a traditional reading party could be like when I went as a wife on a New College party at Sea Toller and listened to the arguments of philosophers.

My social life at Oxford was supplemented by outside contacts, the most important of which were Raisley Moorsom, of whom I have written in the previous chapter, Philip Noel-Baker, and Bill Montagu-Pollock. I had been very taken by Noel-Baker when I met him in Geneva in 1932. He stood for much that I admired. As a conscientious objector he had served in the Friends Ambulance Unit in the Great War and thereafter devoted his life to preventing international conflicts. He was particularly keen to end the private manufacture of and trade in arms. After Geneva we corresponded from time to time and met again two years later when he came to lecture in Oxford. After a romantic evening together, I wrote to say I was in love with him. In reply he assured me of his love, but at the same time he was obviously alarmed by what he had set alight in me, saying he was old enough to be my father and that he was a very happily married man with the most wonderful wife to whom he could not bear to be disloyal. This was an odd way of describing his marriage, for he is said later to have told Megan Lloyd George, with whom he had a long and passionate love affair, that the marriage had been a mistake from the start (1915), had never been enriched by love, and had been kept going only by conscious and strenuous efforts.[14] His wife, Irene Noel, who was ten years older than him, spent a lot of time looking after her estates in Greece, whilst Phil worked in Geneva and London. She constantly complained that he neglected her and their son, and accused him of social dilettantism and philandering. He was in her view deceitful, evasive, and inconsistent.[15] I knew little of this in the nineteen-thirties when we used to meet from time to time to spend the evening dancing, though he told me never to contact him at their London home.

For me our relationship was a great pleasure. I valued his affection, though I never fancied I was central to his life. Moreover I admired his passionate belief in the League of Nations at a time when many people were losing faith in it. I did not consider him a silly idealist for believing that the machinery of the League could prevent wars if governments really wished to use it. I do not propose to pass any judgement on his relations with his wife and mistress, details of which have emerged recently. Those who think one cannot love several people at once, will condemn him as insincere and deceitful, but I think the story shows him as emotionally complex and confused rather than caddish and dishonourable. To me in his political and public life he remains a character of rare nobility. I saw him seldom after the late thirties, and slightly regret not to have acted on his suggestion in 1980 that I should visit him in the House of Lords to talk about the times we had spent together, which he remembered with amazing vividness and obvious pleasure.

During the Christmas vacation of my second year at Oxford (1933), I went to stay in Belgrade with Prue and her husband, Bill Montagu-Pollock. My school friend Katherine Pass came out with me. The experience of travelling out third class on hard wooden seats in a slow train which got bogged down in the snow on the great Yugoslav plain added to the excitement of my first visit to the Balkans. I was totally unprepared for the contrast they offered to the conditions in the West: stations with no platforms, atrocious roads, decrepit cars, people with sacking on their feet instead of

[14] See Mervyn Jones, *A Radical Life*, 1991, p. 269.
[15] See David J. Whittaker, *A Fighter for Peace*, 1989.

shoes, houses which appeared to be made of cardboard like a Potemkin village. That I should have found all this primitive is not astounding, but looking back I am shocked and amazed by my crude reactions to the 'natives'. In letters home I described them as 'wild uncouth creatures', 'scarcely anything but animals', whereas in fact they were perfectly harmless friendly peasants. When on an expedition down south we stayed at the Trepja Mines, run by a British company, I was relieved to be back amongst 'civilised people'.

In Belgrade I met Serbian artists, including the famous sculptor Rosandić. This was particularly interesting as my parents owned one of his bas-reliefs. Otherwise my time was filled by often amusing, informal gatherings with other diplomats and members of the royal family, including Princess Marina, soon to marry the Duke of Kent. At one of these events I had a long serious argument about international affairs with the Minister in charge of our Legation. I found him an unattractive character, and was particularly shocked by his cynicism about the League of Nations. He seemed to me not to understand the principles underlying collective security which he described as 'a forlorn hope'. I now realise that this man was none other than the notorious Sir Neville Henderson who, as British ambassador in Berlin from 1937–9, made friendly gestures towards the Nazi regime and laboured on behalf of the controversial policy of 'appeasement'. However, recent history suggests that he was right in thinking that Yugoslavia could only be held together as a state if governed dictatorially, as it was then by King Alexander.

Throughout my visit Prue and Bill were in high spirits and we all got on well together. He was in no way a typical diplomat, being very unconventional, questioning all received ideas, and more interested in music and art than in politics or foreign affairs.

The next year (1934) they moved to Vienna and again invited me to stay, but this time Prue would not be there, as she planned to spend the summer in England. She wrote pressing me to keep Bill company while she was away; otherwise he would be lonely. He wrote too and offered to pay my fare. I was attracted by the idea, particularly because it would enable me (as it did) to explore Austria, but I had qualms about Prue's attitude, wondering whether she really did want me to come or was just saying she did in order to comply with Bill's wishes. I was also unsure about going, as I felt culturally inadequate in his company. I had never before met anyone who preferred the works of Bartok, Berg and Webern to those of Mozart, Beethoven and Schubert. However Prue was sure I could cope, so I agreed to go. The result I suppose could have been predicted: I was fascinated by Bill and fell completely under his spell. We had an idyllic two months together. These included an interesting trip down south to Carinthia to gauge the extent of Nazi feeling after the rising of July,[16] and a beautiful, leisurely drive back to England through Switzerland and France. Inevitably on our return I suffered, as I knew I would, by having to surrender Bill to Prue, but we were very careful not to cause her any distress. Indeed even if she had known everything, I doubt whether she would have minded, as she did not in principle disapprove of extra-marital affairs, and Bill assured me their relations had not been harmed in any way. Odd though it may seem, I think this was true. In fact Prue, with her generous, romantic nature, seemed almost pleased that he was so fond of me. They pressed me several times to come and stay again whether or not Prue was to be there, but I did not go until Christmas 1935. The visit was not a success from my point of view: Prue was there all the time and I did not usually enjoy the diplomatic parties or if I did, I was, being by then a communist, ridiculously afraid of becoming 'more bourgeois than ever', as I wrote to a friend – so little confidence had I in my integrity. Prue spent the war years in England with her two delightful children whilst Bill was in Stockholm. She asked Bill to divorce her, which he did, and in due course they both remarried.

I also had the good luck during my time at Oxford to get to know Douglas Jay. I met him through a Somerville friend, Peggy Garnett, who became his wife. Douglas was then a Fellow of All Souls, working on the *Economist*. I was immediately attracted by his trenchant, original mind and benefited, as indeed I have all my life, from discussions with him on political and economic matters. Moreover I admired his unusual degree of public spirit, shown in unstinting work for what he believed in. This has enabled me to tolerate what his friend Goronwy Rees described as 'a wild streak

[16] Dollfuss, the anti-socialist Chancellor of Austria, had been murdered by the Nazis on 25 July in an ill-planned attempt at a coup by which the *Anschluss* with Germany would be established.

of personal eccentricity'. One of his unusual characteristics was not to worry much, if indeed at all, about the impression he made on other people, some of whom were understandably critical of his life-style and of his tenaciously held political views. As these coincided broadly with mine, I had no problem, and was able to appreciate his friendship and tremendous loyalty.

The Warden of New College at this time was the historian and politician H.A.L. Fisher. As he knew my father, and his daughter Mary was at Somerville with me, I was occasionally invited to the Lodgings. I found the Sunday teas with undergraduates rather a strain and was relieved when at 5.30 p.m. Mrs Fisher would clap her hands and tell us all to leave; but, though nervous, I greatly enjoyed the dinner parties full of eminent guests. It was here that I first met the philosopher Isaiah Berlin, whose conversation I found so dazzling that, already in an excited state, I was almost reduced to hysterics. Some time later he invited me to lunch at All Souls, where he was a Fellow. Thus began one of the most important friendships of my life.

In my last Easter vacation I went with my father on a Hellenic cruise, despite warnings from my tutors that a three week break from academic work would adversely affect my performance in Finals. I felt the offer was too good to refuse: I had not been to Greece before, and I could go at half price as my father was to be one of the lecturers. Sir Henry Lunn, the founder of the Hellenic Travellers Club, had assembled an impressive array of guests and speakers. They included Harold Nicolson, Vita Sackville-West, Stanley Casson, Hugh Walpole, Sir Richard Livingstone, and Dr Cyril Norwood. I was disappointed to find Vita Sackville-West unapproachable, as, according to a letter I wrote to a friend, she was 'fully occupied with her strange little companion – Harold's sister – who always clung to her skirts and sat in her pocket.' I managed occasionally to talk to Nicolson, alarming though he was. Their son, Nigel, I reported, looked by contrast remarkably ordinary, and seemed preoccupied by reading about the abduction of Charles Lindbergh's son, who was much in the news at that time. 'Norwood,' I wrote, 'didn't speak to anyone – not much to their regret though, and Hugh Walpole made up by vulgar and popular remarks on every occasion.' I was also critical of the ubiquitous Canon Wigram, who adorned his talks at the sites with slightly seamy anecdotes which verged on the pornographic. Stanley Casson disconcerted his audience by suggesting that the famous statue of Hermes by the Greek sculptor Praxiteles was in fact a Roman copy.

When the ship got stuck on a sandbank at the entrance to the gulf of Corinth, Harold Nicolson whiled away the boring hours by giving us an impromptu talk about Byron, pointing out the site of Missolonghi. This mishap lead to a comic incident, for when the efforts made to refloat the boat were at first ineffective, all the passengers were asked to stand on one side of the deck and, at a given signal, to jump. We lost two days in Greece but were still able on the way home to visit Taormina, Pompei and Rome. The whole experience of this cruise was wonderfully thrilling and enlightening, and there can be no doubt that my decision to go was correct. My father too enjoyed it, though he showed some resistance to moving about in a large group and preferred reading Herodotus to socialising.

Many people when reflecting on their time at Oxford describe it as 'a great experience' which opened doors on a wider world, but I cannot write about my undergraduate days in quite such dramatic and ecstatic terms. I was already familiar with the beauties of the place having lived there on and off for two years before coming up, and I was used to the company of academics, several of whom were visitors to my home. This is not to say that my three years as an undergraduate were not of great importance in my life, above all because I became more aware of my intellectual limitations and learnt to admit my own ignorance or lack of understanding. But I could have got more out of my time at Oxford if I had been more involved in University clubs and activities, and had had a wider circle of friends.

It was during this period that I took the momentous decision to have my hair cut short. I describe it thus because as a teenager I had rather fine long thick plaits of an unusually attractive red colour. When I left school I was forced to put my hair up, in compliance with the entrenched convention of those days. I found this experience traumatic, as it symbolised the end of childhood. There were also practical problems: it was hard to prevent the coils into which the hair was twined from falling down, and I never felt at ease with these rather ugly cumbersome constructions. So, encouraged mainly by Bill Pollock, I rushed off one day in 1933 without warning anyone and had it bobbed, leaving the glorious tresses at the hairdresser's. My mother was devastated, and others lamented my action, as can be seen from the following sonnet penned by H.W.B. Joseph.

> The angry Sarah, who, to vex her lord,
> Cut from her head the tresses he adored,
> Yet left them where, when they had stabbed his eyes,
> He still could make of them a secret prize.
> Thee, who by wider-glancing malice driven,
> And on a barber's business hand bestowed
> What once delighted all on whom it glowed,
> Thee shall I dare, who hast this way designed
> To show thy scorn embraces all mankind,
> Still to approach as if thou wert a friend,
> And hitherward entreat thy steps to bend?
> But, if perchance such deed may still be done,
> I pray thee come on Sunday week at one.

Sarah was the early eighteenth century Duchess of Marlborough, the profusion of whose fine hair was said to be the delight of numerous admirers.

How much happier in this respect I would have been if born in a later generation when these dilemmas would not have arisen.

5

Communist

In the summer of 1935 after coming down from Oxford I joined the Communist Party of Great Britain. I have often been asked, especially since the full horror of Stalinism was revealed, how I could have done such a thing. I will explain. The immediate occasion of my joining was the experience of living in a camp for the unemployed organised by the National Unemployed Workers Movement which was, though I did not know it at the time, largely under communist control. I went there at the suggestion of a girl I knew in college. The ostensible purpose of the camp was to give the unemployed a holiday in pleasant rural surroundings, but the organisers no doubt hoped it would provide an opportunity to extend support for the Party. The people attending were a curious mixture of Welsh miners and residents of the East End of London, with a sprinkling of Oxford students. The miners sang beautifully and their leader, Arthur Horner, talked impressively.

I found the whole experience deeply moving, not only because of what I learnt about the lives of those less fortunate than myself. What affected me most was realising to my astonishment that I could relate easily to working-class people. They thought I was odd of course. They teased me for saying things like 'There are three reasons for doing something, a, b, and c', and they could not understand why I received a spate of telegrams when my Finals' results came out, but they accepted me as a product of my bourgeois background and class without envy or contempt. No pressure was put on me to join the Communist Party, but by the end of my stay I was coming to feel that it was the natural thing to do. I was impressed by the tremendous sense of solidarity which the bond of the Party produced among many of the campers, and, perhaps more important, I had an affair with one of them. He was the camp's cook, so he conveniently had a tent to himself. I spent such a large part of the day and night with him that the organisers became worried and suggested that I should mix more with others. My lover, Tom Day, was a six foot tall unemployed milk roundsman from London, much older than me. After I left the camp for a holiday in Cornwall, we corresponded throughout the summer; and in the autumn he settled in Oxford where I was living with my parents for a year whilst preparing for the Civil Service exam. The Party gave him work selling the *Daily Worker* and organising various activities. I used to visit him in his lodgings where I met other working class Party members. I was particularly impressed by Abe Lazarus, a highly intelligent Morris worker, much involved in Oxford politics. I enjoyed this novel and rather exciting life, but I became worried as I came to realise that I meant more to Tom than he did to me. I was, he wrote, 'the finest girl he had met since he could remember'. I was '100 percent'. He saw himself making a new start in Oxford with 'a really wonderful girl'. He had had a hard life, separated from his wife, unemployed for quite a time, and in indifferent health owing to stomach troubles, but with me life would be 'a cake walk'. Previously he had not thought it possible for a bourgeois person to be nice. We didn't discuss marriage, but I think he supposed our relationship would be permanent, whereas I knew instinctively it could not last. Apart from the bond of Party, our interests and experiences were too divergent; the cultural gap was too wide. I decided after some months to stop seeing him, but I recoiled from the embarrassment of telling him this. What to do? At this juncture the Party came to my assistance because, having decided that I should be a secret Party member in the Civil Service if I got in, they saw security risks in my association with well known communists in Oxford. They didn't forbid me to see Tom, but in a rather disgraceful way I used their attitude as an excuse not to see him. He was very indignant and complained that 'the movement' neglected his and my personal feelings. He wouldn't accept the situation 'when the one woman who has done so much for me and who I think so much of shall be just a name and address whom I write long letters to'. I was 'a tonic to him', but he was also thinking of what was good for me in relation to the Party. However I remained adamant, saying that the situation was causing me much anxiety. There was some truth in this, but I fear I exaggerated the difficulties in order to make a break.

I was clearly in a rather confused state during the year 1935–6, torn between working-class and bourgeois cultures. This is apparent not only from Tom's numerous letters, of which two dozen survive, but also from the correspondence I had with some of the other campers. We wrote to each other in very friendly terms for a time. There was even talk of their coming to stay near my family home in Cornwall to visit me. It is not clear whether this was their idea or mine. In either case, if it had come off, there would have been embarrassing problems. I used to complain to them about having to live in a bourgeois household where the class struggle was not understood. They would sympathise with me for the rough time I was having, and would praise me for the wonderful effort I had made to understand the capitalist system and to emancipate myself from bourgeois influences. One of them tried to persuade me to abandon the idea of becoming a civil servant and instead to leave home and take up nursing, working with her as a midwife in London. She was sure I would love the life.

Some psychologists and sociologists have explained the attraction which communist parties had for middle-class persons by their neurotic needs. Thus Gabriel A. Almond in *Types of Communism* (1951) writes that 'emotional conflict and maladjustment appear to be especially significant factors affecting susceptibility [to communism] among middle class Americans and Englishmen' (p. xi), and that many of his respondents displayed 'neurotic hostility i.e. chronic antagonism and need for dominance in personal relations' (p. 255). He does however admit that joining the Party had a kind of plausibility for quite 'normal' intellectuals in the early 1930s, as capitalism appeared to be doomed. It is difficult to determine how far neurotic deviance was a factor in my susceptibility to communism, but it is clear that I was hyper-critical of aspects of standard middle-class family life and that I saw communism as a rejection of these. For instance at a trivial level this would have meant eating in the kitchen instead of in the dining room. Some of my student Party friends were also critical of the deadness of their bourgeois homes, contrasting this with the vitality of life in the camp for the unemployed, but they did not all go as far as me in pooh-poohing comfort and cleanliness. Thus one of them, Peter du

Sautoy, wrote to me in November 1935 when he was moving into a better lodging: 'I expect you think I am a fool to think about being comfortable and clean, but I cannot help the fact that I am in bondage to the bourgeois standard of living to which I have been accustomed.'

Apart from the tensions produced by these rather peripheral issues, there were other problems created by the kind of double existence in which I was living at this time. For on the one hand I was studying hard – history, politics and economics – and greatly enjoying the company of Oxford intellectuals with some of whom I had close personal relations. On the other hand I kept contact with the very different world of the politically committed but poorly educated working class. I was slow to make the break. Indeed I was still corresponding with Tom in the summer of 1936, but all contact ceased after it was announced that I had succeeded in the Civil Service exam.

My reasons for becoming a communist were not wholly emotional and personal. Around this time I read and was influenced by John Middleton Murry's book *The Necessity of Communism*, written in the autumn of 1931. Murry accepted much in Marxism: capitalism involved conflicts, so class warfare existed; competitive capitalism and economic individualism involved ghastly inhumanity to the exploited; we should expedite the historically necessary process in which we were involved. But he thought Marxism had been degraded both in England and Russia by Leninism. He was fiercely critical of Russian communism and of its irresponsible, sentimental sympathisers in other countries who overlooked the inhuman horrors it had perpetrated. So he argued for an English brand of communism which would be humane and not involve a bloody revolution. There should be a revolution in the sense of complete economic change – the extirpation of the system of individualistic capitalism – but this was to be effected by peaceful and legal means, not by a Communist Party nor by the existing Labour Party which he despised. The tool was to be a Labour Party permeated by Marxists.

So my intention on joining the Communist Party was to commit myself to fostering a civilised brand of communism which believed in individual freedom and humane policies. This was undoubtedly naive of me, as most British communists saw the Soviet Union as their ideal, and the Soviet policy of collectivisation and elimination of the kulaks was far from humane. But I felt it was necessary to belong to an organised, structured group if I was to be effective in changing the world, which I passionately wanted to do, for, as Murry pointed out, in the capitalist world individuals, even if humane and decent, were impotent. Indeed I was impressed by the contrast between membership of the Labour and Communist Parties: in the CP every member was important and was assigned a role. This was no doubt partly due to the great disparity in the size of the membership of the two parties – there were in 1935 only 7,000 members of the CPGB as contrasted with 420,000 in the Labour Party – but it also reflected differences in the intensity of their commitment to the cause. Moreover I felt CP members had, with Marxism, a coherent social and economic theory, and a deeper understanding of the capitalist system than Labour Party supporters who deceived themselves about the possibility of making radical changes.

I was also influenced by Barbara Wootton's book, *Plan or No Plan*, published in 1934 and read by me in 1935. She had visited Russia in 1932 with a group of educationalists. She did not have the wool pulled over her eyes as Beatrice and Sidney Webb did later, and she was particularly critical of the Russians' reluctance to recognise shades of goodness or badness, of success or failure. But the book provides a thorough, balanced, undoctrinaire analysis of the achievements and possibilities of planned as contrasted with unplanned economies. It also sets out the conditions of successful economic planning in a democratic country. I was particularly impressed by her belief that the authorities in a planned economy could eliminate our kind of unemployment if they wanted to. She later described the book as 'essentially the work of a democratic socialist, of a liberal mind'.[17] I found equally persuasive the case for some degree of economic planning put forward by Arthur Salter in his book *The Framework of an Ordered Society* (1933), even though his concern was to find an alternative to communism and fascism as well as to unregulated *laissez-faire*.

One authority on British communist intellectuals (Neal Wood, *Communism of British Intellectuals*, 1959), considers that those of

[17] *In a World I Never Made*, 1967, p. 83.

the 1930s who were educated in the 1920s 'came to politics suddenly with little previous political interest or experience' (p. 106). This may be true of some of them, but in my case becoming a communist did not involve a sudden awakening of interest in public affairs. They had made an impact on me from an early age. Thus at five years old I was taken to the Home Office in Whitehall to watch from a window the massive celebration of the Armistice on 11 November 1919. It would be absurd to suggest that I understood its significance, but I think something about the horror of war rubbed off on me. This was reinforced a few years later when my parents took me to see the devastated areas of northern France and some of the endless war cemeteries – a most distressing experience. The impact of the Great War on the French was also evident at school. Several of the teachers at our Lycée in the early twenties were *Veuves de Guerre* dressed gloomily in black, and history lessons often centred on the war. Then in 1929 I saw R.C. Sheriff's famous play *Journey's End* which depicted the realities of war in the trenches. This moved me profoundly, as did a lecture at my English school in 1930 about Toc H, a Christian charity founded after the war to help ex-servicemen. My diary records: 'He [the lecturer] tells us such frightfully painful things about the war. I feel entirely inspired and more confirmed against war than ever. Though the men were so terribly brave and marvellous, God did not make them to be thrown away like that.'

My parents were not pacifists, but my father, an international lawyer, devoted much of his life to working out means to prevent wars, by getting disputes between nations solved without the use of force. I was very fond of him and he was an important influence in my life for many years. He saw the League of Nations as a novel and important institution based as it was on a belief in the collective system. He defined this in his book *Some Aspects of the Covenant of the League of Nations* (1934) as 'an organisation by which the whole international collectivity is actively concerned in the maintenance of the rights and, perhaps, the enforcement of the duties of States'. He took part in several arbitrations before the Permanent Court of Justice at the Hague, one of which I attended. The motto on his bookplate '*Lege lege pacem*' (By Law garner Peace) neatly sums up his ideal.

At home the adults' conversation was often about international affairs. My father thought the reparations clauses of the Treaty of Versailles were unrealistic and that French policy during much of this period was profoundly mistaken. I can remember his coming home to lunch when the French invaded the Ruhr in 1923, fulminating with anger at what he considered an illegal action. In current events classes at school at age 15 I felt superior to the rest of the form because I considered that I knew it all already. At least I acknowledged in my diary that this was bad for me 'as it is only Daddy's cleverness'. When musing early in 1930 over what career to aim at, I contemplated in turn architecture, farming in order to remedy the deplorable state of English agriculture, and town planning in order to tackle the slums; but I finally settled on international affairs. I thought this not so good as the other careers 'from God's eyes', and I was not sure what exactly a woman could do in this line, but my deep interest in disarmament, the League of Nations and international law enabled me to overcome these doubts.

I was also very much affected by my sojourn in League of Nations' circles in Geneva in 1932 at the time of the Disarmament Conference. Many people all over the world saw this conference as the climax of the efforts made during the last ten years to get a general reduction of armaments. It was widely thought that the armaments race which had preceded the First World War was the greatest single element in making that disaster inevitable, and the Covenant of the League of Nations recognised the need to reduce national armaments to the lowest point consistent with national security, in order to achieve international peace. It was also felt in some quarters that it was wrong and unwise to expect Germany to limit her armaments, as required by the Treaty of Versailles, if other countries were left free to maintain their armaments at higher levels. Although the campaign for disarmament was ultimately unsuccessful, in 1935 when I joined the Communist Party I was still a committed supporter of the League of Nations, its machinery and all it stood for, but I felt that international communism would also assist in the prevention of wars, for if the working men of all countries united, as recommended in the Communist Manifesto of 1848, they would not fight each other. Moreover Russia had become a member of the League in 1934.

Whilst quite young I also became a little aware of some social problems. Thus when we travelled, as we did every year, from Paris to Cornwall, we hired one of the many unemployed men who thronged the quay at Southampton to push our large volume of luggage from the docks to the railway station, and as we walked through the streets I was worried by the sight of groups of lean, depressed looking men standing about aimlessly. And in the 1930s I was, when motoring, constantly reminded about poverty by the sight of tramps on the roads, moving from one workhouse to the next, probably twenty five miles away. It was at this time too that, driving through Lancashire to get to the Lakes, my eyes were opened to some of the environmental horrors created in the Industrial Revolution.

Another vivid memory is visiting some London slums in 1930. I can still visualise a woman living in a completely underground dark, damp basement, rather like a coal- hole. I went with a group from my school on the initiative of a remarkable person, Lady Stewart, whom I grew to admire, as although widowed in middle age and left with seven children, she worked untiringly on housing problems in St Pancras, having failed to get into Parliament as a Liberal in 1929. I was also from time to time worried, though only a little I am afraid, by the employment conditions of our servants at home. Their pay was low, their hours long, and, worst of all, they had very little freedom, being virtually tied to the house except for a short half-day off once a week. Even if they were allowed an occasional Sunday afternoon off, they did not escape preparing and clearing up meals for the family. For my mother did not share my worries; indeed she once suggested to my father that we should have more people to stay, as 'it would be good to give the maids a little more to do'.

It was not, I think, the habit in my youth, as it is now, for school children to get some insight into social problems by actually doing voluntary social work e.g. with the mentally handicapped or the elderly, but we had occasional lectures about social and missionary work at home and abroad, and we were encouraged to do voluntary social work when we left school. Girl Guides was also seen as a way of involving us in helping less fortunate people. I interpreted this as trying to discipline ten excruciatingly naughty little boys with a view to enrolling them as Cubs. The result of this ethos at school was to make me resolve to improve the 'spirits and morals' of our village in Cornwall. I wished to reinvigorate the local library, to start up Guides, to enliven the Church choir, and to improve the bell-ringing. Nothing came of any of these rather priggish and absurd resolutions.

At our school's mock general election in 1929, I supported the Liberal candidate, Lady Stewart's daughter Marjorie, backing Lloyd George's manifesto *We Can Conquer Unemployment*. I gave a speech on Free Trade, being, according to the school magazine, much troubled by hecklers. However a few months later I confided to my diary, after listening to a sermon about not being 'stuck up', that I thought I would become Labour, 'for why should some be rich and others suffer in poverty? It seems quite ridiculous. All men equal.' But my egalitarianism weakened a year later when, in the summer of 1930 after going to the Eton and Harrow cricket match at Lords, I was dazzled by what I saw as the virtues of the aristocracy. They impressed me as dignified, well organised and law-abiding, so I felt it was right that they should rule until the lower classes were properly educated. The whole social scene also induced in me unusual pride in the English who alone, I thought, could behave so admirably. These perhaps rather curious sentiments did not override my very real concern about the growing number of unemployed, for at the same time I wrote an article in the school magazine on *The Problem of Unemployment*, recommending drastic action by the Government.

I do not wish to suggest that as a teenager my life was dominated by political, social and economic problems. For one reference to such matters in my diary, there are dozens to the issues which were clearly of far greater concern to me, viz. my obsessive desire to get into various sporting teams, morbid analysis of my character, centering on why I was not more popular, and passionate declarations of love for a succession of girls and teachers. Nevertheless there is evidence of recurrent interest in a wider world, of a social conscience, and of simple ambitions to change what I felt was wrong. However when I joined the Communist Party a few years later, I had had little political experience, apart from that provided by the University Liberal Club and the League of Nations Union. Nor did I as an undergraduate from 1932–5 do any social work except for occasional pathetic efforts to entertain groups of working-class girls on outings organised by the Women's University

Settlement. The aim of the Settlement movement, which started in the 1880s, was to establish centres where University graduates would reside, working among the poor in their spare time, offering art, music and education as well as material help and advice, in order to achieve mutual knowledge and respect between the classes. But I found it difficult on these visits to foster this aim. On the contrary the cultural gap between us was sharply revealed and seemed to me unbridgeable, for when trying to make conversation, I asked one of the girls by which route they had come to Oxford, meaning was it via Henley or High Wycombe, and she answered 'By Cutex and Odorono', referring to the factories which made nail polish and anti-perspirants.

What did I do as a member of the Communist Party? The answer is 'Nothing'. The only specific task assigned to me was Christopher Hill's suggestion that I should recruit Isaiah Berlin as a member, but I knew him well enough to realise this would be impossible although he was friendly with several Party members e.g. Norman O. Brown and Bill Davies. Otherwise I was told by the Party to stay in the League of Nations Union and the International Student Service to which I belonged, and to do anything useful I could there. I saw no way of making my membership of these bodies helpful to the Party.

For at least a year before I became a communist I had decided to try to join the Civil Service. As a result of seeing in the camp the effects of unemployment and poverty at close quarters, and being ignorant of the Party's technique of permeation, I wondered whether I should do some sort of social work rather than become a civil servant. But student friends in the Party said I would be more effective by going into the Civil Service as a secret Party member. I was unclear what, if anything, I as a civil servant would do for the British Communist Party, but I think I supposed that I would occasionally pass them useful information. There were at that time no security checks on candidates for the Civil Service, so my politics were not vetted, and I was not involved in any deception. As I did well in the exam, I was able to choose which Department I wanted to work in. Still ignorant of my role as what has become known as a 'mole', I told the Civil Service Commission that I would like the Ministry of Agriculture and Fisheries as I had strong views about the Government's agricultural policies: quotas and tariffs restricting imports from abroad and the payment of subsidies to British farmers. The Commission presumably took no line on these measures, but they clearly thought the Ministry of Agriculture was an inferior concern; so I next chose the Ministry of Labour, where I imagined I could help the unemployed. The Commission frowned on this idea also, and said I should go into one of the great departments of State like the Home Office. This amusingly enough coincided with the advice being given me at the same time by the Party. So the Home Office it was, and I was welcomed there by my father's old colleagues and friends, for he had worked in the Aliens Branch of the Home Office during the war.

During my first year or so in the Civil Service, I had occasional meetings, probably about six altogether, with an anonymous Party member whose job it was, I suppose, to keep an eye on me. I think these meetings took place mainly in 1937, though as I kept no diary I cannot be certain. To begin with my 'contact' was an Englishman, later a foreigner. The latter, I now feel fairly certain, was hoping to recruit me as a Soviet agent, though this was never mentioned. When we met he went to great lengths to ensure that we were not followed. This, rather ludicrously, once entailed changing taxis *en route* to a restaurant. At first I was amused by the cloak-and-dagger atmosphere he generated, but I very soon felt uncomfortable and stopped meeting him. I particularly disliked the fact that he questioned me about my private life, which I was not prepared to discuss. I was told that there were other communists in the Civil Service, but that I would not be put in touch with them at any rate at present. I was also told, much to my relief, that the Party would not expect me to do anything for ten years. I was simply to appear respectable and to get really well accepted by my department. So I wore a broad-brimmed black hat and walked into the office every day ostentatiously carrying *The Times*. It was also suggested that I should take part in some of the department's social activities; so I joined the Musical Society and sang in the chorus.

I am often asked when I ceased to be a Party member. It is impossible to say, as the process of severance was gradual. There was no exact moment when I resigned from the Party, or tore up my Party card as I had never had one. I just petered out and no one in the Party did anything about this. Certainly by 1939 and indeed probably earlier I no longer regarded myself as a communist.

Several things contributed to my falling off. Being a secret member did not suit me. One of the attractions of belonging to the party was the camaraderie it involved with other communists, but of this I was deprived and left to struggle alone in my bed-sitter with the books I had been told to read: the massive *Handbook of Marxism*, done by Emile Burns, and T.A. Jackson's incomprehensible *Dialectics, the Logic of Marxism*. At one rash moment I moved into the house of a Party member, a friend called Margaret Stewart who had a spare room because her boy-friend was fighting in Spain. The milieu was delightful, but I was soon told by the Party that this was not on: the Security Services would be on my tracks. So I moved out. I occasionally met socially some of my old Oxford friends who belonged to the Party, like Bernard Floud, Wendy Charles, Peter du Sautoy and Philip Toynbee, but most of my friends were not communists, just left-wing in various degrees. They included Douglas and Peggy Jay, Arnold Pilkington, Roger Quirk, Guy Chilver, Philip Noel-Baker, Thomas Balogh, and most important of all Herbert Hart with whom I was living from the summer of 1937 onwards. He was strongly opposed to communism both as theory and practice and thought my involvement with the Party was a silly product of immaturity. Discussions about politics with these friends strengthened my growing dislike of the pressure to conform which was imposed on Party members. I personally was not much irked by Party discipline as I had little to do with the bureaucracy, but I was uneasy when I saw applied the rule that one could not question things once the Party line had been settled, and I disliked the facile way people were called 'social fascists' if they deviated from or criticised the Party line.

Another and important factor which accounted for my apostasy was disquiet about the Soviet trials and the failure of the British Communist Party to protest against them. The trials resulted in the conviction and death of many old Bolsheviks, high ranking Party members, army officers and others who were alleged to be traitors, spies and wreckers, engaged in a vast treasonable conspiracy in conjuction with the intelligence services of hostile foreign countries.

I will digress to explain why I and other Party members did not become disillusioned sooner and defect at once. Indeed membership of the British Communist Party increased by 50% between 1936 and 1939. To understand our frame of mind one must go back to

1933. From then onwards we were deeply alarmed by the spread of fascist ideas and in particular the rise to power of Hitler in Germany, and we felt that only the methods of the Comintern – the Communist International – could provide effective resistance to fascism both at home and abroad.[18] The Party's policy of a united or popular front adopted in the 1930s represented a welcome reversal of the previous line issuing from Moscow which had attacked social democracy as the chief support of fascism. Now the class struggle was suspended and all allies were welcomed by the British CP, which even offered support to the League of Nations.

When the news of the first trial – of Zinoviev and Kamenev – came through in August 1936, the Spanish Civil War had just begun, and it continued during the trials of 1937 and 1938. Spain at this time was central to any left-wing activist. Who was helping Spain? Russia. And who was against Spain? Germany and Italy. Many British communists were fighting with the International Brigade, and a great many of them were killed.

Unease about the trials was expressed by some organs of the British press, but it was difficult to believe that a state could really perpetrate falsehoods on such a vast scale, and difficult to reject outright the Russian version of events as a complete fabrication. Many of us were genuinely puzzled. The prestige of the Socialist State was high; the new constitution of 1936 was reassuring. Most of the accused had pleaded guilty and it was not clear that their confessions were untrue even if they had been obtained by unwarrantable methods. Maybe, we felt, the case against them was exaggerated, but surely not false in every respect. Various British lawyers and journalists found the allegations convincing, as did the American Ambassador as late as March 1938. Even many on the non-communist left tempered their criticism of the trials, or put the best complexion they could on refractory events, if they did not ignore them completely. A great many people across a wide political spectrum were primarily concerned with opposing the National Government's appeasement policy: Hitler's march into Austria in March 1938 seemed more imporant than Bukharin's execution

[18] The Comintern was an association on which all national communist parties were represented.

three days later. It was common at this time for people who were not left wing to denounce totalitarianism as such, not distinguishing between the fascist and communist brands; but the Left argued that the ultimate objectives of communists were better than those of fascists. Even Leonard Woolf as late as 1939, though critical of the treason trials, preferred Stalin to Hitler.[19]

In passing judgement on those who were slow to be sceptical or critical of events in Russia in the second half of the 1930s, it is important to realise that no one then had any idea of the extent of what has become known as 'The Great Terror' or 'The Great Purge'. The Soviet authorities had given publicity to the trials, but they did not reveal that at the same time they were engaged in eliminating many millions of people either by shooting them outright or by sending them to their deaths in labour camps. The world did not hear about these horrendous events until much later – in the 1950s and '60s.

This is not to say that we did not know the regime was authoritarian (at the least) and far from being a liberal democracy on the Western model. As communists we answered critics of the Russian political system in various ways: we said that things would no doubt change in due course; that socialism or even communism did not necessitate dictatorship, and that a fairer social and economic system was more important than political democracy. To illustrate (though not to defend) our standpoint, I cite the following passage from a letter of September 1936 from a very intelligent friend of mine, then an official in the British Museum, who had recently been to Russia.

> I am quite confident in the country and its future, though while actually staying there I felt very anxious about many things. I began to feel more happy about it when I met and talked with Sir Bernard Pares [historian of Russia] on the boat coming back: he seemed to understand it all very clearly and to be quite convinced of the value of what liberals call the Russian experiment, and what's more he appeared ready to give the credit not merely to Russians, whom he loves, but to communists, whom

[19] *Barbarians at the Gate*. Referred to by Duncan Wilson in his biography of Leonard Woolf, 1975, p. 195.

> he has no reason to love. I don't think I misunderstand him if I say that. There is another thing which I didn't realise till I got back here: that is, that all the things that one is inclined to be worried about, restrictions on liberty, a failure to reach our standards of taste in something or other – all the things, in fact, which don't fit in with our oh-so-well-educated lives – simply don't seem to a genuine worker as sources of trouble.

I resigned from the Civil Service at the end of 1947 in order to join my husband, Herbert Hart, in Oxford. In about 1962 I was approached by MI5 who asked if they could interview me, because they were studying communism in the 1930s. They had apparently only recently learnt that I had been a Party member. I agreed to see them and told them my story in full. I felt I had nothing to hide. They appeared to be particularly interested in the foreigner I had met in 1937. They showed me many photographs of individuals, but I was completely unable to identify him.

I was contacted again by MI5 in 1966, when there was a great deal of concern about the infiltration of communists into the Civil Service. I shared this concern, as I took the view that they could not be trusted. So I agreed to be interviewed. This turned out to be a long and rather nasty affair, the interviewers being Peter Wright (as in 1962) and another man. It was also very extraordinary. They produced a long list of people and asked me if I knew them. None of them to the best of my knowledge were communists. Some had been undergraduates with me at Somerville, others were colleagues in the Civil Service, others just friends or acquaintances. After the interview I felt worried. Was I inadvertently causing suspicion to be cast on these people because they knew me? I wrote to Wright to say that no conclusion whatever could be drawn from the fact that they knew me, and that I would hate to think any of them would have this irrelevant piece of information included in their dossiers. I was also annoyed that at the end of the interview one of the MI5 men commented on the fact that I occasionally sat on the Civil Service Final Selection Board. It was common for a few academics to do this, but after the interview I was never asked again. This may have been a coincidence, but was more likely due to a tip off by MI5, for according to Chapman Pincher, the journalist who used to talk with Wright, 'The security men were unconvinced' by my story.[20] Wright in his book *Spycatcher* (1987) does not say he was unconvinced. Instead he indulged in tasteless demeaning.

> Jennifer Hart [he writes] was a fussy, middle-class woman, too old, I thought, for the fashionably short skirt and white net stockings she was wearing. She told her story quite straightforwardly, but had a condescending, disapproving manner, as if she equated my interest in the left-wing politics of the 1930s with looking up ladies' skirts. To her it was rather vulgar and ungentlemanly. (p. 265).

Pincher's book (of 1981) did not mention me by name, but it was clear he was referring to me, although his account of my career in the Home Office was a travesty of the facts, particularly because it stated that I had been an active agent of the Soviet Union. I considered that was grossly libellous, but I decided not to take any action since I felt that the people who knew me would have known that there was no truth in the allegation.

The next year (1982) I again considered legal action against Pincher. There had been references to me in an article by Andrew Wilson in the *Observer* of 8 November 1981, which was inaccurate in a number of respects, and in a book by Nigel West, the Conservative MP, Rupert Allason.[21] West had sent me an excerpt from his manuscript to know whether it was accurate. He was clearly relying heavily on Pincher for his 'facts'. I wrote him a severe letter, pointing out that four of his statements were untrue, and that others were open to objection. West altered his text to meet most of my points, but he left in a reference to a discussion group of civil servants which I had occasionally attended, implying that it had been in some way engaged in illicit activities. In fact the group was of a Fabian type, and entirely innocuous. He also left in a reference to my husband and to the fact that he worked in MI5 during the war, although I had objected to this on the ground that it conveyed the misleading impression that he was somehow implicated in suspect activities.

That same year I was asked by Christopher Andrew, a Fellow of

[20] Chapman Pincher, *Their Trade is Treachery*, 1981, p. 165.
[21] *A Matter of Trust – MI5 1945–1972*, 1982.

Corpus Christi College, Cambridge, to take part in a television programme he was doing for the BBC about Intelligence in the 1930s. He said he was keen to get more historical programmes broadcast. I thought this was a laudable objective, and that my participation would enable me to answer the false allegations made against me by Pincher and others, and to prevent their repetition. The reverse in fact happened.

In my television interview, shown on 27 July 1983, I spoke frankly of my association with the Communist Party. Before it was broadcast the BBC issued various extremely misleading press releases which inspired several newspapers to publish articles saying that I was recruited by Moscow to act as a KGB agent whilst in the Home Office. The most damaging of these was one in *The Sunday Times* of 17 July by Simon Freeman and Barrie Penrose, headed 'I was Russian Spy, says MI5 Man's Wife'. The article included several references to my husband, implying that although he may have known of my 'activities' as a spy for the Soviet Union, he did nothing about this, and indeed that, working alongside Anthony Blunt in MI5 during the war, he might himself have been in some way involved in such activities. I was particularly annoyed with Freeman for writing this because he had rung me up beforehand and given me to understand that he (who had been a lodger in my house) wanted to defend me against the allegations made in the BBC press releases and to set the record straight. I explained to him frankly my ideological position in the 1930s, and he then used what I had said, which was, unknown to me, being taped, to damage my reputation. Herbert and I were naturally appalled by these articles and consulted our friend Lord Goodman who immediately issued a statement to the Press denying the truth of the accusations.

We then took legal advice from Peter Carter-Ruck, the leading libel lawyer. He was clear *The Sunday Times* article was grossly libellous of us both and thought that we could get substantial damages if we sued them. We therefore started proceedings against the paper. We asked them to publish a full apology which we drafted and to pay us damages. An acrimonious correspondence ensued during which *The Sunday Times* argued that as I had admitted being a 'mole' and a 'sleeper' (not terms I had used), it was reasonable to describe me as a 'spy'. They also defended their reference to Herbert on the ground that the extent of his knowledge of my connection with the Communist Party was 'a matter of the utmost public interest'. In the end they published on 18 September 1983 a very brief and wholly inadequate apology. We contemplated taking the matter further, but finally decided not to go to trial. Several considerations prompted this decision. Our legal costs, already huge, were mounting rapidly, and we could not risk the financial consequences of losing the case. Although the article contained a grave and damaging libel, it seemed possible, given the climate of opinion at the time, that we might not win. For there had been tremendous public concern about communist infiltration into government departments and the security services since the Burgess/MacLean affair in the 1950s, followed by the exposure of Kim Philby, Anthony Blunt and others. Much had been published of a sensational and alarming character, suggesting that rings of spies had been operating. Herbert would undoubtedly have stood up well to cross-questioning in court, making it clear that he had always been strongly opposed to communism, that he joined MI5 (in 1940) two years after I had become disillusioned, and that although he was a colleague of Blunt's during the war, he had no reason to suspect that he was behaving improperly.

But doubts began to grow about how convincing my story would look when subject to hostile questioning. I would have tried to give a picture of the reasons which induced me and many other students and intellectuals to join the Communist Party in the 1930s, emphasising our concern about unemployment, and our hostility to fascism and war, especially to old-type wars just for national interests. I would have explained that one could be a member of the British Communist Party without being a Russian agent; that when I went into the Home Office I had no intention of being a Soviet spy, and that I did not agree to become one, although it seemed, looking back, that efforts were made to recruit me. Would this have looked plausible to a jury many of whom would probably not have known much about the 1930s, but who would have been influenced by the anti-communist atmosphere generated by the 'Cold War' between the West and the Soviet Union and by the panic about Russian spies in recent years?

Another reason for giving up proceedings was Herbert's health. Things were getting on top of him. He was already in a state of neurotic worry (totally groundless) about certain income tax matters, when subjected to the strain of the case. We had been harassed by press photographers surrounding our house and waylaying us in the street. The result was that he had a serious nervous breakdown in the autumn of 1983. We had received wonderful letters of support from friends and colleagues, many of them pillars of the Establishment. They were even complimentary about the TV programme which they considered a real contribution to getting the record straight about Communist Party membership in the 1930s, pointing out that this had sinister implications only for those who regarded past membership as a crime of which the guilt is never expiated.

So why had it all gone wrong? No doubt the fundamental reason was, as Isaiah Berlin wrote to me, that I should have known better. I should have been aware that the Press wanted to 'throw intellectuals to the lions of the political pornography-hungry public'. He admired me for being wedded to principles, 'odd though some of them were'; but precipitate action had got me into hot water. Berlin quoted Bishop Wilberforce who when asked why he was called 'Soapy Sam' answered 'Because I am always in hot water and my hands are always clean.' Samuel Wilberforce was an extremely active nineteenth-century bishop who became involved in many controversies. It was admittedly foolish of me not to foresee that the Press were certain to interpret history in the light of current ideologies, and naive of me not to realise what Freeman was up to, but the main cause of the trouble was the sensational notice issued to the Press by the BBC long before the programme was to be shown. The notice was not vetted by Christopher Andrew, and was issued without authorisation from the BBC official in charge of the film. Moreover the programme itself was more sensational than I had anticipated, for it showed Andrew wandering about by Guy Burgess' grave and making constant references to 'Soviet moles'. I had originally understood that I would be able to vet the script, but the BBC did not allow me to.

I don't regret having joined the Communist Party, but I do regret doing the programme, for many people got the impression that I had behaved dishonourably, and I could not go around, for instance in our village in Cornwall, saying 'By the way, if you think I was a Russian spy, I wasn't.'

6

Civil servant 1936–47

While I was at Oxford I decided to aim at a career in the Civil Service. I had always been interested in public affairs, and had all sorts of ideas about how the world could be improved. I understood from talking to my father and his friends, particularly Sir Arthur Salter, that civil servants in the top grade had considerable power and could influence government policies. I did not think of them as obscure little grey men doing routine work. Such a stereotype did not fit family friends such as Sir Claud Schuster, the Permanent Secretary to the Lord Chancellor, or my father's colleagues such as Sir John Bradbury, Sir Andrew McFadyean, or Sidney Armitage-Smith. My decision was also partly due to the influence of a talk I attended given by Hilda Martindale urging more women to try for the administrative grade of the Civil Service. She had spent most of her life as an Inspector of Factories, ending up in the Treasury as Director of Women's Establishments. Women had been allowed to sit the examination only since 1925, in spite of the Sex Disqualification (Removal) Act of 1919, mainly it seems because it was felt desirable to provide as many jobs as possible for ex-servicemen after the war.

So after coming down from Oxford in the summer of 1935, I set about equipping myself to do the exam for the Home Civil Service in July 1936. This consisted of written papers in a wide choice of subjects and an interview before a board. One aimed at a maximum of 1700 marks, 300 of which came from the interview. I was frequently advised to go to a cramming establishment as many candidates did, but I disliked the idea intensely, and instead arranged tutorials with various academics. This was easy as my parents lived in Oxford. I did not relish the prospect of living at home, as I found depressing my father's increasing gloom about the state of the world, and I was becoming more than ever hostile to my mother. She herself was only too painfully aware of the situation, setting out her feelings in a long, obviously carefully composed, letter in the spring of 1936, associating my father with its message. 'I want,' she wrote, 'to ask you to try not to keep us both at arm's length, but to share our interests and let us share yours . . . I am not asking you for confidences . . . but I do ask you not to be quite so grimly distant with us, cutting down your daily intercourse often to less than a Paying Guest would share with her hosts . . . I think you do not realise how we would appreciate a little more human intercourse and a little gentler and more gracious and friendly contact such as you give your friends . . . You cannot imagine to yourself the joy and hope in which you were conceived on a wonderful April night. It makes me very sad sometimes to feel how far away you keep us, and how little use you have for us.' She also complained that I took myself too seriously, urging me 'to give rein to rather more sense of humour with life, even though these are solemn days and times . . . Even a post office official', she added curiously, 'is improved by a sense of humour towards himself.'

I found this letter deeply embarrassing and upsetting, but I was, I am ashamed to say, not willing to alter my behaviour substantially. There was no alternative to living at home and in fact the arrangement had a lot to be said for it. I lived free of charge and was ideally placed to extend my studies. I worked at European History with E.L. Woodward, an excellent tutor who did his best to improve the style of my essays. 'Leave out the scaffolding' was his very good advice. I went to D.L. Keir at Balliol, another excellent tutor, for Constitutional Law, and studied Economics with Ian Bowen of All Souls and with Ruth Cohen. Ian was a clever man who had written a brilliant little book about Cobden in that admirable series *Great Lives* published by Duckworth, but he was wayward and unreliable as a tutor, often failing to turn up. Ruth Cohen, who much later became Principal of Newnham College, Cambridge, was then at the Agricultural Economics Institute in Oxford. I was I think her first pupil. I found the subject difficult and uncongenial, but she was wonderfully clear-headed and thorough, taking me patiently through the works of Alfred Marshall, Joan Robinson and J.M. Keynes, whose startling *General*

Theory of Employment, Interest and Money came out during that year.

The exam itself, involving as it did so many papers, seemed to me to be largely a test of stamina. I was unnerved at first when entering the room in Burlington Gardens to see such a huge number of candidates, but relieved when on closer inspection I realised that many of them were competing only for the Indian Civil Service, which was not open to women. At the interview, I discoursed with unwarranted self-assurance on the differences between French and English education, but could not think of anything to say when asked what I did in my spare time. The woman on the Board, seeing the cross-stitch on my Balkan peasant blouse, tried to help me out by asking if I did embroidery. I reacted indignantly to the suggestion that I should engage in what I considered an unintellectual and feminine activity associated in my mind with my mother. If I had been subjected to the present methods of selection, involving in-depth interviews and psychological tests, I would most probably not have secured the full marks awarded me by the Board, for I would have been considered unbalanced, eccentric, arrogant and intolerant.

I was placed third in the exam out of 493 candidates.[22] This created an enormous sensation. I received numerous telegrams and letters from friends, relations and institutions. What is interesting about these is the note of surprise which pervades them. Christopher Hill wrote that I had been the only subject of conversation at dinner at All Souls, and Douglas Jay (typically) that the report of my success seemed to be 'almost too remarkable to be true'. This astonishment is to some extent understandable, for during the eleven years 1925–35 only eleven women had been successful in the exam, as contrasted with 255 men. The first two years (1925 and 1926) witnessed the success of four outstanding women who all ultimately rose high in the Civil Service – Alix Kilroy (Meynell), Evelyn Sharp, Enid Russell-Smith and Mary Smieton; but after that the flow subsided, and from 1931 to 1934 no woman was successful out of the 40 who sat the exam. Moreover, I had passed higher than

[22] The top candidate was John Cairncross whose autobiography has recently been published.

any woman had before, but the extent of my achievement was exaggerated, and the rather hysterical reaction to it reflects the then current low estimates of women's abilities.

I have described in chapter five the circumstances which landed me in the Home Office rather than in my first choices of the Ministry of Agriculture or Labour. I started in the so-called 'Children's Branch' of the Home Office, the Division which dealt with juvenile delinquency, approved schools, remand homes, juvenile courts, children committed to the care of local authorities, and adoption, all subjects of which I was completely ignorant but found of unfailing interest. I visited some approved schools which impressed me favourably, as they seemed to be much more educational than penal establishments. I began asking myself why there were apparently no middle-class children in these schools. Did they not commit offences? If not, why not? Later I came to think that those who speculate about 'the causes of crime' should give more attention to why some people do not commit crimes.

I shared a room with J.A.R. Pimlott, later the father of Ben Pimlott, historian and political biographer. We got on well together. He had recently read History at Oxford and written a book about Toynbee Hall, a University Settlement in the East End of London where he had resided since 1932. The book was a substantial scholarly work of social history. He was an ideal person to teach me both about the office generally, and my specific work. New recruits to the Civil Service in those days were not sent on training courses as they are now; one was expected to learn on the job, picking things up as one went along. This may seem strange, but there was I think a lot to be said for it, provided one was free, as I was, to ask questions of all the people one worked with, and to discuss with them the thinking behind the Department's policies. One instruction given me by Pimlott was not to tell the public the reasons for official decisions as they would seldom be convinced they were good. This applied particularly when writing to parents informing them that their child could not be released from an approved school. The letter was simply to say that 'The Secretary of State, having carefully considered the matter, could not see his way to comply with their request.' This horrified me, particularly where the parents wanted the child home so that he could take a job and help the family financially; but the practice was understandable, at least in those cases where the reason for keeping the child at the school was that he needed more care and protection than the home provided, for instance in cases of suspected incest. The other instruction which I remember vividly was not to use the standard bureaucratic formulae when drafting a letter to an MP. All letters from MPs had to be answered by a politician, not by a civil servant. The style of the reply was to be informal and simple; and one had to remember that the MP would probably send the Minister's letter on to his correspondent.

My other colleagues were George Porter and C.P. Hill. Porter had started his Civil Service career as a clerk a long time before and had in due course been promoted to the administrative grade. Perhaps as a result of this he tended to accept much too uncritically the proposals and drafts I put up to him. C.P. Hill was very different. He had the skills and critical mind of a classical scholar at Oxford. He handled *inter alia* the obscene literature work which also fell to our Division. This appeared to involve his having on his desk quantities of pornographic material which had been intercepted by the Post Office. At my regular teas in his room, he would ask my advice as to whether or not the mail should be sent on. My instinct was to be liberal, but I tended to sit on the fence, as I did not wish to appear to be devoid of moral standards.

The head of the whole Division was J.F. Henderson. He was a civilised, cultured man, deeply interested in juvenile delinquency, a subject on which he held enlightened, advanced views, focusing on the psychological and social causes of deviance. He thought the courts should, where appropriate, consult psychologists to throw light on what he called a child's 'errors of conduct', and he realised that one could and should recognise at an early age those children who would require special supervision and care, so that effective steps were taken before they became victims of neglect and social failure. This philosophy permeates the 1938 Report of the Children's Branch, which reviewed events since the passing of the important Children and Young Persons Act of 1933. It was a masterpiece, very unlike most official productions, but unfortunately its gestation had been long, for Henderson who was its main author was a slow worker and often had great difficulty in making up his mind. When consulted by juvenile courts, local authorities or approved schools, he would hold endless telephone conversations and make many convoluted points. The files accumulated on his desk; it was said, no doubt unjustly, that some disappeared for good into a cupboard or under the carpet. The other members of the office devised strategies to bypass him, sending papers straight to the very experienced Under Secretary, S.W. Harris; but this could create difficulties. Another device was to use me as a go-between. Henderson was a family acquaintance, having worked with my father, and had pressed me to join the Home Office when I succeeded in the exam. He often summoned me to his room to discuss a case. I would then try to help him clarify the issues and make up his mind, but it was a desperate task as he tended to go round in circles.

The capacity to make up one's mind is an essential ingredient of administrative work. The files turn up in front of one relentlessly. However trivial the issue, one has to decide what should be done, even if this is nothing. At least this was the system, and I think a very good one, in the Home Office. However junior one was, one had, in putting up a file to a superior official, after reviewing the arguments, to make a recommendation, accompanying it when appropriate with a draft answer. This focused the mind; but it can be a taxing process and those not used to having to make decisions can find it wearing. Critics of civil servants have alleged that it leads to the 'Passed to you please' attitude, the title of a book by J.W.P. Mallalieu which achieved notoriety when it came out in 1942. But the system of putting up files through the hierarchy is defensible, provided each contributor has to think of himself as the final decision-maker and put down what he would do. The procedure in effect also provided training, because as the file journeyed back down the ladder, junior officers would see the comments and redrafting which had been made.

The other people I had to work with were the Inspectors. They of course really knew what the approved schools and remand homes were like, and it was very important for the administrators to pick their brains and to be on good terms with them. It struck me as rather curious that these often senior experienced officials were in some sense subordinate to the administrators, whom they merely advised. For instance, it was we who made the final decision as to whether an inmate of a school should be released or transferred elsewhere. The most worrying cases were those where the Inspectors wanted an order made by the Home Secretary transferring an inmate of an approved school to an institution for defectives, on the ground that he or she was a 'moral defective', as defined in the Mental Deficiency Acts, 1913–27. A moral defective was a person with some permanent mental defect, plus strong vicious or criminal propensities, who required supervision and control for the protection of others. These were usually girls in senior schools whose disruptive behaviour and absconsion rates were causing the school serious problems. If a girl had already freed herself from parental control, she resented attempts to reimpose discipline, especially if she regarded the staff as lacking in experience of 'life'. Looking back at what went on, I think these orders were made too easily, for it emerged years later that some quite harmless women remained locked up long after they had ceased to be difficult teenagers. I felt ashamed that I had played some part, albeit a small one, in this process. Some of the Inspectors may quite reasonably have felt that their views were of far greater value than those of a young ignorant new entrant such as me. No wonder that the Chief Inspector, A.H. Norris, who had been in this job for years, appeared to have found means of bypassing the administrators, so facing us with *faits accomplis*.

Although there were very few women in the administrative grade of the whole civil service when I joined, I saw absolutely no sign among civil servants of prejudice against women or of unease at working with them. The atmosphere was totally egalitarian. I felt myself accepted as part of this élite group, though monstrously discriminated against by government policy as regards pay and the marriage bar, for a woman civil servant had to resign on marriage save in exceptional circumstances. Men and women started on the same pay (£275 per annum), but men rose by larger increments to a higher maximum. The maximum for a male Assistant Principal, the lowest rank in the administrative grade, was £655 and for a female £510. In the higher ranks they did not even start on the same pay. Equal pay was not introduced until 1961. My experience with the marriage bar is discussed later. It is possible that the Home Office provided a particularly congenial atmosphere for a woman, since it had employed women as Factory Inspectors for many years, but women who worked in other departments between the wars have recorded broadly similar impressions.[23] This is not to say that women civil servants did not at times encounter problems when dealing with people outside the service, such as chief constables, town clerks, solicitors, who had little experience of women doing high grade, responsible work, for the Civil Service was in the forefront in employing women in such occupations. Anticipating this kind of difficulty, I would not, when writing to such people, reveal by my signature that I was a woman, leaving them to discover this if they telephoned or called in at the office.

The only problem I encountered, and that was not a very serious one, was how to address colleagues. Men at that time used surnames when writing to each other or answering the telephone, but I felt some reluctance to follow suit, partly because they addressed me as 'Miss Williams'. So I timidly wrote 'Dear Mr Smith', not 'Dear Smith'. If we had been on first-name terms, as I imagine they are now, there would have been no problem, but hardly anyone in the office made so bold as to call me 'Jenifer'. Even after I had been Sir Alexander Maxwell's Private Secretary for two years, he still addressed me as 'Miss Williams'.

I was in the Children's Branch for two and a half years. The work was extremely interesting and varied. In 1937 we were engaged with an Adoption Bill. This entailed contact with the Parliamentary Draftsmen, with some of whom I became close friends, writing notes on clauses for ministers and sitting in the official box in the House of Commons to try to ensure that they said the right thing. It emerged in the course of this work that women were not allowed in the official box in the House of Lords, which was inconvenient and rather demeaning. Altogether it was an agreeable life. I was pleased to be financially independent of my parents and, having no expensive tastes, felt quite well off. I enjoyed living in London, particularly exploring its numerous art galleries. Exact office hours were not prescribed, but most people worked from about 10 a.m. to 6 p.m. One had daily to inscribe one's times of arrival and departure in a book, but the luncheon interval could be treated elastically, and I have to confess to abusing the liberty this allowed. One worked on Saturday mornings, but the compensation was six weeks annual

[23] See e.g. Dame Alix Meynell's autobiography *Public Servant, Private Woman*, 1988.

holiday. I acquired several new interesting friends, who belied the common image of civil servants as unadventurous, bleak and boring. I was lucky enough to be introduced to a group who met occasionally to discuss problems which would arise when a Labour Government came to power. They felt they ought to equip themselves with some ideas on how to secure 'the common ownership of the means of production, distribution and exchange', the objective of the famous clause four of the Labour Party's constitution. The group included Edward Playfair and Dennis Proctor of the Treasury, Harry Lintott in the Board of Trade, Charles de Peyer and Roger Quirk in Mines, Andrew Cohen of the Colonial Office, and Anthony Lincoln in Customs. They had mostly been at Cambridge together and were a few years senior to me. They jokingly called themselves the OGPU, the then name for the Soviet Secret Police, but this was misleading and, as it turned out later, an unfortunate appellation because it caused suspicions in MI5. The group was not subversive in any sense, though its members were of a leftist tendency. My contributions on the few occasions when I attended were minimal, as I felt intimidated by this collection of brilliant people.

In the spring of 1939 I was appointed Private Secretary to Sir Alexander Maxwell, the Permanent Under Secretary of State, i.e. the head of the office. This was a great piece of good luck for me, as Maxwell was a superb person to work for, not only because of his sheer intellectual power, but also because he believed fervently that the Home Office had a duty – an important duty – not just to administer 'Law and Order', but also to safeguard liberty. Thus he considered that one should not restrict freedom of thought however unpleasant the thought, or generally freedom of speech, unless this resulted in obnoxious actions or disorder. It was of course not always easy to make these distinctions, particularly when deciding what to do about the activities of fascists and their opponents in the East End of London in the 1930s, but Maxwell's forte was to look at the problem with the classical tenets of Millite liberalism in mind. Similarly, when in 1940 and 1941 many people both inside and outside the Government urged greater press censorship and the detention of the 'offenders', Maxwell argued that one should distinguish between criticism which was loyal and constructive in intention, and that which was fundamentally disloyal and designed to undermine morale.

Maxwell's most important contribution on this issue was probably his minute of 6 September 1940 giving the Home Office reaction to the request from the Security Executive (which was worried in particular about Communist propaganda) that a Defence Regulation should be framed making it an offence to attempt to subvert duly constituted authority. Maxwell wrote that such a regulation would be

> inconsistent with the historic notions of English liberty. Our tradition is that while orders issued by the duly constituted authority must be obeyed, every civilian is at liberty to show, if he can, that such orders are silly or mischievous and that the duly constituted authorities are composed of fools or rogues . . . Accordingly we do not regard activities which are designed to bring the duly constituted authorities into contempt as necessarily subversive; they are only subversive if they are calculated to incite persons to disobey the law, or to change the Government by unconstitutional means. This doctrine gives, of course, great and indeed dangerous liberty to persons who desire revolution, or desire to impede the war effort . . . But the readiness to take this risk is the cardinal distinction between democracy and totalitarianism.'[24]

The proposal to make a Defence Regulation was dropped. If Maxwell's advice had not been taken, essential war production would almost certainly have been adversely affected, for action against communists would have caused resentment among industrial workers far beyond membership of the Communist Party.

Various factors in Maxwell's background may have contributed to his unusual capacity to keep fundamental principles in mind when making decisions. His father was a Congregational Minister, his wife a Quaker and incidentally a doctor in general practice; he had studied with great success Greats (Philosophy and Ancient History) at Oxford; and for much of his official career he had been concerned with the problems of crime and punishment, particularly as a close colleague of that remarkable man Alexander Paterson at

[24] F.H. Hinsley and C.A.G. Simkins, *British Intelligence in the Second World War*, vol. 4, 1990, p. 57–8.

the Prison Commission. Personally Maxwell was gentle and tolerant. His life-style was simple. He normally breakfasted at the Lyons Corner House in the Strand and arrived at the office before anyone else. During my two years in the Private Office I made a few feeble efforts to get there before him, but never succeeded. I did however comply with the convention of not leaving the office before him, which was often very late.

The job itself was fascinating. No papers could go to Maxwell except through me, so I got an insight into the work of the whole Home Office. There was of course not always time to read through them thoroughly, but I was expected to get the hang of the issues and to present the files to him in order of urgency. Sitting in a room adjoining his, I manned a small telephone switchboard and put calls through to him, or not, as I deemed appropriate. I was expected to listen to his telephone conversations so that I could understand what was happening. Anyone who wished to see Maxwell, with a few exceptions, such as the Home Secretary's Private Secretary, had to come through my room, with the result that I met and could often talk with most of the senior members of the Home Office, and various outsiders such as members of MI5, the Metropolitan Police Commissioner, the Director of Public Prosecutions, and other Permanent Secretaries. Sometimes I would take the liberty of trying to choke off visitors if I thought Maxwell was busy or that they were imposing on his good nature. This understandably annoyed him, especially if they were lame ducks whom he wished to help.

Some of the work of a Private Secretary is rather menial, e.g. transcribing alterations on memoranda, but at other times it can be quite taxing. This I discovered early on, when I had to take the minutes of a high-powered meeting concerned with air raid precautions, about which I knew nothing. I made a complete mess of the task, which had to be redone by the long-suffering Maxwell. I confess I enjoyed feeling in the centre of things, though I soon discovered that Cabinet minutes were boringly discreet and uninformative, being more concerned with how to present an issue to the public than with its merits. More exciting were the contents of the safe in my room, for there I found Roger Casement's diaries and a telephone tapping warrant on Mrs Simpson at the time of the Abdication crisis.

The most disconcerting part of the job was witnessing the Department's policy towards aliens. I desperately wanted to see a much more liberal attitude to the admission of refugees from Germany, Austria and Czechoslovakia, and disliked the fact that Home Office policy was to refuse entry to anyone whom the Ministry of Labour, pressured by Trade Unions, considered would damage the employment prospects of British subjects. I even took upon myself to write a memorandum which I presented to Maxwell, arguing that the economic basis of the policy was faulty, as aliens admitted here would increase effective demand for goods and services, and also, if in the right age group, help solve our population problem, for at this time there was a worry that the birth rate was declining. This was apart from the humanitarian case for a more liberal policy, and irrespective of self-interest, as many of the refugees were gifted and interesting people. Maxwell shared my views but saw no way to change the Government's policy. Some of the people to whom we refused entry managed to get to the USA, to the great advantage of that country, but many others undoubtedly ended up tragically in concentration camps.

I was distressed not only by our policy, but also by the inefficiency of the Aliens Branch of the Home Office. It seemed to me that it failed to respond adequately to the great increase in work imposed on it in the 1930s. The result was lost files, massive delays and arrears of work. At times, the more pressure there was about a case from outside, e.g. from MPs or refugee organisations, the slower would the case progress, as the file would be withdrawn from an official's desk in order to incorporate on it a new communication. Civil servants at that time were not trained in office management problems, so the radical reforms which were necessary in the interests of efficiency were not made.

At the beginning of the war I was relieved that relatively few enemy aliens were interned, but of course deeply distressed by their wholesale internment in the spring and summer of 1940. About 26,000 were interned between May and July when a German invasion was feared. With hindsight one can say that it would have been better if the tribunals which graded them into three categories at the start of the war had recommended more of them for internment, so that the panicky measures of 1940 could have been more discriminating, but at least most of the harmless detainees were ultimately released, provided they were not drowned on the *Arandora Star* or deported to Australia.

One of the people I saw a lot of at this time was Frank Newsam who became Deputy Under Secretary in 1941. Newsam had had an unusual career in the Civil Service as he had spent much of it in the Private Office – first in 1924 as Private Secretary to John Anderson, the Permanent Under Secretary, and then as Private Secretary to various Home Secretaries, Joynson-Hicks, Clynes, Samuel and Gilmour. As a result of these experiences Newsam tended to see the job of the civil servant to be service to the minister, not to the public at large. In his view the civil servant's main duty was to keep the Home Secretary out of trouble, by anticipating difficulties and thinking how to avoid them. 'Service' it is true could in his view involve criticising the minister's favourite ideas, but the official's cardinal duty was not to ask himself what was in a broad sense the right policy. His duty was to provide what the minister reasonably wanted. Newsam understood to an exceptional degree the working of the political mind and therefore tended to approach problems from a parliamentary point of view. One could, I suppose, argue that this was a good thing on the ground that it is right in a democracy for the minister to be responsive to parliament, but it is open to objection as leading to short-term policies and to neglect of the general good, which is often not represented in parliament. Newsam and Maxwell were thus poles apart in their habits of mind and also in their methods of work. Newsam was a rapid worker. He made up his mind quickly, wrote brief minutes, and cleared his desk every day, leaving the office in good time to consume some pink gins before going home. Maxwell by contrast would think at length about difficult issues, a habit which sometimes made Newsam impatient. He did however admire Maxwell's intellect. They were also very different in temperament and life-style. Maxwell was quiet and modest, but Newsam was inevitably affected by having been for many years to some extent the power behind the throne. For John Anderson, the Permanent Under Secretary from 1922 to 1932, became less and less interested in Home Office affairs and left much of the supervision of the office to Newsam. Luckily, in a rather chameleon-like way, I got on well with both Maxwell and Newsam, though I had to draw the line at Newsam's sexual advances in the office.

I also became friendly with another Home Office official, a very civilised man with many literary interests, named – curiously enough – Sam Hoare. He was a rather sad character, having entered the Civil Service in 1921 and, as was usual at that time, having taken many years to get promoted in spite of his considerable abilities. We fell into the habit of dining together in modest Soho restaurants, until he was relegated in the summer of 1940 to the Regional Commissioner's office in Leeds, from where he wrote me a stream of despondent letters. We did not resume our relationship when he ultimately returned to London.

One of the unexpected spin-offs of the contacts offered by the job was the appointment of my future husband, Herbert Hart, to MI5. In May 1940 I was asked by Sir Vernon Kell, the head of MI5, if I knew of anyone suitable for them to recruit, as they were overwhelmed with work. I recommended Herbert who, having failed his medical for the army, was still at the Bar, but anxious to do war work. He was immediately taken on by MI5 and was at once doing responsible secret work. This is an instance of MI5's ramshackle methods of recruitment, as I had a few years previously been a member of the Communist Party. About a week later an MI5 officer, Brigadier Harker, came to see me. He said they liked Herbert and thought him very able, but, asked Harker, 'Was he all right?' He wondered, because they had discovered that Herbert was living in a house on which there was a letter warrant authorising the Post Office to intercept foreign mail to that address. I was extremely worried by this information, as I was also living in this house and so assumed the warrant must have been the result of suspicions of me. But this was not so. It emerged when the matter was discussed with Herbert that the suspicious character was Douglas Jay, whose house it was. Douglas, who was at that time on the *Daily Herald*, had been reported to MI5 as having 'sinister foreign contacts'. Herbert, knowing that there could be no question about Douglas' loyalty to this country, managed to calm MI5 down and ultimately to get Douglas' file destroyed. This completely baseless smear on Douglas' integrity prevented his being offered a job in the Civil Service for over a year after the outbreak of war, although his name was on the national register of those anxious to do war work. If it had not been for this curious set of circumstances, the country might never have had the benefit of Douglas' valuable work in the Ministries of Supply and Labour, experience which was also useful after the war, when he held office in Labour governments, ending up as President of the Board of Trade in the 1960s. Why Douglas of all people should have been thought to have undesirable foreign contacts has been a puzzle, for he was generally reputed to distrust all foreigners. The explanation is probably that he attended, at the behest of his friend Shiela Grant-Duff and much against his will, a meeting in Paris, where he happened to be in 1936, addressed by the French communist, Maurice Thorez. The person who had denounced Douglas to MI5 was probably Major Desmond Morton, who was in the nineteen thirties Director of the Industrial Intelligence Centre, a small research unit created by the Government in 1931, concerned with many aspects of intelligence work, foreign and domestic.

Whilst I was with Maxwell I decided that I would like to get married, as I wanted to have a child before too long. In those days the stigma of illegitimacy was much greater than now and I did not wish to flout the convention. So in 1939 I asked the Home Office Establishment Officer if I could be given permission to marry. The marriage bar could only be waived if, on the recommendation of the head of the woman's department, the Treasury agreed it was in the interests of the public service to make an exception. The Establishment Officer said I would have to wait ten years before I could be regarded as indispensable. Maxwell, when I told him this, recommended me to put a notice in *The Times* saying I wished to be regarded as married though barred by the Civil Service. However, by a piece of good luck two years later I was having lunch with Evelyn Sharp – the later famous Baroness Sharp – who was then in the Treasury. She remarked that it was a pity women like us – a flattering concept – did not ask for permission to marry, as it would be impossible in her view for the authorities to refuse us. I said that actually I did rather want to marry. She told me that if my Department applied to the Treasury she would see that there was no problem. I told this to Maxwell who immediately secured Treasury agreement. I got married in October 1941 and had my first child a year later. If it had not been for that chance conversation with Evelyn Sharp, my life would have been very different. As well as being delighted by the decision, I was at the same time worried, feeling that I had been treated more favourably, for no good reason, than the many other women who had been refused permission and who had either given up their careers or hung on in their jobs for years past child-bearing age. However the decision in my case presumably helped other women. I was I think the second woman in the administrative grade to get a waiver, the first one having been a Principal in the Ministry of Labour in 1938. In the war a woman could resign on marriage and be re-employed on a temporary basis, but I was not willing to throw away the security of an 'established' job.

The marriage bar was abolished in 1946 for the Home Civil Service. Years later, in the 1960s when the marriage bar still operated for women in the Foreign Service, I was as a don at Oxford visited by officials in the Civil Service Commission who wanted me to urge more female students to apply for the Civil Service. I told them I could not possibly recommend the Foreign Service as a career for women, because of the marriage bar. We went over all the old arguments, and I was more than ever confirmed in my position when they came clean, defending the marriage bar on the ground that by clearing the women out on marriage, it helped men to get promotion. It was ultimately abolished, but not until 1972.

On my promotion to the rank of Principal in June 1941, I had to leave Maxwell which I very much regretted. I was made Secretary to the Home Office Advisory Committee which heard appeals from people detained under Defence Regulation 18B. These were not enemy aliens, but mostly British subjects, many of them members of the British Union, previously the British Union of Fascists. By the time I took up this job, the appeals of the most prominent detainees – the Mosleys, Captain Ramsay MP, Admiral Domville, Captain Lane-Fox Pitt-Rivers, Prince Henry of Pless – had been heard, so the cases I had to deal with were mostly from minor members of some fascist or pro-German organisation. Although I had been and still was passionately anti-fascist, and had been delighted at the detention of Sir Oswald Mosley (whose detention order I had had, when with Maxwell, to check and initial), I came more and more to feel that it had not been necessary, even considering the desperate situation of Britain in the summer of 1940, to take action under DR 18B against many of the detainees. Several, indeed perhaps many of them, had fought in World War I, had had thereafter a difficult time trying to earn a living, and had been attracted to the British Union of Fascists because in a simple-minded way they thought its policies would prevent another war. However I had no illusions about the character of the fascist movement, partly because I had attended several meetings addressed by Mosley including the famous 1936 one in Oxford. There I witnessed the threatening behaviour of the massed Blackshirt stewards with their rubber truncheons as they were beckoned down the aisles and, on Mosley's orders, pounced on an interrupter for calling out 'Red Front'. Mayhem ensued. Several people including Frank Pakenham (the later Lord Longford) were injured. Terrified, I escaped as quickly as possible. The sequel to this fracas was bizarre: the interrupter, Basil Murray – the victim of aggression – was prosecuted and convicted, whereas no action was taken against the fascists. Less strange was the fact that the whole experience, throwing light as it did on the menace of fascism, precipitated Pakenham's decision to join the Labour party.

My work as secretary to the committee was light and unexacting. Its most interesting aspect was discussing the cases with committee members, who were so very different from the types of people I had been working with in the Civil Service. This was particularly true of the chairmen, Norman Birkett and John Morris, and of the Leicestershire landowner, the thirteenth baronet, Sir Arthur Hazlerigg. Birkett was one of the foremost advocates of his time, connected with many famous cases, skilled in passionate oratory. He was an excellent appointment as chairman of the committee, because basically he felt that no one should be detained unless there were clear grounds for regarding this as absolutely necessary. This attitude rapidly brought him into conflict with MI5, whom he considered illiberal, disorganised and incompetent. John Morris, a barrister, was equally patient, humane, and vigilant to protect the freedom of the individual. Sometimes I felt he did not dislike fascism enough, but looking back I do not wish to defend my facile dogmatism, and am glad that he argued so tenaciously with the Home Office when they did not accept the Committee's recommendation for release. He later became a distinguished judge and in due course Baron Morris of Borth-y-Gest.

It had been nice in a way to work for a time under less pressure than in the Private Office, but I soon felt I was not being stretched sufficiently, and that I wanted to get back to the rigours of a proper administrative job. So I was pleased when in the spring of 1942 I was allocated to the division of the Home Office which dealt with the police, that is, not with crime but with such subjects as police pay and conditions of service, the number and size of police forces, the appointment of Chief Constables, and disciplinary appeals from police officers. One interesting aspect of the job was the opportunity it offered to meet Chief Constables and thus to get some insight into police culture. The ones who called in at the Home Office may not have been a representative cross-section of the 183 separate police forces which then existed, but they were a varied lot; some impressive and sophisticated, often products of the much-criticised Hendon Police College created by Lord Trenchard, the Metropolitan Police Commissioner, in 1932; others much older who, having risen slowly from the ranks, wished to enjoy without too much exertion the perks of high office; and others who had come to the police from the armed forces and tended to distrust 'bookishness' and those they considered 'too clever by half'. This is not to say there was not a lot of talent in the ranks of the police; this was revealed during the war when police officers seconded to the armed forces or to military government in enemy territories showed how well they could do much more responsible and difficult work than had been open to them before. But it is to suggest that the calibre of some, no doubt only a few, Chief Constables left much to be desired. This was revealed by the scandals which came to light in the 1950s, giving rise to the appointment of a Royal Commission in 1960. Some of these scandals are briefly described in my article on the Royal Commission on the Police in the journal *Public Law*, Autumn 1963.[25]

Another interesting part of the work was that concerned with long-term policies. A committee was set up in 1944 to consider not only immediate post-war problems, but also other matters such as the need for a police college to train the higher ranks, and the employment of police women, a subject about which I cared a lot. In 1939 there were only 246 police women in the whole of England and Wales, as contrasted with 60,000 police men, and over half of these women were in London. In most forces there were none at all. Moreover, many forces did not employ women even as clerks or

[25] Reprinted in *Policy-Making in Britain*, ed. Richard Rose, 1969.

typists, sometimes because it was thought they would be shocked or corrupted by the subject matter of their work. In 1946 the Post-War Committee recommended that every force should employ some police women unless the circumstances were totally exceptional. This was a remarkable decision, considering the passionate opposition to their appointment which had existed ever since they were first employed in World War I. All forces immediately complied with the new policy, the numbers of women employed escalating rapidly. Much of the credit for this development should go to the female assistant to the Inspectors of Constabulary who was appointed in 1945. I had the good fortune to share a room with the remarkably skillful woman, Barbara Denis de Vitre who held this job, and we worked closely together.

Less congenial was the work I had to do on police wireless and police pensions. Being scientifically and technologically deficient, I had great difficulty in understanding the experts' recommendations concerned with the regional wireless stations run by the Home Office. Pensions posed different problems, due to the complex statutes and regulations which governed them. Unfortunately I seemed to be regarded as the office expert on this subject, but at least the impact on the police of the Beveridge Report on Social Security gave rise to some interesting issues, as the benefits to which the police were entitled had to be integrated into the national scheme recommended by the report.

Occasionally I was deputed to lecture to foreigners attending a course at some training centre. I was given a sort of official brief which extolled the structure of the British police, particularly the fact that, apart from the Metropolitan police force, the service was the responsibility of local police authorities. This was allegedly the secret of maintaining order without endangering personal liberty. There was and is a lot to be said in favour of our arrangements, particularly the balance we had achieved between the centre and localities, but the situation was far more complex than the Home Office gospel suggested, and I fear that much of what I said in my lectures was superficial, doctrinaire, complacent and clichés-ridden. However I did not fully realise this until a few years later, when I made a more thorough study of the subject for a book I wrote about the police.

In 1947 I resigned from the Civil Service. I felt rather bad about doing this, because I thought that as a woman I had a particular duty to stay in it for life. I was also sad to abandon my ambition to rise to the highest ranks, but I felt I had to move to Oxford where my husband had taken up an academic job at the end of the war. Meeting only at weekends was tending to put a strain on our marriage and on family relationships, for we had by then two children.

I do not in the least regret my eleven years as a civil servant. I was able to learn a lot about the machinery of government which, apart from being intrinsically interesting, stood me in good stead when later I taught at Oxford. I had many impressive colleagues, some cool and wise such as Philip Allen, later Lord Allen of Abbeydale, others delightfully eccentric such as Francis Hemming, whose dominant interest was entomology, which no doubt accounted for the unfathomable complexity of the Fire Guard Orders drafted by him. The most bizarre incident in my official life was being invited to a colleague's room to discuss some problem, and then being asked to choose a pair of gloves from a collection he had in a suitcase. The gloves were cheap and nasty and much too small for me, perhaps reflecting his fantasy about the size of my hands, but I felt it was only polite to comply with his request. Generally there was little pressure to conform, though a few eyebrows were raised when I came into the office after a mountaineering holiday in plus-fours, long wide knickerbockers, with the length increased by four inches to create an overhang. This was at a time when all women dressed in skirts. Moreover I was asked, quite reasonably, to call myself Mrs Hart rather than Miss Williams after it was obvious that I was pregnant.

I enjoyed being part of a public service whose traditions, ethos and integrity I found highly congenial. This is not to say that I was not aware of some of its deficiencies. For instance, there was a tendency to regard Parliament and MPs as, if not the enemy, at least tiresome, ignorant creators of work. Answers to Parliamentary Questions and letters from MPs had to be given precedence over other work. It seemed to me a pity that civil servants did not have direct contact with MPs, for face-to-face discussions would, I thought, have been of benefit to both sides.

Another defect of the system was the often bemoaned tendency to departmentalism, that is too great loyalty to one's department and a blinkered approach to other departments. For instance, the Children's Branch of the Home Office was dogmatically critical of Children's Homes which came under the purview of the Ministry of Health. It was also anxious to prevent the Ministry of Education from interfering with the education given in approved schools. Departmentalism was partly due to the fact that in peace time few officials moved from one department to another. At one time, being bored by police pensions, I tried to move to the Ministry of Labour, but was unsuccessful. I got the impression that the only civil servants who moved were either so brilliant that they were asked for by another department, or so unsatisfactory that their existing department was anxious to get rid of them.

In recent years, indeed ever since the Fulton Report of 1968, many criticisms have been made of the Civil Service and many radical changes introduced, for instance the undermining of job security and the hiving off of work to agencies or to the private sector. My antipathy to these and other changes may be due to hardening of my arteries and therefore not justified. So I will say no more.

7

Herbert and Others 1936–47

AT EASTER 1936 after spending a few very enjoyable days with friends in the Black Mountains at Llantony Abbey (made famous by Walter Savage Landor), I joined a party organised by the Jays at Crackington Haven in Cornwall. Immediately on arrival I went with several others scrambling along the rocks, and I was given my first lesson in the elements of rock climbing by my friend Arnold Pilkington. 'Pilks', as he was known, had been at New College with Douglas Jay who describes him in his autobiography as good looking and 'equally proficient at music, rugger, athletics, foreign languages, rock climbing and economics'.[26] He was also a most amusing, sweet and charming character. As we scrambled along, I fell into conversation with another member of the party, Herbert Hart, whom I had not met before. Rock climbing was clearly not his forte, even less than it was mine, but as we discussed Arnold Toynbee's theory of history, I became immediately aware of the tremendous power of his mind and thought to myself ,'This man is really clever.' So when in May Pilks and I were planning a summer holiday in Spain, I suggested that Herbert, whom Pilks liked, should come too. My parents thought that for a girl to go abroad with two men was even more dangerous than to go with only one, so with some difficulty I arranged for a fourth person, Eve Kisch, whom I had known at Somerville, to join the party. We had to abandon the idea of Spain when the Civil War broke out in July, and decided instead on Yugoslavia. We went from Venice down the Dalmatian coast on a cargo boat, sleeping on the hard deck, then inland by train to Sarajevo which I was determined to see, and up to the

[26] *Change and Fortune*, 1980, p. 25.

mountains on the Austrian border, staying at Zlatorog on Lake Bohin. I enjoyed the sight-seeing and climbing, but the holiday was not a great success. We all found Eve rather trying. She was a brilliant classical scholar, but a tiresome travelling companion, at one point causing chaos by dropping her passport into the sea. We seemed always to be all four together, making close relationships impossible. I did not make things easier by insisting on our living austerely and travelling rough, whereas Pilks and Herbert wanted, not luxury, but greater comfort. My motivation was partly economy, but I was also driven by ideological tenets. I wanted to be nearer 'the people'. Moreover I felt a little guilty at spending three weeks in the company of non-Marxists. When I was planning the trip a friend of mine, Norman O. Brown, who had been teaching me how to be a proper communist, had tried to dissuade me from going, referring to 'the cancer of my prospective unbolshevik summer'; and on my return he was very scornful when I told him that my companions had spent much of their time ridiculing Christianity and all its trappings. He regarded this as infantilism. 'We should be fanatics not just dilettantes,' he said. However he soon went off to the USA as a Commonwealth scholar and in due course settled there; so I lost my mentor.

N.O. Brown was an extraordinary, engaging character whom I had got to know whilst he was at Balliol and I was living in Oxford after coming down from Somerville. He was very concerned with questions about how communists should conduct their private lives. We were both emotionally *petit bourgeois*, he said, and should learn 'emotional communism'. He thought I was attempting the impossible when I tried to acquire a communist approach without living it. It was our duty to help each other with communist ethics. It was all right to admit we liked each other, but we were not to say we loved each other, for complete love absorption was *a priori* impossible for Bolsheviks. His mother understood this when he explained to her that he did not love her, because communism was his mistress. She promised not to interfere. After I had moved to London he decided it would be unbolshevik for him to spend £3 coming up from Bristol to have one night with me, but I could use my right to criticise and object to his decision. The strongest argument for his coming, he said, was that he might be able to do me much good. He had a problem too about helping his mother financially. Would it be a 'right deviation' to give her £10 towards a charwoman, or was it a 'left deviation' to give it instead to the Communist Party? Besides criticising my fundamental 'petit bourgeoisity', he reproved me for having doubted whether I would do well in the Civil Service exam. 'Now that you are pinnacled,' he wrote after the result, 'your modesty becomes positively unbolshevik, since it prevents you exploiting your pinnacle in the way I exploit my stool.' As in the case of so many intellectuals who were attracted to communism in the 1930s, Brown's views changed a few years later when he became convinced that there were better means of transforming people than the political. The succession of his subsequent intellectual interests is revealed in his books: *Life against death: the psychological meaning of history* (1959), *Love's Body*, and *Closing Time* (1973).

It was through Brown that I met another fascinating character passionately admired by him, though not a communist, Jasper Ridley, who is brilliantly described by Philip Toynbee in his book *Friends Apart* (1954). (The other friend is Esmond Romilly.) For a few months in 1936 Jasper, then at Balliol also reading Greats, wrote me numerous letters chiefly about philosophy, and we often met for meals. He was trying to wean me from my simplistic enthusiasm for A.J. Ayer's iconoclastic manifesto, *Language, Truth and Logic*, which had just been published. I could not hold my own against Jasper's arguments, not only because I had not studied philosophy, but also because his strange imagination and extravagant fantasies made obscure to me the workings of his mind. I doubt whether I followed his advice to read the Epilogue to F.P. Ramsay's *Foundations of Mathematics*, but I did, as urged by him, listen to the views about Ayer of Isaiah Berlin to whom Jasper was devoted. I and his many friends were devastated when he was killed in the war, a war which, as an opponent of appeasement, he, like me, supported on moral grounds, keen that its causes and objectives should be clearly understood.

After the Yugoslav holiday I met Herbert from time to time in London to have a meal or to go to the ballet, and at Easter 1937 he joined a party I had organised in my parents' house in Cornwall, while they were away. One of the people who came, besides the Jays and Pilks, was Guy Chilver, an ancient historian from Oxford. I had seen a lot of him during the previous 18 months and had even been away with him for various weekends. On one of these I induced him to come to South Wales to see conditions in the valleys and to go down a coalmine. He was a good companion, equally interested in foreign affairs and Oxford gossip, retailing to me his encounters with figures such as Stuart Hampshire, Isaiah Berlin, Maurice Bowra and Audrey Beecham to whom Maurice had just proposed marriage. Unlike most people, Guy was often bored by Berlin and critical of him. Thus, giving an account of a luncheon party in November 1936, Guy reported 'Shayah [as Berlin was then called by his friends] reached the early life of Marx, a cycle I dislike, at 3.15 and kept to it till 4.35.' On another occasion Guy, who was very promiscuous, was scornful of Berlin's disapproval of promiscuity, not only in the case of married persons but also for what he (Berlin) called 'three dimensional people' who only engaged in promiscuity 'out of a desire to support the cause like most forms of political activity'. Guy considered Berlin was ingenuous about personal relationships and no good as an analyser of character. In fact this was more true of Guy than of Berlin, for Guy's understanding of people was distinctly limited, and his rather doctrinaire approach to personal relations doomed him to frequent unhappiness. It was difficult for women to take his emotions seriously. For instance he proposed marriage to me one night in Cornwall and, on my refusal, he proposed to my sister Judy the next night, also with no success.

My relations with Guy came to a crisis in the summer of 1937. He was trying to organise a party to travel abroad. I was anxious Herbert should come on it. Guy wanted his car driven out for him and so lent it to Herbert and me on condition we should meet up with him and various other people in Czechoslovakia and spend two or three weeks together. Unfortunately for Guy, by the time we arrived rather late in the Tatra mountains where he had been waiting for us in appalling weather with Eva Hubback, her son David and my sister Judy, it was obvious that Herbert and I were deeply committed to each other and that Guy was 'out'. We all spent one dreadful, tense evening together, and early the next morning Guy turned up in our bedroom and asked for the keys of his car, in which they departed. I felt guilty at causing him so much distress. It emerged later that what chiefly upset him was not so much the realisation that he had so to speak 'lost me', but anger with himself for feeling jealousy, as he considered it an elementary condition of mind of which he was deeply ashamed. It had been one of his tenets that jealousy in the ordinary sense was unknown to him, though he once confessed to having experienced it for one hour, adding that it was unpleasant but interesting. 'It must be wildly disagreeable to experience it often,' he once wrote to me in one of his innumerable letters, 'but its unfamiliarity made me certain that I had exorcised it almost completely.' Guy was an unusually honourable, noble, high-minded person, but in a sense at sea amongst his less worthy circle of friends. His fate was brilliantly but cruelly encapsulated in one of Maurice Bowra's verses which included the lines:

> Chilverplaited, Thistlethwaited,
> A penny for the poor old Guy.

Guy had been fond of an undergraduate at Queen's College called Richard Thistlethwaite.

Between Easter 1937 in Cornwall and the Czechoslovak expedition in the summer, my relationship with Herbert had, as I saw it, 'progressed'. For in June he took me to Glyndebourne, and in the interval, walking round the garden, he said he could demonstrate that it would be logical for me to marry him. I was so excited by what I took to be a proposal of marriage that I could not concentrate on the second half of *Figaro*. But the next day after spending the night respectably in a modest boarding house in Lewes, I was rather disconcerted when, walking on the Sussex Downs, Herbert withdrew the offer, on the ground that he was not suitable for marriage. Later he explained in a letter what he was getting at. This was that he had so long suppressed the physical expression of his feelings, because he thought they were all homosexual, that his whole faculty for expression had atrophied and was only gradually coming to life; the effect of all the mistakes he had made or which were made for him had been to render him on the surface and for a good many layers underneath instinctively suspicious of his own heterosexual feelings. I refused to accept that his diagnosis was an obstacle to our relationship; we saw a lot of each other and were very happy. However I did not at that time want to commit myself in marriage to anyone, as I felt it would be the end of independence and freedom. There was also the problem of the Civil Service marriage bar. So we agreed that I should move into his lodgings in Hampstead in the autumn.

Herbert lived in rather primitive conditions in two sparsely furnished rooms, looked after by an eccentric landlady who liked to be called 'Coucou'. She adored him and was at first rather thrown by my arrival. However a reasonable *modus vivendi* was established and she greatly regretted our departure two years later on the outbreak of war. We felt rather bad at leaving her, but were keen to accept Douglas Jay's suggestion that, as his wife and children had been evacuated, we should move into his house nearby. This proved a wonderful arrangement and made life in the war in London not only tolerable but actually enjoyable.

Others joined the household. There were two stables: Christopher Cox, who had been Herbert's and Douglas' tutor and was then working in the Colonial Office as Educational Adviser, and Francis Graham-Harrison of the Home Office, an old friend of mine. Others came for shorter periods. The Hungarian economist Thomas Balogh did not last long as his habits were found objectionable. He summoned the nice Czech peasant girl (Anita) who cooked for us to bring him books in the bath and was inclined to leave them floating in the water. Moreover his girlfriend's underclothes left about in the dining room upset Christopher, as did Balogh's defeatism in the summer of 1940 and his derogatory remarks about Churchill. Nor did Tommy appreciate Christopher who, largely because he had read and taught Greats, came to symbolise for him the defects of the British Civil Service, which he saw as stacked with Greats men. Patrick Reilly of the Foreign Office was a more acceptable member of our community. Oliver Franks, who lived near, sometimes spent the evening with us. Listening to his conversations with Douglas, with whom he worked in the Civil Service, enabled me to appreciate his outstanding gifts as an administrator.

I hated the blackout and was terrified in the Blitz. Sometimes I almost wished I was going to spend the night safely on the underground platform at the very deep Hampstead station, in spite of the stench created by its occupants, but I knew it would be delightful after struggling home from Whitehall to join this lively, amusing group of friends. When the bombing was bad we all lived in the semi-basement which created the illusion of safety, sleeping on mattresses on the floor, some of us in the disused coal hole, Anita in the kitchen unperturbed by the ants. Occasionally I had a good night's sleep in the deep basement of the Home Office, insulated from the noise of anti-aircraft guns, but it was inevitably stuffy and dispiriting. I found it essential if I were to remain sane to get out of London at weekends as often as possible. We were lucky to be able to stay with my sister Judy who was evacuated to Newbury and with various friends, including most memorably Victor Rothschild in his cottage at Tring. I was impressed by *inter alia* his talent in playing jazz on the piano, but rather disconcerted by the pleasure he took in stirring up trouble, particularly between me and his then wife Barbara, by goading me to say things which would shock her, such as that I would not stand up if the Queen came into the room. Victor called this 'putting people at their ease'. On one occasion he summoned his son Jacob, aged five, and asked him in front of all the guests whether he believed in God, and if not why not.

Unlike me, Christopher positively flourished in the Blitz. It seemed as if the outward danger it involved relieved him of his inner worries and even enabled him to open and tackle at least some of the huge quantity of files and correspondence he brought home every evening. Indeed when there was a respite in the bombing of London, he jokingly but half seriously contemplated going down to Dover for the day to enjoy some shelling; and later in the war when it was nearing its end he would try to re-create his earlier emotions by reading at breakfast the *Evening Standard* of the 1940s which he had carefully preserved. I was perpetually fascinated by this extraordinary character whose reactions to ordinary events were unpredictable; but our relations were not always absolutely easy. He was very careful with money and sometimes complained that I was asking him to contribute too much to the household's finances, which I had the invidious job of managing, and he was understandably upset when I officiously cleared great piles of newspapers out of his room in order to get it cleaned. He dubbed me and my sister Judy 'Bleakers and Starkers'; I am not sure which was which. I think Christopher related more easily to men than to women. He never married, though at one time he toyed with the idea, light-heartedly making a list of possible wives. They included Audrey Richards, Margery Perham and Mary Fisher. Margery Perham was an expert on African affairs. She and Audrey

Richards remained unmarried, but Mary Fisher married John Bennett. Christopher's rather convoluted attitude to women is illustrated by the fact that when talking to Herbert he usually referred to me as 'the virgin bitch' and on one occasion as 'the mastiff Queen'. As an example of his bizarre fantasies, I cannot do better than quote the letter he wrote to me on the birth of one of my children. It ran as follows:

> Well well well – I hear you've had a little bicycle. *What* an extraordinary thing, but the doctors tell me it happens once in every 999000 cases and I'm sure you're taking the right line in making the best of it and not keeping it quiet. There's nothing to be ashamed of – it's quite natural, only rare. A rocking horse would have been much less useful, and most angular. [This was an allusion to the fact that one of my other children longed to have a rocking horse.] But it does mean that you can't call it Gossima Gravida Vagina as you would, I hope, have called a little girl.

Living in the same house as Christopher Cox was a great experience, for apart from the amusement provided by his idiosyncracies, it was a wonderful opportunity to observe the mind and working habits of an important public servant who was convinced that education was the key to our colonies' future well-being. I think we also helped him, in spite of little local difficulties, by providing him with a base, and listening whilst he talked freely about both public and personal problems.

Before the war Herbert had joined the Cavalry Squadron of the Inns of Court Regiment, being attracted mainly by the opportunity it offered of learning to ride. So he was on the Officers Emergency Reserve, and when hostilities broke out he presented himself for enrolment in the Field Security Police. He learnt to ride a motorbike, charging dangerously round the streets of Hampstead, and I equipped him with a large stock of warm underwear and some steel rimmed spectacles; but all these preparations proved useless as he failed to pass the army medical exam on account of a mitral murmur in his heart. I confess I was pleased he was not going to be sent on active service, and after initial panic about the state of his heart, we were both relieved when a Harley Street specialist declared the murmur to be innocuous. But the army would not change its mind and Herbert subsequently joined MI5, as recounted in the previous chapter. So apart from occasional periods he had to spend outside London e.g. at Blenheim Palace, the MI5 HQ, we had the great good fortune of avoiding separation during the war. Moreover he enjoyed his time in MI5 enormously, both because he found the work fascinating and because he had many interesting colleagues some of whom, such as Victor Rothschild, Tess Mayor, Guy Liddell and Dick White, became our friends. He was concerned with the double-cross system, which involved 'turning round' German spies and getting them to work for us, thus misleading the enemy. When Herbert went to MI5 in May 1940 it was in a low state, though the double-cross system was already evolving. Two years later MI5 was virtually certain that all enemy agents operating in this country were under its control. The Germans thought they had a good espionage network in Britain when none actually existed.[27] Herbert was the MI5 link with 'Ultra' which deciphered intercepts of German communications, and he took part in evaluating and deciding what to do with the material it provided.

A curious but ultimately important side effect of this job was that it rekindled his interest in philosophy, as it gave him the chance to meet and talk with some of the philosophers concerned with Ultra, particularly Gilbert Ryle and Stuart Hampshire. He was utterly discreet at the time – I only knew in very general terms what his work involved – but he later revealed that there were fruitful opportunities for philosophical discussions when, as sometimes happened, the Ultra material went dead whilst the Germans were changing the setting of their machine codes. Even when he was a busy barrister he had been reading philosophy as a part-time hobby – I remember him being absorbed in H.W.B. Joseph's *Introduction to Logic* whilst travelling daily to work on the underground – but these wartime contacts were an important ingredient in his decision in 1945 to accept an appointment as a philosophy don at Oxford.

The story of how this change of career occurred is remarkable. Before going up to Oxford (in 1926) he had wanted to be a barrister and so, after reading Greats, he went to the Chancery Bar where in the 1930s he had a successful practice with high quality cases. At

[27] See F.H. Hinsley and C.A.G. Simkins, op. cit.

the time he enjoyed this life and the affluence it allowed, turning down the offer of a job to teach philosophy at New College in Oxford in 1937, and if it had not been for the interruption of the war, he would, I am fairly certain, have remained in the legal profession. Away from the Bar for four years and moving politically towards the Left, he reflected on what he was doing with his life. His feelings were graphically expressed in a letter to Isaiah Berlin in the summer of 1944.

> I view return to the Bar with disgust not to mention nausea . . . My main objections to it are (a) the profoundly anti-social or at least a-social character of my sort of legal work (taxation and the like); (b) dislike of other lawyers, judges, lawyers' clerks, solicitors (Jewish solicitors – *o monde immonde!*) [O vile world] and of the legal mentality in all its narrow superficial and reactionary manifestations; (c) horror of the dishonesty of the legal underworld on which barristers batten like gaily coloured fungi. I mean the company directors, the issuing houses, 'cost-making' solicitors, dishonest deals (and dealers); (d) the likelihood that if successful, the volume of my work would submerge all other intellectual interests, narrow the understanding and corrupt my life; (e) the conviction that at the end of a life as a successful or unsuccessful barrister I shall be unable to look back on it without disgust.

I must observe that in writing this rather hysterical letter, Herbert seems to have forgotten that he greatly enjoyed the company of several lawyer friends, particularly Richard Wilberforce, John Sparrow and Duff Dunbar. Anyway, he was wondering whether to give up the Bar for philosophy, taking a job at Oxford if one were offered, which he had reason to think it might be if he showed interest. But he was terrified at the prospect, being tremendously doubtful about the adequacy of his abilities, in particular having difficulty in understanding the whole linguistic approach to logic. 'I am,' he wrote, 'I fear, a hack like Ewing and fear of revealing the deutero-Ewing in me might just absolutely stultify me.'[28]

[28] A.C. Ewing, (1899–1973), was the author of many articles and books on moral philosophy.

Isaiah Berlin's fully argued answer was reassuring on every front. 'Of course you must accept', he wrote from the USA. 'How can you hesitate? The only point of the Bar I should have thought is fame and money. If you don't mind too much about the latter you must certainly abandon it since the death of the soul it produces is automatic and inevitable.'

So Herbert's decision to change his career was not as strange as it then appeared to some people, especially lawyers. But the circumstances in which the offer was made were unusual even at that time. He had not written a thesis or published anything on philosophy, and had had nothing to do with academic life for 16 years. The job was not advertised and was in effect engineered by the Warden of New college, A.H. Smith, his old tutor. Smith thought that Herbert would be a valuable and formidable opponent of the new trend in philosophy towards radical empiricism of which he (Smith) held a low opinion; but he was wrong, for Herbert was in the process of abandoning Cook Wilson, Joseph and Platonism and being converted to linguistic analysis.

Herbert was still doubtful whether he was sufficiently *au fait* with the subject to teach it adequately; so he decided to give it a try for two years, leaving open the option of returning to the Bar if it was a failure. We agreed that I should stay at my job in London with the children. Because the Japanese war ended sooner than expected, he had less time to read up the subject than he had anticipated, and he used to say that, faced with the alarming influx of keen and mature undergraduates, he would take the cleverest, such as Geoffrey Warnock and Ian Little, on Mondays for their tutorials so that he could repeat what they said during the rest of the week. At intervals he felt so overwhelmed by the amount of teaching he had to do and the feeling he would never be competent if he had so many pupils, that he thought seriously of throwing it up. But it is clear that he soon became an excellent tutor. Support for this view was supplied recently by one of his early pupils, Alec Gordon-Brown, who was contributing to a debate about the value of the Oxford tutorial system in *Oxford Today*. 'My time at Oxford would have been well worthwhile for Herbert's tutorials alone,' he wrote. 'He was a teacher of the highest calibre who taught us how to think.' Herbert was no doubt assisted by the fact that philosophy at Oxford was in an exciting state at this time. He became deeply absorbed in the subject and decided to remain in academic life for which he was admirably suited. It was one of the best decisions he ever made and (*pace* Isaiah Berlin) probably brought him greater fame than would have come his way had he remained at the Bar.

I realised at the time that Herbert was finding stressful his first years as a don, but it is only recently with the discovery of his diaries that the extent of his agonies has been revealed. Thus, early in his first term (October 1945) he recorded that going to Waismann's class on advanced symbolic logic 'finally extinguished his confidence'. But he braced himself not to give way to the panic which the sense of his complete inadequacy engendered, and not to go over the old topic of the insanity of his choice. He wondered whether he had constitutional blind spots which were peculiarly disqualifying for philosophy. He constantly felt himself to be a fraud, wanting to keep up appearances and failing to do so. 'To be a fraud is bad enough, but to be an unsuccessful one is too humiliating.' By the end of the month his spirits had sunk to new extremes. 'Tommy Balogh brought this emphatically and perhaps salutarily home by saying I must stop this Jewish wailing and that it was now too late to have a conscience.' But Herbert clearly could not change his nature. He continued to write of his ignorance, inadequacy and sense of shame. One pupil in particular was a nightmare. 'Browne plainly thinks I am (a) a fool (b) philosophically reactionary and can scarcely conceal his contempt. I try to keep cool but find it difficult to state clearly what I mean and doubt I really know what I mean.' A week later Browne announced he was not coming to further tutorials but would be reading Bertrand Russell's *Principia Mathematica* on his own. Herbert also felt he was a failure with Ian Little, writing: 'He distrusts and despises my whole approach to the subject. He also hates Moore whom I gave him to read. Bad and depressing. He has obviously discussed me with Browne and is pretty contemptuous. If he drops out too, the Warden will begin to be a bit uneasy.' Ian Little later became a brilliant political economist and a quite close friend of ours.

Herbert regretted the 'foolish remarks' he had made at Henry Price's seminar, and after attending a discussion by Bertrand Russell at the Jowett Society, he wrote: 'I had to keep a firm hold on myself to prevent myself speaking. It would have been worthless and confused if I had. This must last for a year.' But the next day, after an evening in college talking with colleagues, he had doubts about this policy. 'My maxim is don't speak about philosophy unless you can do so clearly but this at present means not speaking at all which would be odd.' On New Year's Day 1946, he resolved to try to shut out tantalising day-dreams of the happy, successful and stimulating life he could have had at the Bar 'but for a choice which appears wantonly eccentric'. But shortly afterwards he was in a state of hopeless gloom, speculating whether he could get out of 'the hell of Oxford' without losing face. 'How I would welcome release from these too great burdens of responsibility and how fearful I am of my interest vanishing. What a nightmare at times this is.' He constantly recorded fatigue, despair and panic. It is not strange he felt exhausted, considering how he drove himself. A typical diary entry records four hours steady thinking out what Russell meant by 'implication' and why as defined by him inference is tautologous. Later that day he read the first chapter of Ayer 'with minute care'.

Things improved in the spring of 1946 when Isaiah Berlin returned to Oxford from America. Talking to him made Herbert 'think and talk better' he recorded, 'so I must nerve myself and do it more.' But it also made him feel inept and dizzy. 'I can sometimes follow the revolutions of the dynamo, but often not. There is no doubt of the power of the machine as well as the grace and speed of its effortless revolutions. I do a lot of chores for him (writing notes) as payment for the illumination.'

At the end of his first year as a don, in June 1946, Herbert was still doubtful about staying on. On the credit side were 'rare moments of comprehension over some portions of the field', but he felt the gains were exiguous, and there were long tracts of depression mainly generated by the sheer difficulty of the subject, and a hankering after non-academic life. He doubted whether he was by nature academic or a scholar. He resolved to give the job another year, but already at the beginning of the next term (Michaelmas 1946) he fell victim to all sorts of despair and was again wondering whether to return to the Bar. He was in the same state of mind at the end of that term after teaching 19 hours a week, but he began to detect in himself the faint beginnings of some faculty in handling philosophical notions. Although his doubts continued, six months later he decided to stay. Within only five years from this decision, he had been elected Professor of Jurisprudence at Oxford, and by the time of his death he was considered the outstanding English-speaking philosopher of law in this century. The contrast between his low evaluation of himself and his subsequent brilliant career and world-wide fame is staggering.

Reading these diaries has been a painful experience for me, not only because they made me empathise with his agonies and suffer with him, but also because by implication they suggest that he had, perhaps rightly, little confidence in my capacity to help him through a time of strain which was due partly to the intrinsic situation, but also to his determination not to let anyone at Oxford know what he was feeling. If he had been able to confide more in me, he might have remained calmer and been less paranoiac.

Before we married (in 1941) our respective parents had not met, but soon afterwards my mother ventured up from Cornwall, where she lived during the war, to be introduced to Herbert's parents in Hampstead. We wondered how the meeting would go, as the families came from widely different backgrounds. 'My ancestors were robber barons on the Borders,' my mother had told Herbert, when they first met briefly in 1939, to which he replied, 'Mine were robber tailors in the East End.' Herbert's parents were descended from Polish and German Jewish immigrants to this country in the nineteenth century who worked in various branches of the clothing industry. His father was a master tailor and furrier, his mother in the same business. No wonder that when asked how she got on with my mother she replied: 'No problem; she was just like one of our customers,' for in 1900 they had moved from the East End of London to Harrogate, which was then a fashionable spa where the upper classes stopped off to have some clothes made on their way to Scotland for the summer. There is no record of my mother's reactions to this culturally strange milieu, a house where pretentious ornaments took the place of books and where non-U words abounded. However she was so pleased I was getting married that no doubt her normal snobbishness was stifled, and my father was delighted to have a son-in-law who, like him, had been at New College and the Chancery Bar. Herbert's parents too were pleased that he, then aged 34, was getting married, and welcomed me warmly to their home, though I suspect they slightly regretted that I was not Jewish, especially when I failed to do justice to the lavish fare of rich dishes and *gefilte fisch* which his mother pressed on me at meal times.

In retrospect it seems to me strange that we should have decided to have a child in 1942 when it was still not certain that Britain would win the war. How did we justify bringing a child into such an insecure and dangerous world? I can't answer this question. All I can say is that, given my age (28), I did not want to wait much longer before starting a family, and that our decision was not unusual, for, contrary to expectations, the birth rate rose during the war years. In England and Wales it went up from 14.7 per thousand of the population in 1936–40, to 15.9 during the years 1941–5. Our practical problems were solved: the child was to be looked after by my sister Prue who was living with her two children and a nanny in my parents' house in Oxford, whilst I worked in London. I never had any intention of giving up my career. There were often other people in the Oxford house, such as Peggy Jay and her children, but still room for Herbert and me at weekends.

Before my daughter (Joanna) was born, I was disgracefully ignorant of everything to do with babies and children and, what now seems unbelievable, even thought they were of no interest until the age of seven. I soon learnt how wrong I was, but I continued to delegate the prime care of all my children to a nanny, Edith Thomas, who acted as a stable, substitute mother. From my point of view the arrangement was and remained admirable for she turned out to be a remarkable person – wise, compassionate and competent. As well as looking after the children, she gradually took on more and more duties, and virtually ran our household for 36 years before she retired. For much of this time she did all the shopping and cooking with varying degrees of help from *au pair* girls. I just handed over some money to her every week for the housekeeping, and so avoided having to think about domestic matters. Some of my contemporaries have to my amazement managed to do a full-time job outside the home as well as running the house, cooking, often exquisitely, and coping with children, but I have never been able to concentrate on intellectual work if I was also responsible for domestic affairs. This life-style of course necessitated a large degree of delegation and non-interference. Once when I ventured to suggest that nappies should not be ironed in war-time in order to save fuel, Nanny was deeply upset. I saw the red light and thereafter forebore from making any criticism of her ways. However I always aimed, after my initial crazy, indefensible attitude, to maintain close contact with the children and to be involved with their activities. This would not have been possible if I had remained in the Civil Service with its then inflexible hours, but was much easier after we moved to Oxford.

I have of course asked myself what effect these arrangements had on our children, particularly whether they suffered from maternal deprivation, or felt confused by having in a sense two mothers. The easy but nevertheless correct answer is that the system had good and bad sides. There is an important difference between regimes involving a succession of nannies and child minders, and one where, as in our case, one nanny provided continuity and stability and became in effect one of the family. Our children now say they would have liked to have seen more of their parents, and in retrospect I myself regret not having seen more of them; but if I had been in daily charge, I suspect the household would have suffered from lack of routine, and that boredom and frustration would have detracted from whatever talents I had as a parent. Nor would my regime have been suffused with so much kindness and patience – what I considered at times deleterious 'spoiling' by our nanny; but if one looks at the end product and at how our children have brought up their own, I feel our arrangements were far from disastrous.

When my daughter was a year old I suggested to Herbert that we should have another child, as she was such a delight and needed a sibling. He complained I had not warned him I would want more than one, but in the end he agreed, though reluctantly, as he thought one should not contribute to the over-population of the world. Adam was born in 1944. By then we had moved from Douglas Jay's house at 42 Well Walk, as his family had returned from the country, and had taken a lease of the two top floors of the large house opposite, number 21, which belonged to Peggy Jay's parents, the Maxwell Garnetts. We lived in what had been the servants' quarters with access by the back stairs. Other families lived below. It was rather like a tenement. On the ground floor were William and Clement Glock with sundry children, and in the middle Hugh Gaitskell with his family, his Austrian in-laws and often Evan Durbin. Glock was then chief music critic on the *Observer*. Later he became Controller of Music at the BBC. Gaitskell and Durbin were then civil servants. Both became Labour MPs in 1945. It was a wonderful set-up, providing as it did varied and interesting company, besides the occupants of our section: Christopher Cox, Francis Graham-Harrison and his wife Carol (Stewart). One could wander down and listen to William playing the piano or even play duets with him, or talk politics with Hugh and Evan. I found their deep commitment to equality and social justice most congenial, and in later years I never subscribed to the image of Gaitskell as cold blooded and rightist, or to the allegation that he was corrupted by some of the company he kept. He seemed to me to exemplify the important truth that rationality does not kill the deeper emotions. Evan tragically died in 1947, drowned in Cornwall, and Hugh too died prematurely (in 1963) after having risen to be leader of the Labour Party.

Clement Glock was a colourful character, related to the famous acting family of Forbes Robertson and previously married to the literary critic John Davenport, about whom she told entertaining stories. She also regaled us with the latest news from Covent Garden where she was the chief screen painter and clearly brilliant at her job, as she knew how to preserve the feeling of artists like John Piper and Chrétien Bérard whose original small designs she had to enlarge. At the Glocks' large kitchen table, mysteriously covered with food, one could meet musicians and writers, such as the composers Michael Tippett and Priaulx Rainier, Gwenda David and Eric Mosbacher, the versatile translators of many books including the works of Ignazio Silone, the orientalist Arthur Waley, and Elias Canetti, the author of a famous novel, *Auto da Fé*. Clement was amazingly energetic, perhaps presssing herself too hard, for she tragically died of a brain haemorrhage a few years later.

Our quarters were distinctly spartan. The roof leaked and the primitive gas geyser in the unheated bathroom produced an inadequate supply of hot water which became tepid by the time it had slowly trickled into the bath. During the 1947 big freeze-up, none of our waste pipes worked for six weeks. There was no larder or refrigerator. As a result of marrying in war time, and refusing the marriage settlement offered to me by my father, we had few possessions and little furniture apart from some loans and the items we qualified for under the Government's excellent Utility scheme.

But we were very happy, and I contemplated with anxiety the day when we would have to become a nuclear family and possibly succumb to the pressures of materialism and of house-proud friends. Francis was always cheerful and amusing, and Christopher got on well with the depressed single mother who cooked for us, finding in her a kindred spirit. She was a quintessential Londoner with such a pronounced accent that we never knew if her name was Mrs Day or Mrs Doy.

Before Adam's birth we planned to install the children and Nanny in London with us, but the V bombs made this impossible. By 1944 the Oxford house was no longer available and I did not at all like the idea of their staying far away in Cornwall, which seemed the only alternative. I was greatly relieved when by some strange good fortune, we were offered the loan of Mrs H.A.L. Fisher's delightful cottage near the Devil's Punchbowl in Surrey. I stayed there on maternity leave for two months and then came down from London at weekends, as did Herbert. After a time Mrs Fisher moved in with us. At first I was alarmed at this prospect, wondering how we would all get on. I knew her only a little, but enough to realise that she was quite a 'character'. In fact all went well. She really adored babies and children, and her idiosyncracies tended to coincide with mine. We both valued economy in the management of the household – she was what Virginia Woolf, who was related to H.A.L., described as 'cheese paring' – and she displayed a healthy disregard of elegant clothes. She was alleged to have nonplussed people sitting beside her at grand meals by asking them to guess what she had paid for her hat – her triumphant answer being two shillings and sixpence at a jumble sale. She also embarrassed them by talking about 'my illegits', meaning the (most useful) society she had founded to help unmarried mothers and their children. At dinner one evening at Rock Cottage she claimed with pride that her dress dated from pre 1914. Looking at it carefully she noticed she had got it on back to front, 'and inside out' added her daughter. She was rightly proud of her husband who had been a Cabinet Minister and Warden of New College and whom she referred to as 'Herbert – I mean the great Herbert', to distinguish him from my husband.

I enjoyed this rather strange interlude in our lives and was in a way sad when it came to an end with our move back to London in the spring of 1945. But life in Well Walk was still very agreeable.

Herbert came there from Oxford at weekends. Christopher Cox stayed on with us as a lodger, and the assortment of people who lived downstairs provided interesting company and a diversion from family life. Indeed I became dangerously fond of William Glock.

By the summer of 1947 I decided to leave the Civil Service and move to Oxford, but not before I had landed a job there. In this I was once again fortunate, for Herbert had told me of David Cecil's famous warning: 'Bringing a wife to Oxford is like bringing her to the Gold Coast – conditions are colonial.'

8

Oxford Again 1947–52

THE PROSPECT OF finding employment in Oxford had been rather daunting. I was not qualified for anything except administration, a field which offered few openings at that time. I applied for a job which involved running the University Department that trained students for social work. I was interviewed by the chairman, Sir Frederick Ogilvie, a gentle high-minded man, then Principal of Jesus College, who had had an unusual career which included being a professor of Economics, a University Vice-Chancellor and Director-General of the BBC. He asked me what was the difference between public and social administration, a question which floored me and revealed my unsuitability for the post. It was given to Leonard Barnes, Lecturer in Education at Liverpool and author of various books on the Empire. He was succeeded in 1962 by the sociologist A.H. Halsey, who raised the Department's academic level.

I had better luck when I applied for an administrative post in the Delegacy of Extra-Mural Studies. This was the Department of the University concerned with adult education. I was interviewed first very informally by Thomas Hodgkin, the secretary, i.e. the administrative head of the Delegacy. I already knew him a little, having gone occasionally at the invitation of his brother Teddy to his parents' house at Queen's College where his father was the Provost. The 'interview' with Thomas lasted typically a whole long evening at his home. It consisted mostly of his giving me a fascinating but rather bewildering account of the history and present condition of adult education. His wife, Dorothy, whom I knew a little through Somerville and the Communist Party, sat there throughout obviously thinking about her own (scientific) work. (She was later awarded the Nobel Prize for Chemistry, and the O.M.). Thomas may well have had general doubts about my suitability for the job, but he was, I suspect, favourably disposed towards me knowing I had been a communist. He had joined the Party in 1936 and although, I believe, not still a member, he was sympathetic towards much of what the Party stood for.

None of this was mentioned that evening, but may have been a factor in his decision to recommend my appointment. I was interviewed more formally by the Delegates, a board of dons who were responsible for the Department. One of them was my old tutor Lucy Sutherland. She was, I think, inclined to be in my favour, but obviously faltered when one of the things I had included in my curriculum vitae – work for the International Student Service – turned out, on probing, to be grossly inflated, consisting, as it did, mainly of attending briefly one conference in Paris in 1937. However I was offered the job with the rather grand title 'Supervisor of Studies' in the Extension Lecture side of the Delegacy's work. Although the salary of £700 p.a. involved a considerable drop from what I had been earning in the Civil Service, I accepted the offer without hesitation, and after moving the children to Oxford in the autumn of 1947, started work at once.

In spite of what Hodgkin had told me, I had really little idea of the curious world I was walking into. The most salient fact about it was the overwhelming hold which the history of extra-mural education had over the structure of the Department's activities, a hold which made me feel we were to a great extent living in the past. I will explain. University Extension work was pioneered by Cambridge in the 1870s. Oxford followed in the 1880s and London in the 1890s. By then Oxford operated in centres scattered over most of England, except East Anglia, Yorkshire and London. In due course Oxford's 'empire' was encroached on by the new redbrick universities, but when I joined the Delegacy, Oxford still functioned in many disparate areas including Kent, West Sussex, North Staffordshire, Lincoln and Flintshire, besides regions nearer to Oxford. This seemed to me rather crazy, involving as it did time-consuming travel by our staff and any Oxford don who worked for us; but the entrenched view of the Delegacy was that we should resist all attempts by other universities to intrude into our territory. North Staffordshire was particularly sacred, as it was there that Oxford had established the first of the original Tutorial classes in the early twentieth century and where a splendid galaxy of tutors had functioned.

I soon realised that the most important part of the Delegacy's work was the Tutorial classes which it organised, some in conjunction with the Workers' Educational Association (WEA), though, for some reason which I did not understand, our relations with them always seemed contentious. These classes were serious affairs, lasting up to three years and requiring the students to do written work. Many people had benefited and were still benefiting from them. However I had, unfortunately, nothing to do with this side of the Delegacy's activities and was only involved with the Extension Lecture side. This tended to be despised by the Tutorial class people, because they considered the lecture audiences to be dilettante and predominantly middle class, though they had to admit (sadly) that most of the students at Tutorial classes were not working class either, as they had allegedly been in the glorious past. It took me some time to figure out what I thought about the Extension Lectures which I had to organise or at least consider organising if a centre asked for a course. I was worried by the ease with which a high proportion of the cost of lectures (75% I think) was borne by the Ministry of Education if we certified that the audience at the second session came up to a certain figure. Even if it dropped off thereafter, we still got the grant. The theory was that the courses should be 'of a University standard'. This seemed to me an impossible aim given the varied level of education in any audience, and the fact that many of the lecturers were themselves not academics. This was inevitable, as busy university teachers could not spare the time to give a course some distance from Oxford. We did our best to promote a high standard by supplying books relevant to the course; so 20 or 30 volumes were despatched in an enormous strong wooden box to the centre where the lectures were to be given. I never discovered to what extent the books were read. It was also a hallowed principle that the education we provided should be non-vocational, whereas I thought there was nothing wrong, and indeed perhaps some advantage, in for instance helping school teachers to get a greater knowledge of the subject they taught, or local government officers a better understanding of public administration.

My duties also involved organising the International Summer School run by Oxford University for foreign students, of whom usually half were American. It lasted six weeks and involved serious work with tutors as well as a full array of lectures. For me it was instructive and interesting: I acquired some understanding of the American educational system and it brought me into contact with many academics. But I soon realised that my relations with some of them could become delicate, for in effect I decided whom to employ as tutors, lecturers and staff. We paid quite well and I considered it incumbent on me to drop anyone who was slack. My boldest move was to cut down the honorarium paid to the President who was none other than the formidable Maurice Bowra, Warden of Wadham College, as I judged that £250 was excessive compensation for his input of one short welcoming speech. From the point of view of the Delegacy, the School was a useful fringe activity as it contributed to our income and enabled us to improve our stock of books.

During my second year in this job, I became more and more doubtful whether I was suitable for it. I could not see the point of attending meetings in, for instance, Burton-on-Trent or Sussex, even if accompanied by the Dean of Christ Church, one of the Extra-Mural Delegates, to discuss or exemplify what appeared to me to be a fictitious 'partnership' between the local authority, the WEA and Oxford. Indeed these doubts had occurred to me from my first day in the office when I discovered to my astonishment that my predecessor, who was a poet, put his correspondence loose in a drawer. This practice transgressed the sacred principle, inculcated into me in the Civil Service, that all letters and documents should be allocated to a file, and that one did not act without the file and what was known as the 'Previous Papers'. When I recommended a similar procedure, I was regarded by some of my colleagues as bureaucratic. We remained nevertheless on good terms, and I enjoyed getting to know some admirable people, especially Thomas Hodgkin, whose engaging personality and complex mind I found fascinating. There were some unresolved problems in his *Weltanschauung*, due, I think, to the continuing influence of a Quaker background combined with undogmatic Marxism. His wide cultural and intellectual interests made him into a multi-layered thinker, always ready to listen and to talk, particularly about ideologies. I admired his total, unselfish commitment to adult education, which contrasted with my ambivalence, my heart, as he sadly put it, not being 'in the movement'. For I had begun to realise that I wanted to leave the fringes of academia and, if this were somehow possible, myself to become an academic. However I was relieved, when I told him this, to hear that he too was going to leave the Delegacy soon to pursue his interests in African studies.

Soon after my return to Oxford, I had on the initiative and recommendation of my friend Audrey Beecham acquired some teaching for Barnett House, the Social Training centre, for their course on Public and Social Administration. The only subjects I could claim to know anything about were the Civil Service and the police, so I had rapidly to mug up the others. I enjoyed doing this and even more the novelty of trying my hand at tutoring. Moreover I soon saw that the literature on the police was scanty and out of date, so I decided to fill the gap. Allen and Unwin, the publishers of the useful *New Town and County Hall* series accepted my proposal and I set to work at once. This entailed leaving my office ruthlessly at 5 p.m. every day and migrating for the rest of the evening to libraries for the necessary research. The book, published early in 1951, was entitled *The British Police* by J.M. Hart. I decided not to reveal that the author was a woman, as I thought that to do so would diminish the readership and the book's influence. Some reviewers assumed I was a man, as did the Bodleian Library who catalogued it as written by James McKnight Hart, whose identity I have never discovered.

The book described not actual police work but the history and organisation of the police service, constitutional topics such as the powers and functions of local police authorities, the ways in which central control was exercised, and the unique position of the Metropolitan Police. I also contrasted our arrangements with those in 'police states'. The book's approach was dry and analytical, so much so that one reviewer complained it lacked life and colour and was devoid of human values. So I was astonished and worried when I was sent for by a high ranking Home Office official who told me I was 'naughty' to have written it, that the Office took exception to some of the contents and were considering what action they could take. I had admittedly aimed to get behind the official jargon and to describe what happened in practice and not just in theory, without infringing the Official Secrets Act. I defended myself by saying that I did not think I had revealed anything which could only have been learnt by someone who had worked in the Home Office, and that I considered I was entitled to express my views on issues such as the limited value of the published reports of the Inspectors of Constabulary, the need for some democratic control over the Metropolitan Police, and the dangers of corruption. I doubt whether my interrogator was appeased, but at least the Home Office took no further action. The book received some nice reviews and sold well, remaining the standard work on the subject for many years before becoming out of date.

Meanwhile I applied for a studentship at Nuffield College. I was interviewed by one of the Fellows, D.N. Chester, who told me I was too old to be a student and more or less offered me the Research Fellowship which he had been involved in creating for civil servants or ex-civil servants. Thus I became in 1951 the first Gwilym Gibbon Fellow of the college. I worked on various aspects of nineteenth-century police history, particularly relations between central and local government. Chester hoped that I would produce a comprehensive study of this subject, and I fear I disappointed him, for the outcome of my research was only two articles: 'Reform of the Borough Police 1835–1856', published in the *English Historical Review*, July 1955, and 'The County and Borough Police Act 1856', in *Public Administration*, Winter 1956. However from my point of view, the opportunity given me by Nuffield was invaluable, as it enabled me to do some very detailed historical research, using a wide variety of material: Home Office and local records, the Press, criminal statistics and parliamentary papers. My subjects were admittedly not of central interest to most historians, but they were of use to specialists in administrative and criminological history; and, as Professor Kenneth Wheare once remarked sardonically to me, people of my generation who, as was common, had not written theses, had to show that they could 'do this sort of scholarly thing'.

Moreover belonging to Nuffield enabled me to meet many social scientists and other academics, and, later, outsiders such as politicians, civil servants and journalists. The atmosphere at first was informal as our premises were various North Oxford houses, the college's building not being yet completed. Snooty arts people have tended to denigrate Nuffield as a philistine institution, but for me the social and intellectual life it provided whilst I was a Fellow and indeed thereafter for many years was of enormous benefit. Among the Fellows were such civilised persons as Michael Oakeshott, John Plamenatz, Kenneth Wheare, Nigel Walker and the Irish historian K.H. Connell, though I have to admit that Plamenatz was never happy at Nuffield and was pleased to leave it for All Souls in 1967. Apart from anything else I was delighted to belong to a coeducational college. It was the only one in Oxford at that time and indeed until 1962 when St Anthony's, another graduate college, admitted women. Such was the chauvinistic, demeaning attitude of the University that it was not even possible for dons in men's colleges to ask a woman to a meal in Hall or into the Senior Common Room. These restrictions on social life were not significantly relaxed until the 1980s, but at Nuffield sex equality reigned from the start. In recent years I have heard women academics appointed to previously all-male colleges complain when they found themselves in a small minority, but when I was one of the few women in Nuffield, I did not feel any difficulty. I was treated just as a person, not as an oddity, and was neither side-lined nor harassed.

When I joined the college, Herbert mentioned that it had recently acquired a new Fellow from Cambridge, the political philosopher Michael Oakeshott, whom he thought I would find interesting. He was more than right, for Oakeshott and I rapidly fell in love. On meeting him I was at once fascinated by his darting, twinkling eyes and his boyish bohemianism, and I found there was much about his way of life which appealed to me: he was unconventional, rejected ostentation and was an incurable romantic. But this in a sense posed a problem, for I was not in sympathy with his political views and his way of thinking which deviated profoundly not only from mine, but also from those of my friends. Moreover as he once wrote to me, 'I haven't got anything *you* would call a mind.' I had told him that when falling in love, I was usually attracted first by the other person's mind. He was anti-rationalist, for rationalists were, he considered, people who worked out theories and then applied them to politics. In his view, experience of men and affairs was a far better guide to action than trying to apply an ideology. Government was the art of knowing where to go next. So how, I asked, should a government decide what to do, assuming it should do something? His answer was that it should see what existing institutions 'intimated'. In considering whether to make certain changes, one should study tradition, history, customs. For instance he thought

Burke, whom of course he admired, was right, at the end of the eighteenth century, in his hostility to most of the reforms proposed by the parliamentary reformers such as extension of the franchise and equal electoral districts, but correct in supporting what was known as 'Economical Reform', i.e., cutting down the number of placemen, and measures against bribery and corruption, because these were the kind of reforms 'intimated' by the history of Parliament. One should only move along the lines implied by its past development.

I could not of course move Oakeshott from his dislike of general or abstract principles as a basis for action, or, more specifically, from his hostility to the ethos of the Attlee Governments which I supported enthusiastically. But I enjoyed our many discussions which stimulated me to think more thoroughly about conservatism and the arguments used by its protagonists. Several years later I attacked what I saw as an offshoot of the Oakeshottian position in an article I wrote about a Tory interpretation of history in relation to nineteenth-century social reform.[29] In this I argued that there is no learning from experience except by reference to some principle or standard, and that historians who denied this when they belittled the role of Benthamite ideas were wrong. In spite of the deep intellectual gulf between us, we remained close friends, as was exemplified by his bequeathing to me, when he left Oxford, the remainder of the lease of the place where he had lived – typically a small snug pad – to provide me with a private refuge from family life. When explaining why he was attracted to me, Oakeshott threw perhaps as much light on himself as on me. What he admired, he said, was 'your intolerance of being side-tracked by what you consider unimportant – and your admirable sense of what is important. With a scornful gesture, you sweep luxury aside as a substitute not to be considered. Hot baths, food, wealth, reputation. I have never known anyone less accommodating to "the long littleness of life" . . . It's the quality of being unbribable, even by yourself, which belongs to children and to real adults, and since most of the world is without it, you can't blame me for admiring it when I see it.'

During this period I also had great good luck in picking up some

[29] See *Past and Present*, July 1965.

solid teaching. I had helped the New College Politics tutor, James Joll, with a revision class, but I was astonished when he asked me to take over, whilst he was away, a whole year's tutoring in Political Institutions and Modern British History. I fear my students had a rather raw deal, though I did my best to equip myself for the task by attending lectures and seminars – Professor Wheare's were particularly useful – and by discussing the more theoretical side of the work with Herbert; but from my point of view the experience was invaluable, and not only because it led to my doing similar work the next year for Exeter College when their Politics tutor, Norman Crowther Hunt, was out of action. There followed a bleak year when I had only a straggle of pupils from assorted colleges to whom I had boldly written offering my services. That I was still very green in the ways of Oxford is illustrated by various incidents. For instance I revealed ignorance of an important sporting event by asking why the undergraduate I was teaching would after half-term be unable to attend any more tutorials as he had to be at Henley for rowing practice. He was training for the Oxford & Cambridge boat race. On another occasion I inadvertently caused considerable pain to a student by not realising that my report on his work, which contained some patronising, supercilious and uncalled-for remarks on his origins and background, would be read out to him. Another of my end-of-term reports got me into trouble with the Master of University College, Arthur Goodhart, who had been Professor of Jurisprudence, for in it, trying to be helpful, I advised that, as a certain student's work on Politics lacked depth, he might think of becoming a lawyer. I too was shown as lacking depth when a brilliant pupil from Somerville, Sybil Wolfram, who later became a Philosophy don, informed me triumphantly that she had not been able to write her essay, as the question I had posed was meaningless.

On moving to Oxford we lived at first in the famous New College Barn. Built in the fourteenth century to provide stables for the Warden's horses, it had later been converted into accommodation for students and in due course for Fellows. We were delighted to occupy such a romantic and unusual dwelling, but when more spacious quarters became available on the other side of New College Lane, we decided to move out of the Barn. I could hardly believe our good fortune, as years earlier I had gazed at this beautiful Queen Anne house and thought it would be the nicest place in Oxford in which to live. It was as ideal as I had imagined. The children – three of them by then – had ample space and could play safely in the streets around, as well as in the garden. We could take them to school on our bicycles or they could go on their own. Our position in central Oxford meant that friends would drop in as they were passing by, and it was a great help for me to live so near the Bodleian Library.

I was particularly delighted to be able at this time to see a lot of Isaiah Berlin, who was then a philosophy don living in New College and later in All Souls. Herbert and I had both been devoted to him for years – since our respective undergraduate days – and all our lives we realised how lucky we were to have as our closest friend this brilliant raconteur whose conversation never fails to illuminate any of the diverse topics over which it freely roams. I am of course not in a position to say anything of value about his contributions to intellectual history and political philosophy, which have been much discussed recently, but I can testify to his unusual capacity for being both deeply serious and vastly amusing, to his remarkable humility, lack of side, and what I can only call emotional integrity. His reaction to the enthusiasm which greeted the publication of *The Hedgehog and the Fox* was typical. 'I think I'm rather better than some writers, but nothing unusual,' I recorded him in my diary as saying in 1954. Later we acquired in his wife another superb friend, who had by a curious coincidence been, as Aline de Gunzbourg, a school-mate of mine in Paris.[30]

So nuclear family life, which I had rather dreaded, was in fact quite agreeable. Herbert was relieved from the tedium and stress of coming to London at weekends, and enjoyed seeing more of the children. He began to feel less harassed by the weight of tutoring and was very much enjoying Oxford philosophic life, particularly his contacts with J.L. Austin, who was, he said, the cleverest man he knew. They ran a class together in 1948, concentrating on legal concepts associated with action and responsibility, and Herbert was one of the original attenders at Austin's famous 'Saturday mornings' which started in 1947. These weekly meetings of invited philosophers were quite unlike other academic gatherings. Austin wanted

[30] Since writing this, Isaiah Berlin has died, to the great grief of his innumerable friends and admirers.

to do something new, or to try looking at things in some new sort of way, particularly by convincing philosophers that collaboration and agreement were possible, replacing the usual combative atmosphere. He hated aimless talking. If they could reach agreement, maybe they had actually got something right: the truth had been established. One term was devoted entirely to enquiring into the concept of a rule, to which Herbert contributed many examples from the law.

I was of course not a participant in these discussions, but I mention them because Herbert's close association with Austin for over a dozen years had an indirect influence on me and even, I venture to think, on the general atmosphere at home. It strengthened Herbert's already existing passion for rigorous analysis and his detestation of vagueness, obscurity, pretension, rhetoric and jargon, and I learnt to admire these values. Indeed I myself saw enough of Austin to come under his spell, even before I had the great good luck of being twice, some years later, one of his colleagues as an examiner in the Honours School of Philosophy, Politics and Economics. I then savoured his astringent wit and formidable personality. He hated wasting time and persuaded us to be better organised and more rational, so that contrary to usual practice, we could finish our business at 1 p.m. each day. All candidates had at that time to be given a *viva* even if, as was the position in the vast majority of cases, their class was already determined. Some examiners liked using the occasion to converse with candidates about their papers or more generally, but as Austin thought the system absurd, he was, when Chairman of the Board, adamant that formal *vivas* (as they were known) should be despatched with maximum speed, and that his colleagues should be particularly careful not to ask the candidate a question which might suggest that he had been put in too high a class, it being an entrenched principle that candidates should not harm themselves at a *viva*. I saw the logic of Austin's guidelines, but I confess I felt a twinge of sympathy for those candidates who, having perhaps come a great distance, felt they were on a conveyor belt and that the occasion was an anticlimax to their academic studies. When we were conducting serious vivas, he would keep us on our toes by sending a note down the table asking the examiner whether he could not now make up his mind. This could be daunting, but was, I thought, a legitimate exercise of his authority. He appeared to some as a remote and even cold personality. This must have been the impression made on the colleague who in the war, rashly addressing him as 'John', was told 'Austin is also a first name.' But I felt in sympathy with his dislike of facile genialities.

Austin also played a significant part in our family fortune (in the widest sense) by urging Herbert to think of himself as a suitable holder of the Chair of Jurisprudence when this fell vacant in 1952. Even more important in this matter was the philosopher George Paul who had got to know Herbert well since 1945 when they both turned up in Oxford. I had the impression – though this may be stating it rather crudely – that George was a sort of secular missionary, wishing to spread to other disciplines the methods and insights of linguistic philosophy. So if possible they should be infiltrated. Light would then be thrown on their tangles and muddles; and bogus questions would be eliminated or dissolved. Herbert did not regard himself as a participant in any such campaign, though he certainly came to see that many philosophical distinctions could with profit be applied to law. So, being doubtful of his talents as a philosopher, he let his name go forward for the chair, though only after some initial hesitation. The main rival candidate was the Oxford law don, Norman Marsh, with whom I had collaborated as an undergraduate in the Liberal Party and the League of Nations Union. As Herbert had no law degree and had published almost nothing – one article and one book review – his election as Professor of Jurisprudence surprised many people and gave rise to quips such as, 'It's Goodhart [his predecessor] without the good.' Judging by the letters he received at the time, members of the Law Faculty were less enthusiastic about having good done to them than the philosophers were about their annexation of another province and the regeneration of what even one of the lawyers described as 'the intellectual slum of English Jurisprudence'. I am of course not in a position to pass judgement on his appointment, but the great value which has been widely placed on Herbert's contributions to legal philosophy suggests the electors were not at fault. The fact that such an appointment could not take place today ought to raise doubts about the publication requirements which are now insisted upon in academia. The best short assessment of Herbert's work is Tony Honoré's memoir in the *Proceedings of the British Academy* 84 (1993).

As a result of becoming Professor of Jurisprudence, a post

attached to University College, Herbert had to resign from New College, which meant that we had naturally, but much to my dismay, to leave our superb New College house. However once again we were extremely lucky, acquiring with minimum effort the lease, and later the freehold, of a house in an ideal situation near the centre of Oxford but in rural surroundings. I plan to remain there for the rest of my life.

I too acquired a new job in 1952. I was becoming worried about the possibility of getting an academic post, as openings for women were scarce. There were only five women's colleges, and being poor, they could not afford to appoint as many tutors as most of the men's colleges. But by a stroke of luck, the Modern Historian at St Anne's, Mary Leys, decided to retire early. I would not have thought of putting in for this job if I had not been urged to do so by solicitous friends, as I saw myself more as a Politics than a History tutor. Once again 'connections' came in useful. I had known the Treasurer of St Anne's, the historian and journalist Elisabeth Munroe, since my Geneva days, as she had been a member of the Secretariat of the League of Nations. She recommended me warmly to the Principal, Eleanor Plumer. The committee which interviewed me included my old friend Guy Chilver, and others whom I knew to be well disposed towards me. There was, it seemed, one understandably doubtful member, the historian G.N. Clark. At the interview he elicited from me that my German was weak and my Latin rusty. I put a brave face on my capacity to brush up my knowledge of seventeenth- and eighteenth-century history and, with rather more confidence, I assured the committee that my domestic and family duties would not impede my academic work. Married women tutors were still rare at that time, though more numerous than before the war when there were hardly any; hence the anxiety. There was, I think, only one other serious candidate, Agatha Ramm. She had already published scholarly historical work and would certainly have got the job in preference to me if she had not conveniently been appointed at that moment to Somerville. After the session with the committee, I had to run the gauntlet of the rest of the Fellows. This turned out to be hilarious, for over tea in the Senior Common Room, one of them suddenly declared that I must be appointed because my red hair looked so good against the decor and furnishings of the room, for which incidentally she had been responsible. I knew I had made it.

9

Don 1952–81

WHEN I JOINED St Anne's College in 1952, it had not yet completed the process of transforming itself from being the Society of Oxford Home Students into what can loosely be called a proper college, that is, a self-governing institution based on a residential central site. So life there was in many ways different from that which obtained in the generality of Oxford colleges. For the senior members (tutors and lecturers) the lack of a dining hall and the paucity of funds meant that we did not meet each other every day all the year round for free or subsidised meals at a common table, which is one of the most agreeable features of Oxford college life. Our nearest approach to this was lunch together, three times a week in term-time. Nevertheless the atmosphere was friendly, and the tutors, of whom there were only nine, prided themselves on the exceptional harmony which pervaded their relationships with each other. Although a great deal was happening, in particular the development of our site, the administrative machine was simple and the procedures were informal. At tutors' meetings we sat relaxed in armchairs. Brief minutes of the proceedings were written into a book in longhand and read out at the next meeting. Business at Council meetings was rather more formal. We did not receive full collegiate status until 1959, which meant that there were five 'outside' members on the Governing Body. These male dons, who included Guy Chilver, J. D. Mabbott and John Lowe, the Dean of Christchurch, were a great help to us, as had been several others in earlier stages of our history. One excellent result of their presence was that meetings did not, as in later years, last interminably. They were all busy people and we knew better than to exploit their goodwill.

During my first year the Principal of St Anne's was the Hon. Eleanor Plumer. Whenever she is mentioned there is usually a reference to the fact that she was a Field Marshal's daughter, and much though I dislike labelling women in relation to some man, I have to admit that in her case this is a relevant piece of information. She admired her father (Herbert Charles Plumer, 1857–1932), being proud of his distinguished career both as a soldier in many wars and as Governor of Malta and High Commissioner in Palestine in the 1920s – service which gained him a peerage. Eleanor Plumer either inherited or made her own many of his characteristics. She presided skilfully over St Anne's at a crucial time in its development with energy and robust common sense, despatching business with brisk military precision and generally diffusing an air of authority in her dealings with people. Well-educated and widely read, but not an academic, she reputedly took a rather low view of the capacity of dons to run a college, and I suspect that her conception of the role of Principal would have led her into trouble if she had still reigned in the 1960s. For instance, students had to sign a book if they were going to return to their lodgings after 9 p.m., although they did not have to be back until 11.15. Miss Plumer would go through the book at the end of the week and send for students who had in her view been out too often after 9 p.m. I am not clear whether this was due to concern for their work or their moral welfare.

In 1953 a new Principal was elected to succeed Miss Plumer. As I was still on probation I had no vote, but was allowed to attend the interviews. I was, I am ashamed to say, wrong in my doubts about the person who turned out to be the successful candidate – Lady Ogilvie[31] – applying to her, as I did, a rather narrow academic criterion of 'cleverness'. Later I came to think that it could be misleading to use the word 'clever' by itself, and that one should if possible think in terms of 'clever at' or 'clever with'. For Mary Ogilvie, who had lived almost all her life in academic circles, had a bold vision of what the college should be and was brilliantly clever at realising her aspiration. One of her first proposals was that we should have a dining hall so that the students could meet together and talk to each other more than was possible in their dozen or so separate houses. She was also very much aware that a hall where

[31] Mary Helen Ogilvie, née Macaulay, 1900–90.

tutors and other staff could take their meals would greatly enhance the social and intellectual life of the college. She secured the necessary funds for this project by talking to her friend Keith Murray, the Chairman of the University Grants Committee, and by persuading the University to withdraw in our special case its opposition to the acceptance by colleges of direct grants from the UGC. Some people thought this would be dangerous, fearing that if we took what was in effect Government money, our academic freedom would be at risk. No such disaster occurred, though we had of course to comply with UGC building specifications. The initial grant was £50,000. The first architect we approached said he could not do the job for less than £85,000, but Gerald Banks, a friend of one of the Fellows, was willing to undertake the task, though he forecast (wrongly) that his building would not last more than 20 years. Lady Ogilvie also landed several further grants from the UGC before there was a change of the general policy which prevented direct grants to colleges.

When she was interviewed for the Principalship, Mary Ogilvie said, with perhaps rash frankness, that she could not understand a balance sheet and was 'no good at finance'. She was probably right about balance sheets, but she was wrong if she meant, as she no doubt honestly did, that she was inept at raising money. For it was largely, if not wholly, due to her initiative and skills that the college received substantial grants, used for new buildings, from the Isaac Wolfson and Max Rayne Foundations, helped in the case of the Wolfson by her capacity to talk with a Glaswegian accent.

We consolidated and extended our site in many other ways during the 1950s and '60s, assisted *inter alia* by the generous support of alumni, very few of whom could be described as well off. But it would be a mistake to view Mary Ogilvie solely as a 'building Principal'. She has many other claims to fame, the most important of which was her concern for the intellectual life and achievements of the college. She was determined not only that St Anne's should no longer be academically the Cinderella of Oxford colleges; it was to be nothing less than the best of them. And somehow, *mirabile dictu*, this happened. For by the early 1960s we came top of the league table of exam results, and maintained a high position for several years. How to account for this dramatic change is not easy, but I have no doubt that Mary Ogilvie's role in the process was vitally important. She raised Fellows' morale by telling us, sometimes to our embarrassment, that we were a distinguished band, and impressing on us the need to aim for the highest when adding, as was necessary, to our numbers. She had no qualms about informing people in the outside world that St Anne's was the best college in Oxford, and we acquired the reputation of being unstuffy, liberal and generally go-ahead, with the result that a stream of interesting, gifted girls came to us. The fact that one of our fellows was Iris Murdoch no doubt enhanced our image, for she had already published her book on Sartre and seven of her novels before she left us in 1964. Moreover she was (rightly) reputed to be a stimulating teacher, partly because she neither offered nor accepted clear final answers to philosophical problems. Another fellow who contributed to the attraction of the college was the colourful Economics tutor 'Peter' Ady, whose activities included fox-hunting and work for several international organisations.

We were, I think, more flexible and more willing to take risks than the other women's colleges. For instance we accepted a brilliant student, turned down by another college because she was married, and we allowed one of our undergraduates at the end of her first year to marry her tutor, a divorcé with children. He was not, of course, a member of St Anne's. In both cases our decisions were vindicated, at least by the test of academic success. It may be difficult years later to visualise why anyone thought a married undergraduate posed risks, but such an attitude was quite common at the time. It was assumed that marriage for a woman was incompatible with academic interests as she would be enveloped by domesticity. It may also have been feared that the college would find it difficult to secure her compliance with their rules and regulations.

During Mary Ogilvie's principalship (1953–66), the college embarked on many excellent novel schemes as a result of the lead she gave us. A nursery for dons' children was started on the site. A graduate centre run by us jointly with Balliol, where her son was a tutor, was established at Holywell Manor. This venture enabled us to increase our intake of graduate students, many of whom were a great asset to intellectual life in the college. We created a Middle Common Room, i.e. a common room assigned to graduates, a new idea at that time. We welcomed students reading for diplomas in education and social administration, courses despised by academic snobs, and we were the first women's college to sponsor school teachers for a sabbatical term in Oxford.

We had also at this time to decide whether to have a chapel, like all other Oxford colleges except St Anthony's and St Catherine's. The situation at St Anne's was complicated and unusual. A terminal service was held for the college at the University Church and, until it was pulled down in 1961 to make way for a new residential building, there was on our site an Anglican chapel in the hostel (Springfield) run by the Wantage Sisters, but it was not the college chapel. Religious services were also held at another of our hostels, Cherwell Edge, which was run by Roman Catholic nuns. Some of our alumni urged the college to include in its development plans a chapel for Christian worship. This gave rise to interesting discussions in Governing Body. The pro-chapel party argued that as we provided things like tennis and squash courts for our students, we should also cater for their other not strictly educational interests such as religion, to which the anti-chapel party countered that there were in Oxford numerous churches and chapels to which anyone was free to go, whereas this did not apply to sporting facilities. The decision went against building a chapel and was maintained in spite of continuing pressure from some Old Members. We also decided not to appoint a chaplain even when offered funds for this purpose. These issues needed delicate handling, as we wanted to minimise the distress our decisions caused in particular to the Misses Butler (R.F. and C.V.) who, as tutors and in other capacities, had been pillars of the Home Students for 40 years.

For me, as for many others, this was an exhilarating period. It was also instructive, for I was getting to understand the nature of this rather curious institution, an Oxford college, to visualise its ideal form and to think out how to realise this. Observing our Principal, I saw how important was her capacity to know and to relate without side to the many and diverse persons who were part of our community – not just academics and students but all the administrative, domestic, maintenance and gardening staff. Walking about the site, as she frequently did, and visiting our various hostels without any formality, she exuded warmth, friendliness, support, praise, encouragement. To some she may at times have seemed insincere or to empathise indiscriminately, showing too much of a 'warm shoulder', as Maurice Bowra said of Lord Redcliffe-Maud, but no one could doubt that she fostered in the college a great and valuable sense of community.

Lady Ogilvie's previous life as the wife of a tutor, Vice Chancellor and Head of an Oxford college, and her position when a widow as Dean of Women Students at Leeds equipped her admirably for the St Anne's job, provided, that is, one did not object to her slightly cavalier attitude to constitutional niceties. In fact any incipient opposition usually faded when she came to the Governing Body 'in a white sheet' as she disarmingly put it, having embarked on some project or even made an appointment during the vacation; but I and several others were more than disconcerted when she went ahead on her own to invite the Queen to open the dining hall. It was obviously impossible to withdraw the invitation, so we had to engage in the amazing palaver which surrounds a royal visit. Three months of tedious preparation was required for an event lasting less than an hour, but we did not feel we could accept Lady Ogilvie's offer to meet the (not inconsiderable) cost of the visit from her own income.

I had a problem deciding whether or not to attend the proceedings and be presented to Her Majesty with the other tutors. Curiosity overcame my republican instincts and I was glad I relented, for I was able to observe an amusing incident. When a third tutor told the Queen she taught English (meaning English literature), HM assumed that if we needed three tutors for English, we must have many foreign students, but I cannot vouch for the truth of the story that when the Queen heard the tutor was called Mrs Bednarovska, she exclaimed, 'Oh, how clever for a Pole!'. Dorothy Bednarovska was in fact English by birth, married to a Pole. I also enjoyed talking over tea with Harold Macmillan, who was present as Chancellor of the University. I became aware for the first but by no means the last time of the profound impact made on him by the tragedies of the First World War, about which he reminisced most movingly.

Dons in Oxford colleges have to concern themselves with many matters besides their academic work, for they are all members of Governing Bodies responsible for the buildings, finance, staffing and general administration of the institution. So during my first years at St Anne's I had to try to learn various new skills such as how to understand architects' plans and to interpret their rhetoric like 'Buildings should tell the truth', and how to advise on investment policy. I began to feel like a Jack of all trades and master of none. But my overriding concern was how to cope with the teaching I had to do. My appointment was as a Modern History tutor, but it seemed to be generally accepted, though not made clear, that I would also take charge of the Politics side of the PPE school, for St Anne's, like most colleges then, had no separate Politics tutor. The subject was taught by political historians not, as later, by experts in government or political and social theory. When, years later, I was due for retirement, the college appointed a separate Politics tutor as well as a Modern Historian, so I was replaced by two people. Although the double job added to my workload, I was happy with the arrangement: I was interested in political institutions which, unlike some people, I regarded as a genuine subject, and I enjoyed the chance this gave me to teach a wider variety of pupils. At one end of the spectrum there were mavericks such as Hilary Wainwright who amongst her many radical activities founded the journal *Red Pepper*, and Rose Dugdale who unfortunately landed in prison as a result of her involvement in Irish affairs, and at the other pole Edwina Currie who became a notorious Conservative politician.

Being a member of two University Faculties was illuminating, for it was not hard to detect among some historians vestiges of an antediluvian hostility to the Social Sciences. The PPE school – originally called Modern Greats – had started in 1921 and had become a popular though rigorous course, but 40 or so years later it was not uncommon to hear remarks from historians directed particularly against philosophers and the influence of philosophy, but also implying that the study of Politics could not be conducted in the sort of scholarly and unbiased way in which history was taught.

At first equipping myself to teach those reading history, of whom there were no fewer than 55, was a greater problem than handling the Politics work, for I had to cover English history from the year 1660 onwards, although I had not for a long time thought about anything which happened before 1832. I often panicked about how to get through the tutorial hour, particularly if the student had finished reading out her essay after only ten minutes. I resorted endlessly to asking the two questions recommended to me by

Herbert, namely 'What do you mean?' and 'How do you know?' or 'What is the evidence for that statement?' This helped, but it did not solve one of my problems which was not knowing whether to reveal that I had not heard of some character mentioned in the essay, in case they were famous. For comfort I clung to the doctrine that the purpose of a tutorial was to teach the student to think for him- or herself, not to impart knowledge, which can be acquired from lectures and books, but I was aware that the study of history, as indeed of many subjects, requires information about a corpus of facts before one can start the thinking. I am afraid my early pupils, and indeed later ones too, suffered from my ignorance. However teaching helped me to learn, not so much because my pupils knew more than me, though they may well have, but because I found that asking them questions to which neither I nor they knew the answers stimulated me to try to find them. I also learnt a great deal by having to lecture, the fruits of which are described in the next chapter.

Thinking about my experiences as a tutor has made me see why tutorials had in the past sometimes been described as 'reading with the pupil', a concept which would puzzle many people today. What it reflected was the notion that tutorials consisted of a discussion between equals, a joint enquiry in which the pupil was treated as a partner – albeit a junior partner – in the search for understanding. This was no doubt an unrealistic account of what often took place, but it remains valuable as the ideal at which to aim.

When Lady Ogilvie retired as Principal in 1966 (to my regret a year early), some of my friends saw me as a suitable successor. Although deeply interested in college affairs, I did not in fact want the job because it would have meant giving up teaching and most academic work, both of which I tremendously enjoyed, but I have to confess that I was disappointed by the almost total lack of support for me amongst my colleagues, only one of whom, and she was a peripheral figure, thought I should even be considered. My ignorance of this low estimation of my capacities should I suppose have made me think about my personality defects, but I shrank from indulging in such a painful activity and soon recovered from the blow to my pride. College chose for the post Miss Nancy Fisher, who quite soon became Mrs Trenaman. She came to us from the Civil Service, where she had had a distinguished career in the Board of Trade. She adapted quickly to a different milieu and soon learnt to cope with the idiosyncracies of the dons, some of which must have surprised her. We valued her clear head, administrative gifts and loyal commitment to the college. Helped by an excellent memory, she took a lot of trouble with students, especially in advising them about their careers. Her involvement in University administration was also an asset to the college.

Although in the 1960s St Anne's was, as I have described above, a flourishing and successful college, I began to think some aspects of college life could be improved. I was aware of a desire among the students – graduates and undergraduates – to get to know dons other than their tutors, and I was keen there should be more contact between undergraduates and graduates. These types of association seemed to occur more often in other colleges, at least in the ones I had an opportunity to observe: Balliol, New College, and University College where Herbert was a Fellow. So I and some of my colleagues thought up various schemes designed to produce more contacts at all levels. One was to allow a limited number of graduates to join the High Table on some days, not as guests, but as of right. This worked well for a time, but it petered out after a while partly because of opposition from the least sociable dons, some of whom even wanted their meals provided elsewhere in order to avoid having to make the effort of conversing with graduates. Another of our schemes was to have every day, in one of the big common rooms, tea provided for students and any don who wished to come. The administrative staff were also welcomed, in order to break down the existing stratified structure of the college. This was a success for a time, but also petered out through lack of support by members of the Senior Common Room. Another of our ideas was that dons should, when they felt so inclined, eat in an informal way in the body of the Hall with the students instead of at High Table. This never really took off, partly because it was not well supported by the Junior members when a separate table was unfortunately set aside for participants; the wits said they did not wish to be seen as 'don fanciers'.

The most ambitious innovation devised by the reformers was to have what we wanted to call a 'Forum', that is an open meeting twice a term which could be attended by anyone who worked in the college: dons, students, administrative and domestic staff. It was to be an arena for the discussion of matters of general concern, whether academic, educational, disciplinary, or to do with any aspect of the running of the college. Individual cases could not be raised. It was to have no powers. Votes were not to be taken or resolutions passed, but the subjects discussed were to be reported to Governing Body. The chairmanship was to rotate. College agreed to go ahead with this proposal, but the title 'Forum' was not adopted, as our classics Fellow considered it a misnomer. Instead it was given the clumsy and misleading name 'Consultative Committee'. Nevertheless in its early days it functioned as I had hoped, except for the absence of the domestic staff. We had useful, informal, frank but good-tempered discussions on such matters as the substitution of classes for tutorials (to which I was hostile), visiting hours, the use of the college crèche by graduates and staff who had children, whether the college should become co-educational, and access by students to their files. During the period of the Great Student Unrest, some students feared that we kept notes on them, with newspaper and police photos of those who had taken part in demonstrations, by means of which we meant to ruin their careers for ever. I think we reassured them about this. Unfortunately after a time the procedure became more formal and the atmosphere confrontational, particularly when the college's finances and maintenance fees were the issues. After the students secured representation on Governing Body and college committees, the function of the Consultative Committee was less clear, but it continued to exist, as it still does.

In the late 1960s I and some of my colleagues were keen that the college should go mixed, i.e. admit men at both the senior and junior level. We were worried by the often small number of applicants for our tutorships, and wanted to widen the field from which appointments could be made. At the junior level our arguments centred on the creation of a more agreeable and normal social life. This was a difficult time at which to make the case for a women's college to admit male undergraduates because many people were anxious to increase the number of women students at Oxford, or at least to make fairer their chances of admission. In the mid sixties only 16% of undergraduates were women. However, encouraged by the fact that some men's colleges declared they wished to admit women, albeit sometimes for discreditable reasons,

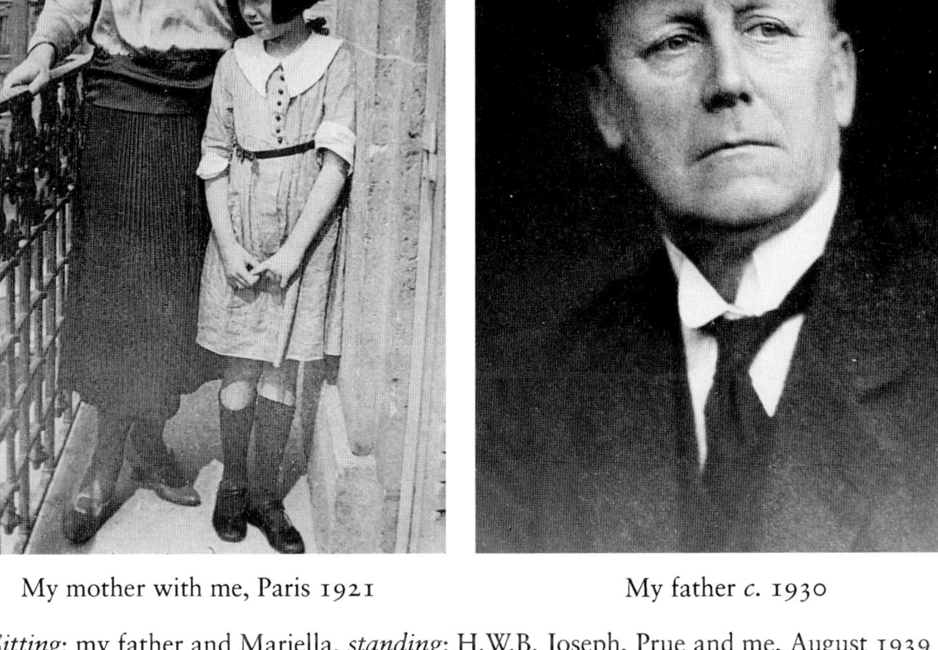

My mother with me, Paris 1921

My father *c.* 1930

Sitting: my father and Mariella, *standing*: H.W.B. Joseph, Prue and me, August 1939

Above: At the Cours Fénelon: Jenifer Hart middle row third from left; Aline de Gunzbourg back row second from right. *Below*: VIth form at Downe House with Miss Willis: Jenifer Hart back row second from left

With Raisley Moorsom, Geneva 1932

Elliott Felkin 1932

Philip Noel-Baker 1932

Prue and Bill Montagu-Pollock at their wedding 1933

Tom Day at the Unemployed Camp 1935

Above left: On the Finsteraarhorn in the mid-1950s; *above right*: with George Paul in the Lake District 1961; *below*: Herbert with Charlie, Adam and Joanna (in front), *c*. 1951

Lamledra from the Dodman

Joanna

Adam

Charlie

Jacob

With Jacob

Herbert, thinking

Above left: Isaiah Berlin; *above right*: Herbert under portrait by Derek Hill in Brasenose 1977; *below*: Stanford 1984, Tanner Trust

such as a desire to teach pretty girls, we pressed ahead and secured in 1969 a vote in favour of our proposal, but it fell short of the two thirds required for a change in our Statutes. Ten years later we became a mixed college at both senior and junior level. By then five men's colleges were already admitting women and most of the others had decided to follow suit. I and many other women dons would have preferred a more gradual transition from single sex to mixed colleges in the University as a whole, but we welcomed the fact that both the number and proportion of women students at Oxford had increased and that this trend was likely to continue, as indeed it has. In St Anne's the effect of the change at senior level seems to have been altogether good: many excellent appointments have been made, and our science side has been strengthened. At the junior level, I am more doubtful. Maybe the sum of human happiness has been increased, but the drunken and yobbish behaviour of some of our male undergraduates has made me feel I had been rather starry-eyed when putting the case for going mixed.

Many people, especially women, are disappointed that the advent of mixed colleges has not resulted in the appointment of more women dons in the former male colleges, but they were in my view unrealistic in hoping that the composition of the fellowship would be changed rapidly. There were, and no doubt still are, pockets of male chauvinism at Oxford, but I do not feel as gloomy about the situation as do my ultra-feminist friends. It inevitably took time for vacancies to occur and a change to take place. All the former men's colleges now have some women fellows, and at the time of writing three of them have women as Heads. Many more women hold research fellowships than in the past when few such posts were open to them, so the pool of applicants for full fellowships is potentially much larger than it was. Moreover the University has introduced various procedures to counter discrimination against women and to improve their chances of appointment. It would however give a misleading picture of the situation if I did not also mention that many men, including two Heads, have been appointed to jobs in the former women's colleges. This has received much adverse comment in feminist circles. Some of this criticism was unwarranted, because many of these appointments were necessary to strengthen the science teaching in these colleges. Nevertheless on the face of it the overall position looks strange, and indefensible if one believes in fairness, as about as many men have been appointed in the four previous women's colleges as women in the 25 previous men's colleges; but at least women academics now play a greater part in the running of the University than they did previously.

During these years many of us at St Anne's, and indeed in other colleges, were resenting the relentless escalation of administrative business which was occurring. I began to calculate the man-hours spent by the Fellows on the Governing Body and our numerous committees. It seemed to me more and more absurd that so much of tutors' time should be occupied in running such a small concern as a college. I felt afternoons could be better spent on academic work or, as in times past, walking in the fresh air with an agreeable companion rather than sitting in smoke-filled rooms. So I and a few others proposed a radical restructuring of our arrangements, the main feature of which was that Fellows should in rotation delegate the management of the college to some of their colleagues for a few years, with the long stop of a General Council which anyone could attend. The scheme was turned down. Although complaining about the bind and boredom of committees and four-hour long Governing Body meetings, the majority of the Fellows were unwilling, even when they understood the concept of man-hours, to surrender the possibility of having a say in all decisions. They feared the governance of the college would become oligarchic instead of democratic.

In the 1970s the college acquired rather unfortunate notoriety by being the scene, as described in the Press, of the first ever strike of domestic staff in the 800 years of the University's existence. The circumstances giving rise to this extraordinary event were as follows. In the spring of 1972, the National Union of Public Employees (NUPE) enrolled as members some of our maintenance and domestic staff, and asked that the Union should be recognised as having sole negotiating rights for all the maintenance and domestic staff. The college said it was not in principle hostile to recognition, but was unwilling to grant it unless a majority of the staff wanted it, which at the time they did not. In early October, before term had started, one of the maintenance staff, Mr Keen, was given notice. He was told that his post had been dispensed with as an economy measure. The college was at that time concerned about its running costs, and the students, in order to help with the problem, had suggested that the standard of domestic services should be reduced, though they later said they had not contemplated that this would mean the dismissal of staff. Trouble then started, for Mr Keen was the shop steward of NUPE at St Anne's. NUPE asked for his reinstatement. They doubted whether the sacking was really due to financial considerations, and suspected that he had been singled out because of his trade union activities. College of course denied victimisation but the circumstances looked suspicious. There was deadlock and NUPE members went on strike at the end of October. For two weeks the college refused to negotiate and was in a state of siege, surrounded by pickets. Left-wing students in the University formed a Strike Support Committee to show solidarity with the workers. Essential supplies were cut off from St Anne's and only got through with the help of strike breakers – some dons and non-unionised staff. Food was thrown over the wall and collected by the chef, who was hostile to NUPE. The central heating was turned off to save oil. Laundry could not get in or out. Life for the resident dons was distinctly unpleasant. The atmosphere was extremely tense as the college was deeply divided. Sympathetic strikes were held in a few other colleges and dustmen came out for a day, leaving 4,000 houses in Oxford with their bins unemptied. In the end college agreed to go to arbitration and the strike ended. The arbitrator did not accept that Mr Keen had been sacked because of his trade union activities, but was not convinced that his dismissal on economic grounds was reasonable, an astute judgement giving, as it did, something to both sides. College complied with the arbitrator's recommendation to reinstate Mr Keen. A year later, after endless negotiations, recognition of NUPE was granted. Some of the participants enjoyed this bizarre affair, but I think it damaged the college's image for a time, as we were thought foolish and inept.

Reflecting on my time as a don, I am clear that I had a much more enjoyable life than I would have had if I had stayed in the Civil Service. The work of a civil servant can be, and often is, interesting, but it can also be boring, though difficult. What I valued above all in academic life was the large degree of freedom it allowed me to think about and work on subjects of my choice, and the intellectual stimulus provided by a rich feast of lectures and seminars. Turning from what I found enjoyable to the much more difficult issue of whether students enjoyed or benefited from my teaching, I can say little of value, the mechanisms of appraisal and feedback having not yet been instituted, though I am clear I was often deficient as a supervisor of graduates. My knowledge of the subjects they were working on was frequently inadequate, and they were often discouraged rather than helped by my criticisms. Some of my undergraduate students, who formed the bulk of my teaching, no doubt also felt I was too hard on them, pernickety about language, putting too high a value on clarity of thought and expression. Some, I suspect, felt I lacked objectivity and the imaginative understanding of ideas to which I was antagonistic, but at least I made clear my position as an entrenched atheist and socialist, so they knew where they were. Looking back I realise that I did not see that adults need a steady diet of favourable comment as much as children, but I hope that on balance, if it makes sense to strike one, I did less harm than good. It is possible that the main impression I made on pupils was that of mild eccentricity, at least in my choice of clothes. During one of our entrance exams a candidate was heard to remark as I walked along a corridor where they were all sitting 'She won't get in, dressed like that.' In the 1950s candidates came for interviews often wearing hats and gloves. Later on the convention was to dress down, even in one case to coming in a boiler suit. The bright colours of my socks featured prominently in the speech made by a pupil on the occasion of my retirement.

Besides teaching I took seriously my duties as a 'moral' tutor, seeing individually the students allocated to me at the beginning and end of every term – not to supervise their morals, but to check up on how their work was going and to discuss any problems they wished to raise. There is a danger of idealising this long-standing Oxford practice; it can become formal and empty, but at its best it seems to me invaluable, and I can but hope that it will not lapse. There may be a danger of this now that more tutors than previously do not live in Oxford. Without prying into the private lives of my pupils, I would try to picture their home circumstances. If these were difficult I would, remembering my own experience, advise them to be realistic and not to tax their capacities of being agreeable and dutiful at home for the *whole* vacation. The other advice I felt confident to offer was to aim at a career when leaving Oxford rather than to mess around for a year or so as girls often did; to get a training and to work before marrying and having children, so that if they gave up work outside the home, they had something to go back to. I also advised them not to marry too young. I felt less well equipped to say anything useful when asked by an undergraduate how she could be less boring.

If it were not presumptuous to claim credit for the subsequent achievements of one's pupils, I would point out how many of mine have had great careers, as academics, public servants, lawyers, school teachers, journalists, in television and radio, and even as novelists, often combining their work with family responsibilities. I wished I had been able to get to know personally more of my students. The pressures of work and family life made this difficult unless, as some did, they lived with us in Oxford or Cornwall. These have become life-long friends and I am very aware how lucky I was to be able to recruit new faces from the younger generation into my circle of friends to take the place of those of my age who are inevitably dying off.

Another aspect of Oxford life which made it particularly agreeable when I first returned there were the informal dances held in the houses of youngish and indeed middle-aged dons. Unlike traditional Oxford balls, these were quite simple events where dancing, usually to a record player, was more important than food or drink. The hard core of the participants included not only what were mockingly dubbed 'the dancing economists' – Halls, MacDougalls, Littles, Worswicks, Peter Ady – but a variety of others: Chilvers, Warnocks, Dawes, Robinsons, Nowell-Smiths, Butterworths, Deightons, Chesters. Nothing similar had, as far as I know taken place in Oxford in the 1930s or even in the gay twenties – the golden age of dancing. I was sad when these enjoyable events petered out in the sixties.

10

Academic Work

UNDER THE SYSTEM instituted at Oxford after the war, I, like most tutors in Arts subjects, was appointed a Lecturer of the University with an obligation to give 16 lectures a year. It was an excellent arrangement, as it both helped colleges financially by supplementing tutors' salaries from University funds, and stimulated research and academic work. Cambridge, to the regret of some people there, did not adopt a similar scheme. This is one of the many ways in which the two Universities, though often lumped together, are in fact different in their arrangements.

At first the only subject I could offer for a course of lectures was the History of the British Police, which even when given the more enticing title 'Crime, Public Order and Police' attracted inevitably a small and ever-declining audience.

My next course, on the history of the Civil Service from the late eighteenth century onwards, was better attended, for there was considerable interest in administrative history at this time, and I treated the subject very broadly, bringing out whenever possible the light it threw on politics and society generally. The mid-nineteenth century proposal to abolish patronage as the method of appointment to the Civil Service and to replace it by open competition stimulated a long-drawn-out and interesting debate. There were fears that without patronage the government would not be able to control Parliament and that open competition would, as one nervous contemporary said, let in 'quick-witted youths without breeding'.

In my lectures I discussed how far one could rely on the colourful and amusing accounts of life in public offices given in contemporary fiction. How typical was Barnacle Junior in the Circumlocution

Office in Dickens's *Little Dorrit*, 'singeing his knees by the fire and gaping his weary way on to four-o-clock'? Or Charles Tudor in Trollope's *Three Clerks*, who could 'hardly be said to have worked at all', and who, with five other young men, rendered the life of 'the wretched Mr Snape as unendurable as possible for five hours a day, forcing him to certify that an extra hand was necessary to do their work'? This got me into the whole question of how safe it is, when writing history, to use contemporary fiction as a source, and I later made a study of the literary image of Utilitarianism, showing how unreliable it was.

The term 'administrative history' makes the subject sound boring, but the more I studied it over several years, the more unfair and misleading I found this judgement. For the mid-nineteenth century was the heroic age of the civil servant who was also a reformer. A new type of public servant was emerging who was not just a superior clerk, neutral and anonymous. Men like James Stephen, Edwin Chadwick, G.R. Porter, Kay Shuttleworth, Charles Trevelyan, John Simon, had strong views about what needed to be done, even at times trying to influence public opinion to get support for their policies. I showed how the famous Northcote-Trevelyan report of 1853 on the Civil Service was a trap for historians giving, as it did, a distorted picture of the public service at that time. Carelessly drafted, it asserted in general terms and ringing phrases that the Service was a haven for the unambitious and indolent, for men 'of very slender ability and perhaps questionable character', for 'sickly youths' who acquired rights to a pension upon early retirement. This led me on to think about and criticise the models of administrative history postulated by revisionist historians in the 1950s and 1960s. Their thesis was that many improvements in social conditions in the nineteenth century were the result of abstractions such as 'impersonal forces' and not due to human agency. This to my mind was not an adequate explanation of why certain things happened.

Parts of my lectures were based on what historians call 'original' or 'primary' sources, for when preparing them I had managed to get hold of the papers of Sir Charles E. Trevelyan, the main author of the Northcote-Trevelyan report. The story of how this happened is not without interest.

I first wrote to Charles Trevelyan's grandson, the famous historian George Macaulay Trevelyan, asking him if any such papers existed. He said he had no idea whether they did or not, which I thought strange, as he had written a book on Britain in the nineteenth century.[32] However he suggested I should contact his brother, Sir Charles P. Trevelyan, with whom incidentally I knew he was on cool terms because of their political differences. C.P. Trevelyan had been a member of the Labour Governments of 1924 and 1929–31, whereas G.M. Trevelyan was a Baldwinite. Sir Charles, to whom I wrote, sent me a small book written by his gardener, saying that it would tell me all there was to know about his famous ancestor. But he added that there were some volumes of letters which I could come and look at if I wanted to, though he doubted whether they were of any interest. I accepted the offer with alacrity and took more or less the next train to Newcastle-upon-Tyne. When I arrived at Wallington, the ancestral home, Sir Charles had clearly forgotten I was coming, which was rather disconcerting, but having recovered from the shock of my appearance, he showed me the treasures of his house, especially his great-uncle Macaulay's desk. When I finally got him to focus on the purpose of my visit, he took me to the bookshelves containing 59 volumes of C.E. Trevelyan's correspondence while he was head of the Treasury and in India. A quick glance at the contents made me realise this was a magnificent find, and that it was essential, if I was to be able to work on the papers, that they should be transferred to Oxford. Sir Charles was at first reluctant to part with them, but, after a day's thought, agreed that they should be lodged temporarily in the Bodleian Library. He left me in no doubt that he trusted the papers would be used to enhance the reputation of his grandfather. I returned to Oxford and sent him a large trunk in which he most nobly packed the bulky Letter Books. I was thrilled at the successful outcome of our negotiations, especially as I knew that previous efforts by historians to get access to the papers had been unsuccessful. They are now, very suitably, lodged in the library of the University of Newcastle-upon-Tyne.

As I worked on the 11,000 pages of the correspondence during the next six months, I found that it was concerned with a great

[32] G.M. Trevelyan, *British History in the Nineteenth Century (1782–1901)*, 1922.

many matters besides the Civil Service. Of particular interest was the light it threw on Trevelyan's attitude to the Irish famine of the 1840s, an appalling event which resulted in the death of millions of people. He insisted that the recipients of relief could easily be demoralised, but that, if properly handled, the crisis could become a blessing, as intended by Providence; for deaths by starvation were in his view a discipline through which good could be obtained for Ireland and the whole British nation. I wrote an article which put forward a revisionist evaluation of Trevelyan's general administrative skills, and which emphasised that he was far from being a model humane philanthropist; but I had difficulty in getting it published. It was turned down, on the ground that it would hurt the feelings of his grandson (G.M. Trevelyan), by both Peter Quennell, the editor of *History Today*, of which G.M Trevelyan was a founder, and, what astonished me even more, by Richard Pares, the editor of the *English Historical Review*. However after Pares' death, it was accepted by the EHR and published in 1960.[33] I was relieved that it was generally well received, though one or two people thought I had been unduly hard on Trevelyan and wrong to imply that his views, particularly about famine relief, were unusual at the time.

I also lectured on Local Government since 1830, having been asked to do this in the absence of Brian Keith-Lucas, the expert on the subject. I had never subscribed to the view held by academic snobs that local government was a dim subject, unworthy of study. For government done in local units gives rise to many of the same questions as government organised on a national basis: Who had power? How were they appointed or elected? What were they like? What role was played by political parties, local families or pressure groups? Moreover English local government in the nineteenth century is particularly interesting as it was a period of great change. Local authorities were coming to be regarded in a new light, less as trustees of rates and more as providers of services; they were judged more by their enterprise than their frugality. This raised constitutional and legal questions such as: could they only do things specified in legislation, or, as in most foreign countries, could they do anything not specifically forbidden? Was municipal trading

[33] Vol. 75, pp. 92–110.

legitimate? Should it be allowed to threaten the livelihood of private traders? Contemporaries discussed the case for having local government at all, and, if it existed, how it should be financed, how far it should be controlled by the central government, and whether local authorities should be democratically elected. John Stuart Mill in particular made a thorough and illuminating survey of these issues in his book *Representative Government* (1861). Much of what he said about the value of local government could, incidentally, have been studied with profit by recent British Governments before they made the nefarious decision to weaken the role of local authorities. Exploring all these questions confirmed me in my view that the subject was many-sided and fruitful.

At about this time I became one of the 12 University representatives on the Oxford City Council, being one of the three members elected by Congregation, that is MAs with college or university appointments. Six of the others were elected by heads of colleges and bursars, and three were aldermen elected by the University representatives. This arrangement had existed since 1889, though for centuries previously the University had been deeply involved in the government of the city. I wanted to serve on the Council partly to learn how Local Authorities worked, but mainly because I felt that academics should take more interest than most of them did in the problems of the town in which they lived and worked. The dons and college officers who sat as University representatives were the exceptions. Far more typical were those whose attitude was exemplified by the comment I received that they supposed I was standing as a candidate because I was 'interested in drains'. My three years on the Council (1961–4), especially my time on the Housing Committee, were not without interest for me, but I felt I had contributed little towards the proceedings or to the welfare of the city. This was partly because I was not a member of any caucus, and so was ignorant of what was happening behind the scenes. I was not good at fraternising with other councillors, though I attended most conscientiously boring ceremonies, as when the Lord Mayor welcomed foreign visitors and we were served with a dark sweet British sherry. The University quite rightly did not brief its representatives, and although I was a member of the Labour Party and anxious to help them if I could, they did not allow me to come to their meetings because I had not been 'democratically elected' to the

Council. University people should, they argued, stand as candidates in local government wards, as had famous figures like Dick Crossman and Frank Pakenham in the 1930s. I realised that this remnant of corporate representation was anachronistic and indefensible on standard democratic principles and that it was bound to be abolished, as it was finally in 1974. I nevertheless felt a tinge of regret at the decision, for both City and University had benefited from the previous arrangement facilitating, as it did, closer links between Town and Gown than exist today. My experience on the Council, brief as it was, supports the verdict expressed in the *History of the University of Oxford*[34] that 'University councillors had usually justified themselves as disinterested contributors to city government, offering experience through long service but not standing for a particular University interest nor acting in concert.' As an instance of this I can cite my solo vote against a road across Christ Church Meadow, when on one occasion in this long drawn out affair, the other University members were amongst the 59 who voted for the road.

My next course of lectures was an ambitious examination of nineteenth-century social reforms, taking each week a separate subject or problem: factories, mines, the poor law, public health, crime and punishment, housing, drunkenness. I was interested in finding out who was primarily responsible for such improvements as were made. This involved assessing the influence of Jeremy Bentham and his followers, the part played by officials, such as inspectors, and by philanthropic individuals, the role of the churches, and the controversial question whether the supporters of reform were predominantly Whig or Tory. I also identified the main opponents of the reforms which were proposed, and analysed their arguments, particularly to estimate whether these were what I rather simplistically and tendentiously called 'valid'. When progress was slow, was this, I asked, due to contemporary disagreement on the facts, e.g. were long hours prejudicial to the health of factory workers? Did children suffer from working in the mines? Were prisoners reformed by solitary confinement? Or was progress slow because of disagreement over the remedies proposed, e.g. the best type of drain to improve public health? Or were the obstacles

[34] Vol. VIII, 1994, p. 554.

genuine administrative problems, such as the inadequacies of local government or the lack of expert officials? How far were ignorance, apathy, selfishness, or inhumanity the obstructions?

This work led me on to dig more deeply into the influence of Christianity, not on people's private lives, but on public affairs, social, economic and political, in nineteenth-century England. I had long been interested in the wider, controversial and topical question whether Christians should try to apply Christ's teachings to secular problems, or whether they should think of his message as concerned only with spiritual matters, involvement in politics being particularly dangerous. It was of course not for me as an atheist to have a view on how Christians *ought* to behave, but it seemed legitimate and important to study how churches and individuals have *in fact* interpreted Christian tenets, and, because of my interest in social reforms, to test the often held view that Christianity had without doubt been a force for social progress. So, after a great deal of research, I gave a course of lectures, examining each week one of the churches or main religious movements: Methodism, Evangelicalism, the Oxford Movement, mainstream Church of England, Christian Socialists, Nonconformists, Roman Catholics. This involved trying to find the answers to many questions. Were the people in each group interested in social problems and social policy, or were their main concerns different, e.g. theological, doctrinal and liturgical issues, church building, ritual, defending Christianity against attacks from scientists and sceptics? If they were interested in secular matters, what was their attitude to the main social problems of the day? The picture which emerged was very complex, and I suspect that my analysis was at times rather crude, categorising the various groups as reformist and even politically radical, or conservative and reactionary, condemning as they did the values of the eighteenth-century Enlightenment. But what could not be disputed was the profound differences of opinion which prevailed. Was poverty God's will, or should it be attenuated? If so, how? Had the poor a right to be educated, or was education of the working classes a danger to the social fabric? Could social conditions be changed by a moral reformation of the individual, or was state action necessary?

At one time I thought of turning these lectures into a book, but in spite of encouragement from a publisher, I abandoned the idea, thinking it beyond my capacities, and I confined myself to making a more thorough study of the political and social doctrines of Church of England clergy in the mid-nineteenth century. So I examined a cross-section of the vast mass of surviving sermons and pamphlets to see what social and political messages, if any, they contained. These were uniformly to the effect that the existing social structure was the creation of Divine Providence. Poverty was endlessly justified on numerous different grounds. Afflictions, private and public, were declared to be signs of God's love, or punishments for sin. Government had a divine origin, so rulers should be revered and obeyed without question. War was usually justifiable. Immersed in this literature, I became deeply depressed. I also found it difficult to cope with the large quantity of material I had collected from the abundant resources of Oxford libraries. But not wishing my labours to be entirely in vain, I later embodied the fruits of my research into a chapter of a book which applied the concept of 'social control' to the study of relationships between rich and poor in nineteenth-century Britain.[35] In this I showed how a great many Church of England clergymen used religion to maintain and reinforce the social order. My contribution to this book was received contemptuously by reviewers, but I still think my project was not valueless, even though, inevitably, it was impossible to estimate the *influence* of the clergy's teachings.

Whilst I was working on these problems, an eminent Cambridge historian, Dr G.R. Kitson-Clark, delivered the prestigious Ford Lectures at Oxford on 'The Making of Victorian England', published as a book in 1962. I thought some of the things he said were questionable, for he belittled the role of men and ideas, and put in their place, as organs of change, concepts such as 'the historical process' or 'blind forces'. This stimulated me to examine the works of various other historians (Oliver MacDonagh, David Roberts, W.L. Burn and R.J. Lambert) on some of whom Kitson-Clark relied, and in due course to write a rather sharp article characterising their interpretation of history as 'Tory'. I used this label in order to contrast their attitude with the much derided 'Whig' interpretation of history which required human heroes and villains in the story. In my article I argued that the social reforms made in nineteenth-

[35] *Social Control in Nineteenth Century Britain*, ed. A.P. Donajgrodzki, 1977.

century England did not take place, as was suggested, 'naturally', as a result of impersonal historical forces, but were the result of conscious human effort to control what happened. In particular I showed how important were the principles and ideas of Bentham and his followers, dismissed by the historians I was criticising as 'mere philosophers' with virtually no influence. I saw these views as dangerous because they lead imperceptibly to the notion that social progress would take place in the future, as in the past, without human action: all would turn out for the best if we just drifted in an Oakeshottian boat. This is a reference to certain passages in Michael Oakeshott's inaugural lecture, *Political Education* (1951).

Soon after the publication of my article in *Past and Present* (July 1965), I received a long, distressed but polite letter from Dr Kitson-Clark, complaining that I had been unfair on him, and that I had misconceived and misinterpreted much of what he had written. He was also critical of my grouping together a number of different historians and labelling them with the same political standpoint. However he said he did not propose to reply to my article, partly because this would take up too much of his time, and partly because public controversies were in his view fruitless. He hoped therefore that I would reconsider what I had written. I trust I replied to him politely, but I did not offer to retract. I felt I had shot my bolt and that it was for others to discuss the thesis I had advanced if they thought this was worthwhile. And this is what happened. I had many supporters including some of Dr Kitson-Clark's colleagues at Cambridge, and in due course, inevitably, critics, the most damning of whom was Professor G.R. Elton, who wrote: 'A debate which was already lively enough, was needlessly exacerbated by Hart, who saw nothing but political prejudice in the new view, and discovered a Tory conspiracy against the liberal gospel. That however is nonsense.'[36] The new view referred to by Elton was that reforms occurred simply because they were necessary. Other commentators were stimulated to do some further research in order to test my contentions, so there are grounds for saying that the controversy was not (*pace* Kitson-Clark) fruitless. I was pleased that my article was reproduced (in 1974) in a book of

[36] G.R. Elton, *Modern Historians on British History 1485–1945. A critical bibliography, 1945–1969*, 1970, p. 121.

Essays in Social History edited by M.W. Flinn and T.C. Smout; but looking back on the whole affair, I feel I should perhaps have delivered less of a broadside, clothed my views in more temperate language, and have made it clearer that I was not attributing party-political affiliations to the historians I was discussing. In using the term 'Tory' I was merely trying to show the ideological implications of their explanations of social reform. That these reinforce conservative philosophy, I have no doubt.

My next venture into print was a chapter in a book on the growth of government in the nineteenth century.[37] My contribution, on *The Genesis of the Northcote-Trevelyan Report*, reflected my continuing interest in the differing types of explanation offered by historians when discussing why certain things had happened. In relation specifically to Civil Service reform in the mid-nineteenth century, there was a contrast between writers who saw reform as due chiefly to pressure from the middle classes, anxious to find more outlets for their educated sons, and others who focused on Sir Charles Trevelyan and his associates wishing to provide a more efficient and economical public service. The difference of approach seemed to me of interest, not only as part of the history of the Civil Service, but more generally, illustrating as it does different kinds of explanation, some focusing on groups, social classes and economic motivation, others emphasising the roles played by individuals, particularly great men, and the influence of ideas and of practical experience.

In the early 1970s, taking advantage of the wonderful freedom allowed to Arts faculty members to lecture on anything they liked, I launched boldly into a topic largely new to me – the history of women in England from Anglo-Saxon times to the twentieth century. Some members of the University were understandably sceptical about my capacity to deal with pre-modern periods. One professor, Hugh Trevor-Roper, even sent his secretary to find out what went on at my lectures, but I was undeterred by the implied criticisms of my enterprise, and greatly enjoyed the research involved. I compared the position of women in different periods, discussing the impact of Christianity, feudalism, capitalism, and the

[37] *Studies in the growth of nineteenth-century government*, ed. Gillian Sutherland, 1972.

industrial revolution on their roles and status. I dealt very fully with the growth of feminism in the nineteenth century, that is the demand for the removal of discrimination against women whether it was based on law or convention. Some members of my audience inevitably considered me an old-fashioned feminist, for the Women's Liberation movement was gathering momentum at this time in England as well as in the USA and elsewhere, and the flow of books about women, which later became an avalanche, had already started with key pioneering works by Sheila Rowbotham, Juliet Mitchell and Kate Millett. I familiarised myself with some of this literature, but continued to lecture throughout the seventies on traditional lines, little influenced by the vast industry of Women's Studies. It seemed to me still worth recording in some detail and acclaiming the success of the hard and long battles fought in the nineteenth and early twentieth centuries to get secondary and higher education for girls, access to the many forms of employment which were closed to women, and to win the right to vote. In doing this I was distancing myself from those who, in order to emphasise that women were still discriminated against and oppressed in all sorts of ways, wrote disparagingly of the early feminists because they were mainly middle class and concerned with attacking only the 'superstructure' i.e. formal employment and the suffrage.

I also took the opportunity to argue in my lectures against the thesis advanced by some historians, including Professor O.R. McGregor, that progress in the fields of employment and education owed little to pioneering feminists; rather it was in their view the result of other things like 'the technological and social diversification of industrialism' and the need to satisfy the demand for cheap labour, or the need for school teachers after the passing of the 1870 Education Act. I saw this theory as an example of my *bête noire*, namely the notion that changes happen more or less spontaneously, as a result of impersonal forces, without allowing that what people, even single individuals, do is or can be important, that is that they can affect 'the historical process'. In taking this line I was encouraged by reading a vigorous article by Tony Judt criticising much modern social history.[38] He bemoaned the fact that, in the hands of

[38] 'A Clown in Royal Purple: Social History and the Historians'. *History Workshop*, spring 1979. pp. 66–94.

many social historians, past human society takes on an oddly impersonal quality. He was keen one should remember that people have ideas and ideals and that they are not just passive pawns pushed around by impersonal causality. He hoped that 'real people, with opinions of their own, would re-emerge from the heap of taxonomological wool under which they have been buried'. However he saw the need for Women's History, whilst regretting the quality of much of the work in that field. I am not in a position to evaluate this work and suspect that my attitude towards Women's Studies is warped by the fact that, although I regard myself as a feminist, I am not whole-heartedly in sympathy with Women's Lib.

Thinking about women and linking this up with my long-standing interest in criminology, I became interested in the vast subject of Women and Crime. This led me on to look into the explanations which have been offered by criminologists, who are mostly male, to account for the fact that women and girls commit, and it seems always have committed, many fewer, and many less heinous crimes than men and boys, both in this country and indeed all over the world. The most common explanations have referred to fewer temptations and opportunities, unequal physical strength, and lack of certain skills, in effect, to put it colloquially, 'they would if they could'. It is also said that the official figures in this country under-represent female crime more than they do male to such an extent that the lesser criminality of women is more apparent than real. These and some other explanations struck me as suspect, that is prompted by male chauvinism. More sophisticated thinkers emphasise the influence of social and cultural factors, especially differences in the upbringing and socialisation of boys and girls, and the role models to which they are exposed. The more I studied and wrote about this subject, the more I felt it did not receive enough attention when thought is given to the prevention of crime. For if social and cultural factors have prevented the female half of the population from committing many crimes, the moral is surely that we should reconsider the conventional forms of the upbringing and socialisation of males. I realise that this is a mammoth project, requiring a fundamental change in attitudes and behaviour throughout society, but I continue to hope that more attention will be given to the significance of the figures illustrating the marked lesser criminality of women, and that when tackling 'the problem of crime' we should not be daunted by the difficulties involved in a revolutionary approach to the subject.

I enjoyed preparing courses of lectures, but I cannot pretend that I liked lecturing. Indeed I often dreaded it. My heart would sink as I walked along the corridor towards the lecture room, wondering if anyone would be there to listen to me – no lectures in Arts subjects at Oxford being compulsory – and I was relieved if a small group were still attending. I think my material was often quite original and interesting, but I was not a natural lecturer. I did not relate to my audience, being too nervous to look at them lest I should see boredom or incomprehension on their faces. Once I was bold enough at the end of a lecture to invite questions, but I never did this again as I did not know the answer to the only one which was asked. Towards the end of my career I attended a day's instruction on the art of lecturing and found this useful. In recent years the University has, I am glad to see, taken seriously the need to improve the lecturing technique of its staff, as snobbish indifference to lecturing skills has been a scandal at Oxford. I wished I had been given help earlier in my career.

A few years after I retired, with more time at my disposal, I got around to writing a book which was published by Oxford University Press under the title *Proportional Representation: Critics of the British Electoral System 1820–1945*. Ever since my childhood I had, through the influence of my father, been interested in electoral systems. He was a committed advocate of Proportional Representation, a pillar of the PR Society from 1905 for many years and the author of two brief books on the subject. I too became convinced that electoral systems which did not represent voters' views in at least the rough proportions in which they were held were indefensible, and I had often wondered why the advocates of a more logical and rational system had been unsuccessful in this country. So I set about trying to find the answer to this question. I traced the first signs of interest in voting theory shown in Britain to the early nineteenth century, and I gave a detailed account of all the subsequent campaigns for a change from our procedure, known as first-past-the-post, to a less chancy and more representative system. I discussed the numerous difficulties encountered by the reformers, not the least of which was for many years the unwillingness of many people, including prominent politicians, even to think about the subject, believing it to be hopelessly perplexing. But I also showed how some advocates of Proportional Representation presented their case badly and overstated it absurdly, claiming that their proposals were a panacea for all the defects of our political system.

When planning and writing this book, I was of course aware that for several reasons there had been in this country since the mid-1970s a sharp increase in interest in electoral systems and growing doubt about the legitimacy of first-past-the-post, and I had hoped to 'cash in' on this interest by getting the work published without delay. This unfortunately did not happen, for soon after it ultimately came out in February 1992, a general election here had not, as expected, resulted in a 'hung' parliament. Instead one party had an overall majority in the House of Commons, and interest in Proportional Representation declined rapidly. I had never suffered from the illusion that such an unashamedly academic and (alas) highly priced book as mine would be popular reading, but I had hoped it would have attracted greater notice from historians. I had clearly failed to woo them from the traditional lack of interest in electoral systems displayed in British historical writings. My disappointment was a little mitigated by the warm reception of the book in New Zealand and by the laudatory review of it by Professor Ann Robson, one of the editors of John Stuart Mill's Collected Works.[39]

During my 30-odd years in or on the fringe of academic life, I published little on present day standards and requirements: one book before becoming a don, and thereafter, until retirement, only eight articles or chapters in books edited by others. This relatively small output was not exceptional at the time; indeed some Oxford tutors never published anything. Sometimes this may have been regrettable, but in my view far less regrettable than the results of the present 'publish or perish' policy which is being forced on universities by the Government. In my case I produced no book whilst teaching because I saw no subject on which I could make a significant contribution, and I felt I was better occupied tutoring and lecturing. It may well be that my teaching would have been improved if I had managed somehow to cut down my heavy load of

[39] In *Utilitas* vol. 5, no. 2, Nov. 1993.

tutoring and take time off to write more, but the provision of sabbatical leave at St Anne's was for many years inevitably minimal because we were a poor college. Moreover I occupied one of my sabbatical terms having a baby, as the concept of maternity leave did not exist. I admit that I felt a little ashamed of my low level of publication, but I was able to prevent this becoming a worry by absorbing myself in other activities besides teaching: namely, college administration, reviewing, examining, and very importantly, though I mention it last, family life.

11

Family Life

'WHEN YOU DIVORCE, will you put the interests of the children first?' my son Adam asked me when he was about eight years old. My daughter Joanna tells me that she too thought divorce was likely because Herbert and I argued so much. In fact our marriage was never near collapse. The arguments which worried Joanna were usually about Hobbes, Locke and Rousseau, but I can well understand how some features of our family life gave a different impression, making the children feel insecure. For Herbert and I were not physically demonstrative towards each other, and he had a tremendous capacity for detaching himself from everyday life, happy on his own, reading novels and poetry, playing records and above all working. So he seemed self-contained, uninvolved with the inevitable ingredients of marital and family life. Indeed at times he would make throw-away remarks implying that he regretted having abandoned the freedom and pleasures of his years as a bachelor. It is unprofitable to speculate how serious he was on such occasions, though there can be no doubt about his deep almost neurotic antipathy towards babies and all that they involved. I think that at some level he remained fond, perhaps even very fond of me, and I am certain he was never in love with another woman either before or after our marriage. But he was irritated by some of my characteristics. He thought I fussed about what he considered unimportant matters, such as his appearance and for me unparalleled untidiness. He even had a theory that for people to want their surroundings to be orderly was a sign of neurosis and inner chaos. He criticised me for inhuman behaviour towards some people, particularly, and with some justification, my mother, whom I failed to visit regularly when she was getting old and infirm. He thought I was unduly touchy when I alleged I had been slighted and treated as a second class citizen because I was a woman, for he was antagonistic to thinking in terms of women and men. He also complained about my insatiable and in his view indiscriminate love of parties and social life, often implying that he would happily refuse invitations addressed to both of us if I had not wanted to accept them. In fact he usually enjoyed the event almost as much, if not as much, as I did, but he would continue to make this point by, if possible, leaving a party before me.

Herbert was extremely unsentimental and would never have described our marriage as idyllic, but I think he was, on most standards, a happy man, except during his first two years as a don and his last years of illness. We never discussed issues such as this, and in a way, now he is dead, I rather regret not doing so, but perhaps he was wise not to be explicit about his feelings. I see no grounds for thinking that probing away at the subconscious level and resolving some of the inconsistencies between his demeanour and utterances would have added to his or my happiness. Just as he insulated himself against the tedious aspects of family life, so he avoided getting worried about my tendency to have romantic liaisons with other men by ignoring such situations. The most illuminating example of this occurred when, being told by a friend that he was in love with me, Herbert's reaction was to say 'It's not possible.' He was content to see us leading what he called 'parallel lives'. Quoting Shelley, he once wrote to me that he did not wish to be my 'one chained friend and jealous foe' or to restrict what I did, as long as he knew the basis was all right, adding that it would be mad of him to doubt that. This willingness to leave me an unusual degree of freedom was mainly due to the high value he attached to tolerance and liberty.

Nor had I ever any desire to break up our marriage. I realised how lucky I was to be 'partnered' to Herbert, being always conscious of the fact that only one other man had ever proposed to me. This may have been because my first affairs were with married men 20 years older than me, but it was probably significant that my other close friends and lovers who were younger did not fancy me as a wife. In the company of someone with so much intellectual vitality and humour as Herbert had, I was seldom, if ever, bored during our 55 years together. Apart from the fact that he did not share my lingering sympathy for communist ideals, we held similar views on all important political and social issues. We both put a high premium on clarity of thought and rationality, and rejected all religions. Though brought up in the Jewish faith, Herbert had not even gone through a pious phase, as I had. I benefited enormously from discussions with him on many subjects, in particular when I was teaching Political Thought. Sometimes I felt angry that he knew all the answers, dispelling muddles and ambiguities with such consummate ease, and I envied his vastly superior knowledge of literature and poetry which enabled him constantly to come out with the apt quotation; but I was always aware of the numerous ways in which he had enriched my life. Another thing on which we luckily agreed with no hesitation was that he should refuse the knighthood offered him in 1966, on the ground that honours should be given only for public services and not for academic distinction. Neither of us regretted his decision, unusual though it was.

It would be wrong however to depict our marriage as if it was on a par with the perfect relationship of Beatrice and Sidney Webb. Given my over-critical temperament, there were inevitably aspects of our relationship which irritated me. The most important of these was Herbert's unwillingness to share the responsibilities and burdens of household management and routine chores. Like many men he protected himself from participation in these duties by pleading lack of the necessary skills. He considered it convenient that I had somehow acquired these basic skills and that I knew how to do things like work the washing machine and rectify blocked drains. I favoured a more egalitarian regime, not only in connection with trivial domestic matters such as ordering the milk and putting out the dustbins, but also with larger problems involving thought and planning, like holidays, the care of property, houses, cars. My sense of grievance may be considered unjustified given the gap between our intellectual abilities. It could well be argued that he would not have made his great contributions to jurisprudence if he had had to devote time to more mundane issues, and that I would not have achieved more academically if I had not had to make certain the bills were paid, the chimneys swept, and endlessly to look for his allegedly lost possessions. But at the time I could not help feeling it was unfair that he should leave it to others to pick up the pieces both physically and metaphorically.

As an antidote to these rather carping reflections, I cannot do better than refer the reader to the speeches made by Herbert's friends and colleagues at the memorial ceremony held after he died. Extracts from these are reproduced in the Appendix to this work. Whilst inevitably enconiums, paying tribute to his many virtues, they give a very fair picture of his personality and unique charm.

Besides the two children already mentioned, we had two more, Charles born in 1948 and Jacob in 1959. Herbert had never contemplated having a family of this size, but after some initial hesitation, he became interested in the children's development, education and activities. This was very evident when in 1956 he went to the USA for an academic year, felt homesick, and yearned for news of the children. He disliked all games, whether physical or cerebral, so would not play with the children, but he told them brilliant stories on country walks and enjoyed talking and arguing with them. Jacob posed particular problems as he was brain-damaged at birth. These will be discussed in the next chapter.

The three elder ones started their education at a private school in Oxford. It was unusual at that time for the professional classes to send their children to state primary schools, as many of them did subsequently and do now. So we simply followed David Cecil's advice, and excellent it proved to be. For the school he recommended, the Crescent, suited our children admirably. It was run on the principles advocated by Friedrich Froebel (1782–1852), principles which had considerable influence on educational thought and practice in England and elsewhere, but which have come in for much misguided criticism recently as being too permissive and child-centred. Borrowing, as Froebel did, from the ideas of contemporary German philosophers – Fichte, Kant, Schelling, Krause and Hegel – it is not strange to find that some of his thought was obscure. But his aim was clear: children should learn to think for themselves; one should try to set one's charges 'free of their facile disciplinability, and turn them into original, inquiring, restless and adventurous men', into adults capable of critically assessing and if necessary changing the society in which they live. To achieve these goals, learning should not be a grind, but a delight; it should bring joy. Play, especially spontaneous play, was important. Competition was bad. Children should develop at their own pace, though teachers and parents should stimulate the desire to know and provide opportunities for satisfying that desire. This was more important than simply providing information and knowledge ready-made, to be passively accepted.[40]

Some anxious Crescent parents could not believe their offspring were learning enough because they were not pressed, and advised us to take Joanna away at age nine to improve her chance of getting into the High School. But we had complete confidence in the Froebel philosophy and kept her at the Crescent until the last possible moment. Our decision was vindicated when she sailed through the eleven plus exam, even gaining one of the few free places at the Direct Grant Girls High School, which provided an orthodox, academically orientated education. Some of the teaching there was excellent, some rather uninspiring, and Joanna was irked by its sillier rules e.g. when she was told that her socks were not of the exact shade of beige which was prescribed; but the presence of many intelligent, lively girls provided a redeeming stimulus and a congenial atmosphere. Assisted by discussions with Herbert, she was accepted at New Hall, Cambridge.

The boys had to leave the Crescent at the age of eight if they were to go to the Dragon School, to which we had decided to send them, albeit after some hesitation. It was, and maybe it still is, a unique institution, not only on account of its size (about 400 pupils) and its large contingent of clever, gifted day-boys and a few token girls, but also because it combined traditional with unconventional characteristics. The ethos both in work and sports was highly competitive; there was much streaming and grading, and an enormous emphasis on Latin and Greek. But at the same time the atmosphere was relaxed, gay in the old sense of the word and informal, due to a high level of eccentricity and libertarianism amongst the staff. No wonder parents were not admitted to the hilarious end-of-year reviews featuring masters dressed up in drag doing risky sketches. There were few, if any, silly rules e.g. about clothes, and, for day-boys at least, no compulsory religion. Our children did not complain about the exacting pressure of work which was imposed on them, perhaps because there was scope for so many other activities: music, acting, chess, debating, and in Adam's life the Science Club. Run by the charismatic Gert

[40] See Irene M. Lilley, *A Selection from Froebel's writings*, 1967.

Sommerhoff, an adviser to the famous toy-makers Triang, the club was an unusual feature in a prep. school. Creating objects such as tape recorders, radio-controlled boats and aeroplanes, its members learnt how to experiment and to inquire empirically. Looking back over some old issues of *The Draconian*, I can easily understand how the school was a vastly stimulating experience, for a hundred pages of the magazine were usually necessary to describe the term's activities. The only trouble with this was that life thereafter might seem rather flat. But we did not regret sending the boys to the Dragon: it provided them with an exciting ambience and fostered independent thought.

Deciding what secondary school to choose for Adam was a problem to which we gave much attention. Herbert had never found it easy to cope with Adam's idiosyncrasies and had tended to leave it to me to handle any difficulties. I sometimes found these overwhelming. For instance a diary entry of mine when Adam was aged ten in 1954 reads:

> A day of misery so far as Adam's sanity was concerned. I feel more and more convinced he will end in a madhouse. The deepest depressions – a sense of utter hopelessness – a terrifying capacity to see through one's efforts to distract or cheer, and above all the posing of dilemmas, 'I want to sell my football and yet don't', and there's logically no way out. He seems to have an uncanny power of creating frustrating situations – making impossible demands on life and then feeling disappointed

I may well have been over-dramatising the situation because for much of the time Adam was buoyant, enjoying his many successes at school, but his spirits were undoubtedly low at times. He found the church bells of Oxford profoundly depressing especially on winter Sunday evenings, and once, when quite young, asked me if there was a suicide club he could join. He saw us as subjects without objects. Equally worrying, but in a different way, was the fact that he and a gang of friends roamed about Oxford after school looking for adventures, trespassing on other people's property and engaging in various pranks. Although they were not, I think, breaking the law, they were sailing near the wind, and our inability to prevent these activities has made me realise how facile are the homilies of government ministers and others who condemn, and propose to punish, parents for failing to control their teenage children. I did not even know how to answer Adam when he asked where my authority came from – in effect what legitimised my claim to have a right to control his behaviour.

Because I empathised with Adam more easily than his father did, Herbert thought we were too close to each other and that this was bad for Adam. So he should go to a boarding school. I admitted there was a certain case for sending him away, mainly because he was at that time keen on all games, and we did not like the conventional values of the only 'gamesy' boys school in Oxford, St. Edwards. Moreover Adam himself wanted to go to a boarding school; he had announced a few years before that he was hampered by feeling affection for his parents and wondered whether children should not be brought up communally. But at the same time I desperately wanted to keep him at home, for I disapproved in general of boarding schools, and on selfish grounds I did not want to lose the interest of his company. Some of my diary entries reveal my state of mind. For instance:

> Adam has spent a busy two days making electrical gadgets – absorbed in wires and amplifiers etc. He sometimes puts on a bit of the 'genius' turn I think – but a lot of it comes naturally to him e.g. wandering about in his pyjamas all Sunday morning, with no breakfast, deep in a great sea of objects, clothes, books, bottles etc. How shall I ever exist without him? The thought alone is very cruel. (October 1955)

> I expect he is too fond of me – but it's certainly very agreeable. (August 1956)

One solution to the dilemma was to try to get him accepted as a weekly boarder at Westminster, but this fell through when the school said he could not be given a scholarship, which we were hoping for, unless he was a member of the Church of England. Adam, like all our children, had not been baptised, and apart from a brief period, when aged about six, he had, under the influence of a school teacher, maintained against Herbert that Jesus *was* the son of

God and not just a very good man, he could not, if words have any meaning, be described as a member of the Church of England. We were not willing to treat the question as a mere formality and to commit something near perjury. Afterwards we wondered how several Jewish and atheistic parents of scholars at Westminster had got around this obstacle.

We turned down Winchester as being too conventional for a maverick such as Adam, and also rather foolishly Bedales on the ground that it would not train him to become well-organised, clean, and tidy, as if that were possible. In the end we settled for Bryanston which had a reputation as a progressive liberal school. Unfortunately there was a change of headmaster when Adam went there. I feared the worst when we received a letter from the governors asking parents to be loyal to the new head, recommended on the grounds that he was a member of the Church of England and had played tennis for Somerset. The previous head had been of a different type.

It is difficult to say whether on balance we made the right decision. Adam says going to Bryanston was a terrible shock as he was totally unprepared for leaving home. Though by no means 'soft', he found the physical regime harsh, including as it did the traditional public school routine of icy baths before breakfast. He thinks this kind of training gave him some fortitude, but also an unwarranted sense of superiority over, and scorn for, weak characters and less advantaged people – something that took him many years to get over. He disliked being made to attend religious services, and though he ultimately got excused from them, was indignant that the chief result of his campaign against compulsory religion was the banning of all petitions. However the school had redeeming features. Adam did not have to join the Corps. He was allowed to give up most sport in return for enjoyable sailing in Poole harbour; and he was able to spend much of his time building an ambitious radio telescope and baking superior bread in a self-made oven in the woods. There was considerable scope for musical and literary activities, and the science and maths teaching at least seems to have been good for it secured him a place at Balliol. Finally it must be said in Bryanston's favour that it did not push Adam over the brink and lead to his expulsion, as it did in the case of his close friend, Felix de Mendelsohn. He was able to carve out a quite agreeable life for himself with congenial friends and did not mind being sacked after a term as a prefect because he refused to administer punishments.

Like most mothers I suffered acutely when Adam went away to school and it would have been worse if I had known how miserable he was for the first year or so. Sometimes when I was packing his trunk at the end of the holidays, he would upset me (not deliberately I think) by asking why we did not want him at home. Joanna by contrast was rather pleased to be rid of her troublesome brother, though she occasionally questioned why we were spending so much more money on him than on her.

When we had to decide on a secondary school for Charles, the main problem was to resist the pressure applied on us by the Dragon who wanted him to sit for a scholarship at one of the prestigious public schools. Charles himself expressed no wish to go to a boarding school, though maybe we did not even give him the option, for the local Direct Grant Magdalen College School was acquiring a good reputation despite the Dragon's derisive opinion of it. The school's buildings were undoubtedly uninspiring and pathetically inadequate, but the teachers were mostly excellent and the music was good. The fact that scholastically he found himself two years ahead of most of his contemporaries did not make him arrogant. At times I had doubts about whether he should not have gone away to school, not because I thought poorly of MCS, but because life at home was rather dull and cloying. It lacked the stimulus previously provided by Adam who was away either at Bryanston or working his way round the world between school and university, and the tone of family life was to a great extent determined by our Nanny. As a small boy Charles had been rather recessive and timid, for instance worrying even at the age of five, before conscription had ceased, which branch of the armed services was least risky, with the result that he had been over-protected. Another drawback to life at home were the problems caused by the existence of a mentally handicapped sibling. But on the other side of the balance sheet was the fact that Charles, as a school friend of Miriam Rothschild's son, Charles Lane, was taken on fabulous holidays abroad – to Switzerland, Rome, Belgium and Normandy – as well as staying on the family property in England.

In 1960 our three eldest children were aged 18, 16, and 12, so they were inevitably affected by at any rate some aspects of the social and cultural revolution (it is not too strong a word) that occurred in the 1960s. To many of the young, the 1950s seemed stuffy, rigid and conventional. They wanted a more permissive society, less hidebound by the class structure, less competitive, less materialistic, more tolerant of diversity in behaviour. They thought there was much wrong with the world and that they could alter almost everything. They advocated a new life-style, often substituting just existing for the rat race. This led to the novel habit of 'dropping out' instead of aiming at a career.

There was much in this movement which Herbert and I admired. Indeed he was fascinated by some of its manifestations, and his study of it bore fruit when he chaired the committee set up by the University in 1968 to advise on student unrest in Oxford. The report's famous Appendix A, 'Student Radicalism in Oxford', which was written by him, illustrates his penetrating, sympathetic but at the same time critical, understanding of the revolutionary ideas of the young. It drew attention to the great range of abilities amongst student radicals, some scatter-brained and muddle-headed, others gifted and perceptive. It suggested that the root of their unrest was a horror of many features of the contemporary world and that they focused on universities because these appeared both to reflect and to sustain the structure of a corrupt society.[41]

As parents we had always been distinctly liberal – too liberal in the eyes of some other parents who thought our children were a bad influence on theirs. Our policy, as it developed in the sixties, had two main prongs. One was to distinguish clearly important from unimportant issues, which meant in practice not interfering with unconventional behaviour such as growing their hair long, talking with a cockney accent, dressing like a tramp, covering the walls of their rooms with newspaper or black paint. The other principle we acted on was as far as possible to discuss everything openly with them, to argue about the moral and practical implications of their behaviour, making our views clear, but never rejecting them as people, whatever they did. I was determined at all costs to prevent the sort of tragedy which I saw occurring in some families where, as a result of disputes over minor issues, the children completely

[41] Report of the Committee on Relations with Junior Members (May 1969).

rejected their parents, and all contact was severed, in one case for ever.

Our children certainly tested our liberality. It is no use pretending we were not worried particularly about how they would face life after leaving University. Rejecting achievement as defined by their elders, especially a career in the professions, would they ever be able to earn a living? We tried to bring them down to earth by making it clear that once their education was finished, we would not support them financially, which in any case they did not expect or ask for. I admit it was sometimes painful to keep to this line when one saw them living in squalor on a bare pittance, and, looking back on our policy, I think it was rather brutal, but at least they knew they would always be welcome at home. We were of course like most parents at a disadvantage when we argued with them about drugs as they knew more about the subject than we did and maintained that cannabis was less harmful than 'our drug', alcohol, even if consumed, as in our case, at a very modest level. Maybe they were right.

The culture of the sixties had some lasting effects on our family. It reinforced Joanna's feminism, and contributed to her critical attitude to what she saw as the academic establishment, with the result that she resigned after a few years from her fellowship at King's College, Cambridge, in order to live in a wider and for her more congenial world. I am afraid I was not successful in hiding from her my disappointment at her action, as I was proud that my daughter was the first female Fellow of a man's college. I had not yet learnt not to have aspirations for my children – other than basic ones e.g. that they should not land up in a mental hospital or prison. Adam lived in various communes, turned towards Buddhism and discovered the value of meditation which he has continued to practise. Charlie's musical tastes were widened and, abandoning Economics after he had finished at Cambridge, he became set on life as a musician.

The main effect of the counter-culture on us as parents was to broaden our outlooks or at least our behaviour. As one of the children pointed out, I no longer asked automatically, when observing the strange friends they brought to our house, who their parents were, where they went to school, what they did for a living, why they had been in prison. We were never reconciled to their low esteem of rationality, but we became tolerant of much in their lifestyle and indeed found amusement in some of their gestures. We were of course relieved to get through this rather extraordinary period without disaster, but nothing that happened in the sixties or thereafter has ever undermined my conviction that people who have no children, whether by choice or not, miss many stimulating and fruitful experiences.

It would be wrong to give the impression that our family life was perpetually turbulent. I tended to keep a diary only at times of crisis, which accounts for the fact that Adam features in it much more than Joanna and Charles. As a teenager, Joanna's dominant interest for several years was horses. She had learnt horsemanship, riding bareback on Port Meadow, the enormous unique open field on the edge of Oxford, brilliantly instructed by an eccentric elderly lady of German origin, known as Miss Dearing, who claimed she had taught riding to the Austrian cavalry during the First World War. She lived in a garden shed near the Meadow, and though she looked like a 'bag lady', she was highly educated and had a meal every day in the grand Randolph Hotel, paid for allegedly by a well-wisher. One of her more bizarre habits was to shelter under a horse when it rained. Later the ownership of her own pony meant Joanna never lacked an occupation, for apart from being ridden, the animal had to be visited and looked after. She now says the experience was isolating, and the burden of responsibility a worry to her, but at the time it seemed to us as parents that she got much pleasure and satisfaction out of the whole business – the humdrum caring duties, as well as the more exciting events such as gymkhanas and pony camps. We welcomed what we saw as a stabilising influence in her life, and slightly regretted the shift of her interest at age 16 from horses to young men, and not only because we had to pay for the pony's keep for a year after she had given him up; for she was reluctant to sever her links with the loved object, just as smaller children keep their dolls long after they have ceased playing with them.

Charles' main interest was music, and as a teenager he was happily occupied learning and playing no fewer than four instruments. He also enjoyed his time in Ghana where he went between school and university, though he thought it was ludicrous to be teaching Latin to African children, and on reflection I think it was rather irresponsible of us not to vet more thoroughly the arrangements for this enterprise. For, as it turned out, we were wrong in assuming that the British Council would look after him, and I was shocked when, on a visit, I discovered how he was living and that no one was concerned with his health and welfare.

Regular holidays *en famille* at Easter and in the summer played an important part in all our lives. We were fortunate in having access, through friends and relations, to some wonderful places: in the Lake District to Roger and Paula Quirk's property where they gathered together many interesting people; in Snowdonia at my brother-in-law David Hubback's primitive cottage; and in Cornwall at our family house. We were often joined on these holidays by our son-in-law Alan Ryan, even after his marriage to Joanna had ended. Some people, rather curiously, did not expect us to maintain close relations with him after they had separated, but we regarded him as one of the family and enjoyed his invigorating company. I am delighted by his recent return to Oxford as Warden of New College.

Our Cornish parties developed from being mere family affairs into much larger functions with a unique character – unique, at least unusual, because of the great variety and mixture of people who gathered there every holiday. These included, as they still do, besides relations, academics, pupils and ex-pupils, foreign friends especially Americans, helpers of one kind or another often with some hangers-on, children of all ages, and anyone else whom I had come across and thought would fit in and add interest to the company. Because there is so much space both in the house and in the surrounding countryside, it is easy to break up into small groups. Everyone can do their own thing: read, talk, work, swim, sail, fish, go for walks, ride, play games or make music. I always employ someone to cook – often an astonishingly competent student – so domestic chores are kept to a minimum, but I welcome offers of help or advice with the garden, the land and the buildings. Herbert sometimes suggested that I exploited these 'working guests' as he called them, and was particularly worried when they engaged in hard physical labour such as road mending or bramble bashing, but I took a Ruskinian rather than an Aristotelian view of the situation and was confident that they enjoyed making a contribution to the upkeep and improvement of the property. The fact that most of the people who come to stay wish to return suggests that I am not deluding myself. They seem not to mind the absence of luxuries and to welcome the opportunity to meet old friends or to make unexpected new ones. For me there is sometimes a problem in keeping numbers down to a manageable figure, but I like to think the place is used to capacity. Guests who have complained about the weather or who commit the heresy of suggesting that the north coast of Cornwall is superior to the south tend not to be asked again. The only guest not to appreciate the beauty of the landscape was Isaiah Berlin, who on arrival disconcertingly exclaimed, 'How I hate nature.' These Lamledra parties grew up gradually over the last 30 years. I did not originally plan them as an experiment in living and working together, but I have come to see that in a small way they perform a valuable function besides providing family holidays, because one of their side-effects has been the extension of social contacts between people who might not otherwise have met each other. I am always pleased when they result in the making of friends, especially across the generations.

Not all our family holidays were spent in England. One summer we took the three children to Switzerland, staying in a modest pension bedecked with moralistic notices such as 'Arbeit macht das Leben schön'. ('Work makes life beautiful'.) Trying to control the children's exuberant behaviour, so as not to upset the sedate elderly guests who surrounded us, was at times a strain, and financial constraints also created problems: the children felt badly let down when we ruled out an expensive trip to the summit of the Jungfrau Joch. But this experimental holiday was by and large a success. We also one Easter took the two boys to Greece, joining rather boldly in a party of 25 school boys. On another occasion, in 1964, Charles came with us to Israel where Herbert was lecturing. I found the experience intensely interesting, and my ardent philo-Semitism was only a little dented by a rather perverse teenager's greater empathy with the way of life of Arabs and especially Bedouins. Charles was however willing to admit that the trip had taught him a lot, for he commented afterwards that, after listening to the guides who took us round the country, there was no further need for him to work for his University entrance exam, as he had got enough material for a dozen General Papers.

These family holidays went some way towards assuaging my feelings of guilt at abandoning the children every year to go abroad with Herbert. I realised how lucky and exceptional we were as parents to be able to do this, knowing the children were in our Nanny's very responsible hands. Even so I sometimes shed a tear on leaving them, but I have to confess that my bad conscience soon evaporated once I had crossed the Channel and was enjoying the stimulus of foreign travel. We gave up skiing, which we had done before the war, but continued our amateur efforts at climbing mountains and glacier-walking in Switzerland. I had always loved mountains, but frankly did not altogether enjoy being roped to Herbert, as he tended to be casual about his equipment and body movements. But he was an excellent sight-seeing companion. Desperate to travel after the war, we got ourselves to Belgium in 1947. Finding somewhere to stay in Brussels was a problem. There were bugs in the bed in our first lodging, so we took refuge in a cleaner place, which turned out to be a brothel. When I got back to the Home Office and mentioned this to a Chief Constable, he immediately, and I think only half jokingly, asked me for its address. Wandering round Bruges and Ghent in temperatures of 20 degrees below zero, looking unsuccessfully for somewhere to get even a bowl of soup, brought home to us dimly what life must have been like there during the war.

Travelling in Italy in 1948 was also quite tough. In Venice we lodged with a working class family who gave up their bedroom to us and where the only place to wash was under a tap in the living room/kitchen. Trains were packed to overflowing, with people on the roof. To get to Vallombrosa, which Herbert as a lover of Milton was determined to see, we had to go in a cattle truck.[42] Conditions in 1951 in northern Spain and Portugal, where we rocketed around in trains and buses, were easier. The only drawback to going abroad with Herbert was that I became lazy about learning foreign languages. He had a working knowledge of Italian and Spanish and even picked up some Portuguese, so I rather feebly relied on him to conduct all conversations. For him the chief disadvantage of travelling with me was that our standard of living tended on my insistence to be lower than he wished. He also complained in a mild way that, besides avid cultural sight-seeing, I always wanted to look at slums

[42] See *Paradise Lost* I, 303, 'Thick as Autumnal Leaves that strow the Brooks/ In Vallombrosa'.

and the more squalid parts of the places we visited. This ineradicable urge of mine was also deleterious as it resulted in my becoming depressed, sometimes acutely as in Spain, Sicily, Persia and India. I was deeply shocked at the sight of men grubbing in dustbins in Madrid, and never thought I would see this in England, as alas one does now.

Later on we travelled in great comfort, even luxury, especially when Herbert was receiving one of his many honorary degrees. I was able to accompany him on most of these occasions. Sometimes I felt pangs of resentment that I was merely an appendage to a Great Man, but such shameful sentiments were rapidly dispelled by the pleasures of visiting Mexico, Stockholm, Israel and Harvard, as well as less exotic but agreeable places in Britain.

Herbert's connection with the Tanner Trust for ten years was also a great source of interesting foreign travel. The Trust was created by a remarkable American philanthropist, Obert C. Tanner, who was both a professor of philosophy and a business man. We never ceased to marvel at the story of his life. He was the youngest of ten children in a very poor polygamist Mormon family living in Utah. His father, who had six wives and 42 children, abandoned his mother when he was about eight years old. As a boy and young man, Obert worked in many different, extremely hard, rough jobs. In one of these – an ore dump – he became interested in minerals, which stimulated him to experiment with them at home. This was the origin of the O.C. Tanner company, a business ultimately employing 2,000 people with annual sales of $200 million, manufacturing recognition awards, medals, plaques and jewelry. Besides building up this enterprise, Tanner studied law, philosophy and religion, for his remarkable mother was determined to have an educated family. He gained various degrees and held academic posts. Sometimes when propounding his many ideas and ideals on vast subjects such as world peace, freedom, education, religion, democracy, Tanner could appear a little ingenuous, which made Herbert and me wonder how he could be such an astute business man. Clearly our categories and experiences were too narrow to explain this mystery; so we had to content ourselves with admiring his outstanding altruism, generosity, integrity and humanity.

The purpose of the Tanner Trust was to sponsor lectures on Human Values all over the world. The Trustees met once a year in fascinating places in North America and Europe. In true American style, the wives of the Trustees were assigned a role in the work of the Trust, a burden which I have to admit was not onerous. These occasions led to many warm and lasting friendships. They also provided welcome opportunities to deepen my understanding of the USA. In particular I learnt how absurd it was to generalise about 'America'. I had not visited it since my first trip in 1957 when I joined Herbert for three weeks at Harvard. I was then already less ignorantly critical of the American educational system than I had been, though I was startled and impressed when on my arrival at New York, the immigration officer, on hearing that my husband was a professor of Law, began talking to me about Blackstone.

There was yet another spin-off for me as Herbert's wife, due to his appointment in 1973 as head of an Oxford College. The role of spouse in this situation is ill-defined. It seems to me reasonable to expect the partner to play some part in the life of the college, but I was astonished, as indeed was Herbert, when it was assumed by some of the other spouses in this position that I would, on his appointment, resign from my post at St Anne's. They saw themselves, I think, as doing a full-time job and felt that it would be impossible for me to perform my wifely duties if I continued in other employment. I realised that some of them were admirably conscientious and that they did useful work, but I resented the criticism implied by their enquiries about how I was managing this dual role. Maybe I was unduly touchy, and I must admit that I had to work out whether I had duties to the college, and if so what they were. However I soon abandoned a doctrinaire feminist stance, as I realised how agreeable it was to have the chance to meet a whole new set of people who welcomed me into their community. Supplied as we were with excellent college servants, entertaining was effortless. Our policy was whenever possible to mix up the generations, and students with our friends. I even inaugurated informal dancing at our evening parties. Sometimes I wondered whether I had taken on too much and was doing nothing properly. My lowest moments were at lengthy tea parties on gloomy winter afternoons when I was unable to get a conversation going with shy mathematicians or physicists or those whose only interest was computers, but these were exceptional times in an otherwise interesting and enjoyable life.

The Principal's quarters at Brasenose were extremely attractive, but very limited and in no sense a family house. Moving in was out of the question. This did not worry the college in spite of being a departure from a long established Oxford practice, provoking some adverse comments at the time. Our own home was only five minutes away, and indeed Brasenose would have been disconcerted if we had asked them to accommodate all of us. Herbert in fact constantly resided in the Lodgings during his five years there. The college also accepted without demur his unwillingness to attend chapel services except on important occasions.

I was delighted when he accepted the invitation from Brasenose, because he had on several previous occasions refused to allow his name to go forward for the headship of a college, and because when he had finally relented in the case of Hertford, the appointment had fallen through. This was because he was unwilling to live in college. Moreover the fact that he said he would not regularly attend chapel services worried a few of the Fellows. Indeed two of them and the Chaplain felt so strongly about this that they wrote to the Visitor, Harold Macmillan, asking him to veto the appointment. This was revealed to Herbert a few years later by Macmillan who did not know to whom he was speaking. The name of the candidate was not mentioned by either of them. Although pleased about Brasenose, I was also apprehensive about what was yet another extraordinary step in his career. For Herbert was then aged 66, had never held any college office such as dean, bursar, or senior tutor, and had often said he disliked administration. As it turned out he loved the novelty and variety of activities which the post involved, and his reign was widely regarded as a great success. An amusing account of it can be found in Bernard Richards' piece in the Appendix. I was sad when it ended, but he was determined to retire after five years. He then resumed his work on Bentham and on a Postscript to his book *The Concept of Law*.

12

Jacob

For some years before Jacob's birth I had, like many women approaching middle age, longed to have another child, but did not make up my mind to go ahead with this project until 1959 when I was 45. All went well until his actual birth when, with the umbilical cord round his neck, he lacked oxygen for a brief moment. This caused a brain injury. I knew at once that something was wrong, as the midwife would not let me hold or even see him, as is the usual practice. I was frantically worried and deeply depressed. This was one of the lowest moments in my life, but after a few days his colour became normal and I felt less anxious.

Back home he was a 'good' baby, sleeping and eating well. I ceased to worry, but Herbert, who studied medical books, was full of forebodings and after a few months insisted we should get him examined by a paediatrician. The verdict was that Jacob was not developing properly. I was totally ignorant about mental handicap, as was revealed when I said to the doctor that I supposed he would in due course 'catch up'. Like many parents in a similar situation, I found it difficult at first to face up to the facts, but it gradually became clear to me that something was wrong. The most striking thing about Jacob was that he would not play with any toys, as a normal child does from an early age. By the time he was three, indeed before, his behaviour had become difficult to cope with. He threw tantrums at the least provocation. He was abnormally fearful, but also over-active. As he grew older this created strains in the household, for he disrupted social situations and dismantled everything he could lay his hands on. Record players, radios, cameras, clocks, watches, electric appliances were taken apart and ruined. It was not safe to leave within his reach anything he could open, like pots of paint, ink, scent, cleaning materials.

There was a certain difference of opinion between Herbert and me as to what advice to seek. He favoured taking Jacob up to Sheffield to see an eminent consultant, the Professor of Child Health, who had been Herbert's school friend, whereas I believed in sticking to the local medical services. Our two journeys to Sheffield with Jacob aged three and four were nightmares, and the prognosis disheartening. It was in particular dispiriting to be advised that nannies were bad for children such as Jacob, because they were over-protective.

The next problem was education. We were told by the Local Education Authority that Jacob presented an unusual combination of features, being in some ways intelligent with an extensive vocabulary and in some ways handicapped, and that there was no suitable school for him in Oxford. The solution was to create one. The originator of this brainwave was not the Local Education Authority, but the Consultant Psychologist at the Warneford Hospital, May Davidson, who took a special interest in children. She persuaded an acquaintance of hers, Joy Fuller, a school teacher who had given up work, to start a small unit for children who needed a lot of attention on unorthodox lines. Miss Fuller, who lived in a rather ramshackle caravan on the edge of Shotover, a rural paradise near Oxford, added a tin hut on to her rambling attractive site, and started what she boldly named 'The Caravan School'. Jacob was there in the mornings from age five to ten with at times two or three other children, some like him backward and disturbed, and a few normal. Miss Fuller turned out to be a genius. She was familiar with the relevant literature but not doctrinaire. She was good at devising unusual activities and was infinitely resourceful. Above all she managed to get inside Jacob's mind and to see things as he did. This was important, for he displayed many autistic traits.

Autism has been described as 'a feeling of being in permanent jeopardy'. Autistic children do not develop a sense of self which allows them to feel safe in the world. As a result they often do not know how to behave with other people and in particular find it difficult to relate to their peers. They do not like being touched. They are extremely resistant to change, full of unwarranted anxieties, unable to grasp the concept of time. This leads to impatience, for since five minutes or half an hour means nothing to them, they expect things to happen at once, They want desperately to know what is going to take place each day, but have difficulty in following a description of future events. They endlessly ask questions which have been answered. They hear sounds which others do not. High pitched or unexpected noises cause them great distress, even agony and panic. Their frightening sense of powerlessness leads to obsessive rituals in an attempt to order the chaos they feel around them. They have an unusual form of memory, for the items selected for storage do not appear, on any criteria used by normal people, to be of any special importance, and they are stored without being interpreted. The best works on the subject are in my view those of Lorna Wing, and her *Guide for the Parents of Autistic Children* (1971), I found invaluable.

Miss Fuller's technique in coping with Jacob was to give him masses of praise and to make overt statements of affection and admiration for his good qualities and abilities. This was done to reinforce his personality, to build up his self-esteem. But she also talked with him about his worries, as she saw the need for him to express and formulate his problems to help him to come to terms with them. She considered it was important not to present him with anything where he might fail, and he should not feel he was being criticised. Nor should he be punished; this was not only useless but damaging. The tool used to induce more acceptable behaviour was rewards which were also given freely for any achievement. His happiness depended on feeling loved, wanted and useful. He should not see himself as a passenger, but as a contributor to life. So, creative activities were necessary e.g. making Christmas presents as symbols of his having within himself something of value for others. Miss Fuller, who is a Roman Catholic, thought that Jacob would probably be helped if he had some kind of faith in a God who was in control of the universe – a universe which he found intractable. We agreed that she should introduce him to some religious ideas, and promised her not to undermine this project by revealing our own atheism. Subsequent events proved her to be right.

Seeing Miss Fuller almost every day was a great help to us as parents. She kept elaborate diaries and supplemented our discussions with numerous letters. At first I was astonished when she talked about Jacob's 'courage' or when I heard her tell him she was 'proud of him', for I had been more aware of his deficiencies than of his attainments, but I soon came to appreciate her approach to his problems. This enabled me to understand more about how he saw the world and thus how to handle and help him. I saw the need for constant, even effusive, expressions of praise and love, such as Miss Fuller's letters to him in the holidays telling him how she and all her numerous animals missed him and were looking forward to seeing him again. Before Jacob started at the Caravan School, we had felt isolated and anxious. Working with her raised our morale, for she was appreciative of the whole family's attitude and patience. Jacob luckily was an attractive child – good looking and often charming – so those who had to deal with him found him lovable in spite of his trying behaviour.

When he was aged eight, we realised we had to begin thinking about the next stage; so he went for assessment by the local authority's educational psychologist and the experts at the children's hospital. This precipitated a vast wrangle, the story of which is of general interest and thus worth recounting. Jacob's IQ was assessed by one of the people who examined him at 52, which classed him as ineducable. His reading ability was in fact up to average, but, resenting the tests, as he wanted to get home, he refused to co-operate. Miss Fuller was told that there was no suitable place in Oxford for him or some of her other pupils, because they had acquired more skills than was expected of handicapped children. Moreover it was implied that she had wasted her time and their parents' money teaching them, particularly teaching them to read, and that it was useless to try to take their education further. She put up a spirited fight against the authorities, arguing for the right of every child to be educated to his ability, but to no avail. We were told that it was up to us to arrange what we could for Jacob.

We were in despair and deeply resented the implication that, being academics ourselves, we were not realistic about our son's intellectual limitations. Thus one of the experts thought it was necessary to disabuse us of the idea, which of course we did not have, that Jacob would be capable of getting some O levels. The impasse led to tension between Herbert and me, for he began to think that the only solution was to send Jacob away to some residential school. I was totally against this, not only on what were perhaps selfish grounds, for I was deeply attached to him and did not want to lose contact. I also genuinely thought it would be irresponsible to hand the problem over to others, and that it was our duty to care for him at home whilst we could, in spite of the difficulties this caused. Nevertheless I wrote around to various Rudolph Steiner schools. To my relief, none of them had a vacancy.

Once again Miss Davidson came to the rescue. She did not agree with the diagnosis of Jacob made by her colleagues and others. She knew him well and estimated his IQ at 74, which made him educable. We were fortunate that she was willing to disregard the normal bureaucratic channels and to help us informally, just as she had given constant support to Miss Fuller. After studying the relevant local handbooks, she suggested that the Special School (Teasdale) at Abingdon might be suitable. The problem was how to get him accepted there, as it was in Berkshire whose Education Authority had no responsibility for Jacob. We set about trying to persuade the Local Authority and the headmaster of the school to accept him. After further tests, it was agreed that he should be tried there for a term, provided Oxford was willing to pay Berkshire and we did not ask the school to arrange his transport. These conditions were complied with, and we were delighted with what appeared to be a solution to our problem. But our relief did not last long, for at the end of one term, the school announced that he was not fitting in well and that he must leave. After we had pleaded with them, they agreed to keep him for a year. After the end of this trial period, though still doubtful, they thought it would be unfair on him to turn him out. So he stayed. Until his last year, when he developed school phobia, he was on the whole happy there, and we were satisfied with the care and education he was getting, though it was inevitably a drawback that the school was five miles away from where we lived. Getting him there was complicated. He was allowed to go on the school bus, provided we took him to the Berkshire border every morning and met him there every afternoon. This rather precarious arrangement was a help, but it unfortunately resulted in our not having close contact with his teachers. Nor were we assisted by school reports, for in five years we never received one. This would, I understand, not happen today. Occasional informal parents' meetings helped and made us appreciate the teachers' dedication and skills, but they did not constitute an adequate substitute for regular reports, especially as Jacob, who will hardly ever answer a question, was unwilling to reveal anything about what happened at school. This is perhaps an example of how he compartmentalises his experiences. In an effort to find out what went on, I used to ask him every day how Miss Brown was, thinking this was the name of his teacher, only to discover that he had not been in Miss Brown's class for a year.

The next crisis occurred when at age 16 he had to leave Teasdale School. We naturally wanted his education to continue, but there was at that time no provision for the Further Education of the handicapped in the age group 16–19. We realised that ultimately he would need long term care in some institution, and so had been investigating what was available. The charity known as the Home Farm Trust seemed the best and agreed to put him on their waiting list. Herbert, who was much more willing and able than me to face up to the problem of Jacob's future welfare, had already put aside some money to create a trust fund for his maintenance. We were unwilling to rely on action by the Local Authority, in spite of their statutory duty to care for the handicapped. Until the Home Farm Trust was able to offer him a place, Jacob continued to live at home and went to the local Industrial Training Unit. This was a help to us as it got him out of the house every day, and he acquired a few simple, mainly mechanical, skills. On the whole he enjoyed his five years there, for the work was repetitive and the regime easy going, but we were greatly relieved when he settled in with relatively little difficulty at Milton Heights, a Home Farm Trust home fortunately for us near Oxford. Here in a relaxed but constructive atmosphere he is provided with training, work, and a variety of leisure activities. This should ensure that he is well cared for after both his parents have died.

Jacob's existence and the problems he created had a profound impact on my life and indeed on all the members of our family. Some of these can be crudely classed as 'negative', some as 'positive'. Sometimes the negative have seemed to predominate. One of the most important results was strain in family relationships, particularly between Herbert and me when we differed about what should be done. Moreover our other children, in spite of the wide age gap between them and Jacob, must unconsciously, if not consciously, have resented our inevitable concentration on him. Even nowadays I too am troubled that when we are all together, and especially when the grandchildren are there, I have to pay so much attention to Jacob, both because he demands it and in order to keep a watch on his activities. One of his quirks is an intense dislike of babies and small children, mainly, though not exclusively, those related to him. Apart from the difficulties this created for me in handling the situation, it also disconcerts and worries the grandchildren, the objects of his hostility.

I do not regret the fact that Jacob lived at home for 23 years and that I was throughout closely involved with his care and development, but this was inevitably time-consuming and encroached on my other activities. I suspect my academic work was adversely affected. It also meant that I could not contemplate playing a part in University administration, which I had hoped to do. Nor could I be away from home for any substantial length of time. I am by no means suggesting that the brunt of the burden of looking after him fell on me. Many others were involved: primarily his devoted and eternally patient Nanny who knew so well how to empathise with the more childish sides of his nature, and a succession of students to whom we gave accommodation in return for evening help. This became even more necessary than before when, at the age of ten, Jacob started having epileptic fits. As these usually occurred at night, he could not be left alone. Our lodger-carers were remarkably skilful in performing what was for them a novel job. They related brilliantly to Jacob, developing his appreciation of music and occupying him with conversation, familiar stories and games. The four outstanding ones were Karen Armstrong, Heather Milne, Robyn Marsack (now Airlie) and Jane Hyder.

Karen Armstrong, an ex-nun, has given in her book *Beginning the World* (1983) a vivid and at times hilarious account of living in our house and learning to handle Jacob. Though at times highly coloured, the picture she paints bears a close relation to reality, so close that many readers of the book have identified him and us behind our fictitious names. The story she tells has many layers of interest, for Karen was in a state of turmoil, due to her decision to leave the religious order she had belonged to for seven years. Having many problems of her own helped her to understand the turbulence of Jacob's life, hampered as he was by overwhelming anxieties. Ironically during her two years with us Jacob 'found religion', whereas Karen lost most of her faith. When by agreement with us she started taking him to family mass at Blackfriars, the local Dominican church, he was enthralled. It was at once clear that religion gave him great comfort. He felt peaceful knowing that Jesus loved him and was his friend.

Karen was astonished that Herbert and I, whom she knew to be uncompromising atheists, not only did not object to Jacob's going to mass, but actually welcomed his baptism and admission to the Roman Catholic church, of which she gives a moving account. She admired our liberalism and lack of bigotry. She also admired our tolerance in handling the situation when she attempted suicide in our house. She thought my instinctive charity compared very favourably with that of the professional Christians to whom she had appealed for help over her crisis. Another factor contributed to the weakening of Karen's attachment to Christianity. This was anger against God, as she presumed He was responsible for Jacob's handicap. She found him fascinating and felt he would have been brilliant if a senseless birth accident had not occurred. She was also distressed by the dislocation he caused to our lives and the suffering we endured watching him day by day. In fact she retained some sort of basic though cloudy belief in God, but her view of the Church was undermined by the curious and emancipatory experiences she was undergoing as a result of life in our household. So just as Jacob became more and more enthusiastic about going to church, Karen's belief in the central articles of the Christian faith was declining rapidly.

Jacob's baptism and admission to the Roman Catholic church gave rise to an interesting incident. For when the Jesuits heard what was proposed, they contacted us to say that the Dominicans had no authority to perform a baptism. We naturally resisted what appeared to be an attempt on their part to 'get hold' of Jacob, and insisted that the ceremony should take place at Blackfriars where he felt at home rather than in the more forbidding atmosphere of their church, St Aloysius.

Although I gradually learnt how to cope with some of the problems which arise when one lives with a disturbed handicapped child, there have been many occasions when I have suffered from nervous strain. For instance Jacob likes eating out in restaurants and cafés, but sometimes cannot stand a crowded room. He will then become extremely tense and do most embarrassing things, like demanding to be served everything on the menu, or trying to seize all the food and drink on the table. One then has to get him out of the premises as quickly as possible, which is not always easy. Although such incidents occur much less often than they used to, I never feel confident that his obsessive focus on food will not cause trouble. When he was small he would sometimes freak out in a crowded shop, lie down on the floor and scream. On such occasions it was difficult not oneself to be upset when onlookers seemed to be implying that one ought to be able to control one's child. The worst incident I can recall was when he, aged about four, and I were walking in a college garden. We passed some people lying on the grass. For no apparent reason Jacob suddenly kicked one of them heavily on the jaw. The unfortunate victim, a German lady, was naturally furious. I was appalled and at a loss what to do. She obviously expected me to punish him, but I did not believe in slapping, so I simply tried to explain that he was handicapped and that he did not understand things properly. This was luckily a one-off event. Travelling with him can also be a strain, for he gets desperately impatient if the train or car is held up, and he is liable to panic when on a bridge crossing railway lines.

Jacob's eccentricities make living with him trying. Our house sometimes looks as if it had been burgled, for he rummages in cupboards and drawers, strewing their contents all over the place. At other times, instead of creating disorder, he 'tidies up'. This may mean taking pictures down from walls, piling up the carefully segregated papers on desks, or throwing things away. It is not unknown for unopened valuable post to be found in the waste-paper basket. In the winter he will open windows, and in the summer close them. Preventing such tiresome and often inexplicable behaviour is difficult unless he is never left in a room alone, which is impossible. Nor is it possible to lock up everything, the ridiculous solution suggested to us by one of the doctors we consulted. Another psychologist recommended that he should live in a virtually empty room. Neither of these policies, even if practicable, would have helped train him to behave in a more acceptable way. Getting angry, threatening to punish, or actual punishment after the event are useless, for they suggest withdrawal of affection which will intensify his feelings of insecurity. One falls back on making the distinction between continuing to love him, but not always loving what he does, a distinction he cannot easily grasp. I have also made virtually no impact on his light-hearted attitude to telling lies, and have found it difficult successfully to explain to him why this is wrong. I did not resort to my mother's alarming device, when she wished to make me a more honest small child, which was to read me the Bible story of Ananias and his wife who were struck down dead when they told a lie (Acts ch. 5, v. 1–11).

I believe there are people who do not regret, or at least do not allow themselves to regret, that their child is mentally handicapped. I do not class myself among them, but I am not romanticising if I say that what may be called 'the Jacob experience' has had positive spin-offs. His life coincided with a general change in the public's attitude to mental handicap. The fact that certain terms such as 'moron', 'mental defective', 'village idiot', 'half wit' are no longer in common use is itself significant. Indeed even 'the mentally handicapped' has been replaced by 'people with a learning disability'. The impact of Jacob on our family and friends has been a good example of this less stereotyped reaction to mental handicap. For besides the frustration and boredom which his company can sometimes engender, his complex character and bubbly conversation often entrance those around him. His language abounds in original metaphors and similies. Someone he dislikes is described as 'a big black cloud'. A friend with an alert expression is known as 'hawky eyes', for he reminded Jacob of the hawks he watches in Cornwall hovering and swooping on their preys. When I am tired and limp, he will ask 'Are you feeling crumbly?', and when I am pleased with him 'Are you pumped?' He christened our elderly Morris Minor 'Chuckaboom', because of the booming noise it made.

One of my friends who was particularly adept at relating to Jacob was Audrey Beecham. I had not anticipated her success and at first found it difficult to explain. Then I saw that because she herself was so eccentric, she did not think Jacob odd. Nor did he think strange her belief in magic and witchcraft. He loved going to her house, relishing especially her squalid kitchen basement. He even became fond of her three yapping dachshunds, having previously been antipathetic to dogs. He would watch her sing and dance or shoot at the magpie in her garden. He was fascinated by her huge vintage car, and would listen as she read him her poetry.

He must have felt reassured by her enthusiastic acceptance of him as an interesting and normal person.

Jacob has in some sense kept me going and prevented me, as I got older, from getting into too much of a rut. For one is inevitably stimulated by such things as his enthusiasm to visit churches and to explore new places, his deep enjoyment of classical music and his own musical gifts. He cannot really read music, but he can reproduce on the piano tunes he has heard, and can transpose them into other keys. When he listens to music, he can often identify the key in which it is written, and when I play to him, which he constantly demands, he spots my mistakes at once, even in music he is not familiar with. It is delightful to see the pleasure he gets from our joint activities and it is salutary to have to share his optimism that everything is going to be all right. In his company, anxiety, depression, and of course hypochondria are taboo. One of my friends has described me as 'a reluctant saint' in my dealings with Jacob. This is to overdo it. The suggestion of saintliness is absurd, but he has inevitably had the effect of revealing in me a greater capacity for patience than I had previously been credited with. He has also, I believe, made me in general more tolerant of human frailty and of deviance from social norms, less scornful of stupidity, perhaps even more compassionate.

Another beneficial consequence of having a problem child is that one is brought into contact with a wider world, and learns to appreciate the work of many other people: altruistic volunteers who help with all sorts of activities like running play groups and clubs, others who get involved in raising money for charity, a taxing and tedious business, and the devoted staff of the Home Farm Trust who face their difficult tasks with patience and resilience. Moreover although some of our early experiences with the statutory authorities left much to be desired, we were later given excellent help and support by various professionals, including the social worker who was allocated to us, albeit after years of waiting. She introduced us to the device of respite care, which meant that Jacob could sometimes go for a few days to a Local Authority hostel to give us all a break.

Occasionally, at times of emotional disturbance, Jacob's behaviour has regressed in certain respects, but by and large there has been progress. Scenes are rare; his obsessive rituals have decreased;

he adapts more easily to change, and he complies with most of the social norms of public behaviour. All this has helped me to look on the bright side of the situation, and to enjoy the company of someone who feels, as he puts it, 'on top of the world and brimming with life'.

13

Finale

WHEN I RETIRED from St Anne's in 1981 I considered myself lucky to have been able to stay in a job until age 67, whereas if I had remained in the Civil Service my employment would have ended at age 60; but foolishly I had not prepared myself for the inevitable results of retirement. Suddenly my whole way of life was transformed. One of the most agreeable and distinctive things about Oxford and Cambridge is that they provide social and intellectual contacts for their members – because they meet each other daily at meals or in Common Rooms – without the need to plan and arrange this. After retirement such contacts do not occur automatically, and I soon realised how acutely I missed seeing friends and colleagues even for ten minutes a day. I am not referring to the lack of those highbrow inter-disciplinary discussions which some people imagine take place all the time in Oxford Common Rooms, but to conversations about such topics as the latest news, international, national and local, plays, films, holidays, family affairs, and of course academic gossip. I also missed the stimulus provided by tutoring. I did some teaching after retirement, but decided it was necessary to give this up when I began forgetting my pupils' names and even confusing which was which. I knew I had been fortunate, indeed privileged, in my past life-style, but this did not relieve my current depression. So desperate was I to have some contact with other people that I would walk around the streets of Oxford hoping to meet someone I knew who was willing to exchange a few words. On a bad day, this did not happen. I could admittedly talk with Herbert if and when he came home after working all day in college, but he naturally found my company rather dispiriting. Moreover he himself was less cheerful than usual, owing to various worries –

particularly about Jacob and the financial problems posed by his future.

The situation improved when, after a time, the college gave me some Common Room rights including a weekly meal, thus enabling me to see my friends and indeed to make new ones. This was a great boon, but I could not help noticing, and with distress, that my ex-colleagues, though kind and welcoming, saw me in a different light now I had retired, for their usual greeting was to enquire how I was, as if I had on 30 September 1981 put one foot in the grave. However gradually this uncalled-for solicitude about my health faded out and I seemed to become re-accepted as a normal member of their community. For this I am profoundly grateful, especially as I am aware that it can be tedious for busy working dons to have ageing talkative ex-colleagues cluttering up the place.

Many academics manage to fix up interesting projects for their retirement, like lecturing abroad, attending conferences or acting as consultants, but I was not sufficiently eminent to be offered anything like this and in any case it was impossible for me to leave home whilst Jacob was still there. Nor did I feel drawn immediately to some piece of research. This was not because I had completed work on all the subjects I had intended to write about whilst I was teaching. The mountains of material which I had to clear out from my room in college supplied painful evidence of unfinished projects; but I rejected them all as unsuitable for further effort. Nor could I settle down to random reading of the many books in our house which through lack of time or objective I had, as one of my friends put it, 'only handled'.

After a while in this aimless limbo, I decided the best thing was not to try to hang on to the fringes of academic life, but to do something quite different. I surveyed the possibilities, which were not extensive, and plumped for social work, in which I had always been interested. My first experience was in the Probation Service, whose Oxford branch was at that time keen to recruit and employ volunteers, who were known as Voluntary Associates. We had to attend a thorough training course which I enjoyed, except for the, to me, novel device of role-playing, which I found embarrassing and difficult. Volunteers could be asked to do many different things, but could always refuse to take on a task for which they felt unsuited. I was involved in a wide variety of activities: research projects, supervising offenders, literacy work, attending court, transport, even cooking. My first job entailed examining 150 Social Enquiry Reports made by probation officers for the courts, looking at the exact wording of their recommendations as to the appropriate sentence, and then finding out what the court and different types of court had decided. The underlying object of the exercise was to increase the effectiveness of the Probation Service, for there was concern at that time about the falling use of Probation and the resulting rise in the prison population. Putting the probation officers' recommendations or suggestions into categories, such as equivocal, unequivocal, or firm with alternatives, was not always easy, but for me reading the reports was illuminating and an education in itself.

Another project involved me in going through vast tomes of court records to extract from them information about offenders in Drunk and Disorderly cases. Oxford had for various reasons an unusually large population of winos. Most of them were unable to pay a fine, so instead they went to prison for several days. The system was pointless, and was in due course changed to one in which such offenders only went to prison if they had been cautioned three times by the police; so I felt my labours had not been in vain.

Occasionally, under the supervision of a probation officer, I took on the job of 'befriending' some of their clients. I found this a difficult task and realised that they were usually better at getting me to talk about myself than I was at assisting them to face up to their problems. I was, I think, more successful in helping the less literate to improve their reading and writing skills, a job for which I received a very necessary and excellent training. This was rewarding work as most of my pupils – the black ones in particular – realised the need to be more literate and, as they put it, 'to talk posh' if they were to get on in the world. My main problem here was understanding what they said and sometimes in their understanding me, due to the gap between our accents and modes of expression. There was always a call for volunteers to do transport work, especially taking people to visit their relatives in prison. I tried my hand at this, but gave up after a hair-raising drive to London on, by chance, the day of a rail strike, trying to find the way to Holloway Prison. This did not even provide the bonus of a sociologically interesting conversation with my passengers, as I was unable to induce them to talk about themselves, much less about their delinquent daughter, or indeed about anything.

My worst experience with the Probation Service was cooking one evening for the three dozen residents at a bail hostel, when a crisis had occurred on New Year's Eve. I had warned the warden that my culinary skills were very limited, but either *faute de mieux* or because my self-description was not believed – for it is often assumed that all women are competent cooks – she pressed me to oblige, and I rashly agreed. I battled alone for three hours with the unfamiliar and antediluvian equipment of their kitchen with its feeble gas pressure, and somehow managed to produce a meal consisting of the only two dishes in my repertoire: shepherd's pie and apple crumble. Afterwards I wondered who was most disappointed: the hungry young men who were the victims of my amateur cooking – the crumble in particular turned out very peculiar because I made it with cornflour instead of ordinary flour – or me not receiving a word of thanks from them for what I considered to be a valiant effort. They treated me like a skivvy, wolfed the food and left me to clear up.

Being associated even at the margin with the Probation Service was a fascinating experience. In spite of the difficulties posed by some of my work, I enjoyed functioning at so to speak the coal-face, having to relate to actual delinquents and deviants, instead of just speculating about 'the causes of crime'. Moreover there were amusing incidents as when one of my clients, who had a long record of petty thieving, assured me he was going to change his ways on his release from prison, but in the same breath asked me to tell him which colleges had the richest students. I liked being part of a structured organisation and having colleagues again. They came from a wider variety of backgrounds than I had anticipated, e.g. nursing and industry, though they had all had a training in social work, which, contrary to the views of some people, I am sure is essential. They were not like the stereotype of Probation Officers depicted by the right-wing Law and Order lobby, soppy 'do-gooders' taking the side of the criminal and ignoring the victim, but realists anxious to find the best way to stop offenders continuing to offend. This necessarily involves understanding and explaining, but not excusing their behaviour.

After a few years the employment of volunteers by the Probation

Service in Oxford declined, so I moved to the closely related sphere of Victims Support. This involved further training with the inevitable role-play. Our function was to visit the victims of crime and to offer them whatever help seemed relevant. This might be just listening and sympathising, or practical advice about such things as getting their property repaired or insurance issues. We had usually been informed by the police whether they wished to be contacted by one of us, but even when they had not heard of our organisation, I found them welcoming and grateful for the visit. I did not handle serious crimes such as rape, and was chiefly concerned with burglaries. It was distressing to find how often the goods stolen had a great sentimental value for the owner, for instance the wedding ring of a widow, and also to be told by the victim that, as a result of the crime, they would never leave their house again for a holiday or even for an evening. I tried to discourage this kind of reaction to their experience, even though I may thereby have been exceeding my role. We discussed our cases at regular meetings of the volunteers, a practice which I found helpful though also disturbing. It was important not to become obsessed and worried by hearing about nasty crimes. I was impressed by the devoted work of some of the volunteers who did not, like me, call on victims just once or twice, but who kept contact with them for a considerable time. Sometimes they did this because they became involved in helping the victim cope with problems other than those resulting from the crime. This seemed to me wrong, and even more mistaken to advocate, as some of them did, that we should turn ourselves into an organisation to deal with the effects of all disasters, like fires, accidents, deaths. But at least these policy questions produced interesting discussions.

After a time I decided, though reluctantly, to give up working for Victims Support, because I had embarked on writing a book and found this incompatible with sudden requests to visit a victim. Moreover because Herbert was becoming less and less mobile, and could no longer drive a car, it was essential that I should act as his chauffeur to enable him to take part in social and intellectual activities. I did however manage to keep on doing some work for another voluntary body, Parents Anonymous, whose purpose was to help parents who had problems with their children. Before joining I had imagined that my job would be to work with a family in their home, observing how they handled their children and delicately suggesting different techniques when these seemed called for. So I was disappointed to learn during my training that most of our work was done on a telephone Help Line, though we offered to meet our callers if they so wished. Moreover we were told not to give advice to callers; we were merely a listening service, so our role was just to encourage them to talk. One did this by repeating back to them what they had said. So the conversation would go like this. Mother: 'My son is naughty and hits his sister.' Volunteer: 'So your son is naughty and hits his sister.' Or, Mother: 'My husband peeps through the bathroom door to observe my daughter undressing.' Volunteer: 'So your husband peeps etc . . .' I was doubtful whether this helped the parent much, if at all, but the accepted belief was that it did. Occasionally when a parent came into the office to have a talk, I could not resist slipping in a few warnings or words of advice, such as 'You run the risk of losing your daughter altogether if you refuse to have her boyfriend in the house because you dislike him.' Or I would talk in general terms about how small children need to feel secure and loved – implying that it is a bad idea to smack them, or to threaten to throw them in the dustbin or the sea when they are tiresome. We had to record all calls in a book, and so amassed an enormous amount of information about what can go on in family life. Much of this will not be new to social workers, but I could not help wishing that such an excellent source of material could be used for a research project or see the light of day in some form or other, but this is of course out of the question even with strict safeguards to protect the callers from recognition.

As with the experience provided by the world of Victims Support, I was deeply impressed by the selfless commitment of the volunteers who manned the Help Lines for Parents Anonymous, several of them exemplifying Christian ideals at their best. I enjoyed working with them and felt rather guilty when after a year or so I gave up. I knew that a good telephone manner was not my forte: my friends constantly complain about my abrupt answering style. Moreover I felt my contribution to the work of this organisation was minimal, for I was not willing to be one of the volunteers who were rung up at home, so I had only done a few hours duty at the office every week. But I did not wish wholly to abandon the world of social work, which had for me a certain fascination, contrasting as it did so vividly with academic life. So I enrolled as a volunteer to give reading help in schools to children with special difficulties. Even though I was given a thorough training with, to my relief, no role-playing, and was equipped with a generous supply of books and games, I was apprehensive when launched on my first assignment. I was allotted three seven-year olds and spent half an hour with each one separately twice a week. Sometimes I had a problem finding the child whom I had to extract from a classroom, and, what was even more difficult, finding a suitable empty space in which to work, but the staff were remarkably friendly and helpful, so after a few sessions my anxiety decreased. I even allowed myself to think I was of some use, pleased to feel the children enjoyed their times with me.

My next school presented a greater challenge as it was situated on a huge housing estate on the edge of the city and was notorious for the classic problems which arise in such areas. I was shocked by the sense that my pupils lived in a sort of void; things just happened to them with no explanation. Some of them had never been outside the estate, certainly not into Oxford. If they had gone away on a holiday, they might not know where they had been. I could not help thinking how different these children would be if they had received the same stimuli, cultural and intellectual, as had my grandchildren, and I realised once again how lamentably far this country is from even a moderate degree of egalitarianism. I took some small comfort in the thought that my pupils might not have been typical of the bulk of those attending this large primary school, for I had probably been allotted the most deprived and disturbed. This did not go far to raise my spirits, but made me focus on doing what I could on a small front. Apart from working specifically on their reading, using all the standard techniques, I thought it important to get the children to talk freely and in particular for them not to be frightened of asking questions. I also aimed to widen their vocabulary. During our training, great emphasis was placed on the importance of making our sessions enjoyable for the child; so establishing a relaxed one-to-one relationship was essential, as was varying our activities.

The organisation for which I worked, Volunteer Reading Help, provided excellent back-up to its workers. Each of us was supervised by a more experienced person with whom we could discuss our problems, and at the periodic meetings of volunteers one could acquire new ideas and reading material. I did not in fact take to many of the available books. They were certainly not in short supply, as in recent years the output of literature for children has been stunningly large, but many of them struck me as inconsequential or even positively silly. They often lack a story and seem to me rather boring. But I had no success when I tried, no doubt naively, to interest my pupils in some of the books my children had particularly liked. When I brought these along from my home, they were usually rejected as old, grubby, and above all not glossy. Clearly I had not moved with the times.

Apart from the interest of the actual 'teaching', this experience gave me the chance to observe at first hand some of the problems faced by the staff in schools: how to manage large classes, how to maintain discipline without being repressive, how to digest the endless flow of missives from the Government and other authorities. No wonder much of the talk in the staff room at break was concerned with pensions and the hope of early retirement. Compared with these massive problems, the contribution which we volunteers could make was, I realised, minute, but I had no doubt of its value and of the crucial importance of improving literacy. I was disappointed that the Government had decided on grounds of cost not to introduce here the more ambitious Reading Recovery Scheme which has been so successful in New Zealand.

Some of my friends admired me for doing voluntary social work, but they were wrong to regard me as virtuous. In engaging in the various activities I have described, I was motivated less by altruism than by a desire to fill a gap in my life, to have a niche, a role if only a mini one, new stimuli, new colleagues. Social work was a good choice: it made me more disciplined, and, whilst getting me regularly out of the house, fitted in well with my home duties. But ultimately it was clear I had to stop because of the deterioration in Herbert's health and my commitment to his care. In the past when he was perfectly well, he had always said that he would not wish to be nursed by me if he became ill, sensing quite rightly that I was not by nature cut out for such a job. Also, being a kind man, he was concerned with my welfare and wanted to save me from uncongenial duties. But I slipped imperceptibly into looking after him, though, as his problems multiplied and escalated, I had to rely more and more on assistance from others, both professional and amateur including family and friends, with the result that my main function seemed at times to be organising the team of helpers.

The medical and social services provided excellent care and were a good advertisement for our National Health Service and much maligned Welfare State; but after Herbert's death (in 1992) I felt more and more that I had during his last years been deficient in offering him emotional and psychological support. I found it difficult to do so because he evinced no desire to reveal his feelings about his present condition or to discuss the past, with the result that I felt unable to try to counteract his inevitable gloom over his physical afflictions by stressing his virtues and achievements, not only in the academic field, but as husband and father. This has left me with a sense of unfinished business, a sense that we should somehow have wound up our joint life by talking about the best things in it.

Herbert, to my astonishment, was quite in favour of my writing an autobiography, but I did not start to work on it until after his death. It has therefore not benefited from the kind of help he gave with my book on Proportional Representation, the text of which he scrutinised with extreme care, in spite of the fact that he, like so many people, found the subject strange and puzzling. This is by no means the most important respect in which my life is impoverished by his absence.

Having regrets is not a profitable activity, unless by expressing them one can help younger people to avoid one's mistakes or to lead morally better or happier lives. But I find it impossible not to reflect on my life, and this necessarily involves recognising failures as well as possible achievements. My main regret is that I have had so little, if any, impact on public affairs. When young I wanted, as is common, to 'change the world', in particular to eliminate war as an instrument of national policy and to reduce social and economic inequalities. These ideals were clearly too grandiose, but even my more modest aim of influencing some Government policies became less realisable after I left the Civil Service, which I had joined in the hope of making a contribution to the betterment of the world. After I became a don, I vaguely hoped I would in due course be appointed to some committee or body concerned with public issues, perhaps the police or penal policy. But clearly I had ambitions above my station in life, for all I ever achieved was occasional membership of the Final Selection Board for the Civil Service – which ended in the circumstances described in chapter five – and brief membership of the Advisory Council on the Misuse of Drugs. I and Ruth Runciman were appointed to this body by the Home Secretary, Roy Jenkins, to replace Barbara Wootton after she resigned from it in 1974. She says in her book *Crime and Penal Policy* that her resignation was due to pressure of other obligations, but it seems possible that her disagreement with Government policy on cannabis was also a factor in her decision. She did not favour the legalisation of cannabis, but thought it less dangerous than alcohol, and if smoked in moderation, not more dangerous than tobacco. She had recommended without success that penalties for the possession of cannabis should be reduced, with magistrates' courts being stopped from sending anyone to prison for mere possession. I tended to agree with these views and was hoping in due course to help shift opinion ever so slightly in their direction, but this was not to be, for at the end of three years my appointment to the Advisory Council was terminated by a subsequent Home Secretary, Merlyn Rees. I was naturally disappointed at being dropped, and could not help wondering whether my removal was due to the Home Office's distrust of my views as too liberal, for I had attended meetings assiduously and moreover was at that time in the middle of a piece of research, working with Ruth Runciman to find out what happened to drug addicts in custody.

I also regret that I was never a magistrate. I did not try to become one, as I thought, wrongly, that their work was largely concerned with traffic offences. I would probably not have been appointed if I had applied, but if I had succeeded, I think I would in some sense have enjoyed the work. I say 'in some sense' because I would surely have agonised when deciding on the appropriate sentence, and found much of the experience depressing. Moreover differences of opinion with colleagues would no doubt have sent my blood pressure soaring, for, being imbued with Bentham's view that 'All punishment in itself is evil', I would have seen the role of the court not to punish offenders, but to try to prevent the repetition of crimes by other means.

I think I gradually came to realise that I was not able to have any influence on world affairs, that nothing I could do would prevent or mitigate the many terrible things which were constantly occurring – civil wars, famines, terrorist acts, repressions, tortures, hijackings, global environmental disasters – and that it was essential to be realistic, which meant thinking out what, if anything, I might achieve on a narrower front. The front would be narrower in two senses: the issues to concentrate on would be those concerned with personal and intellectual values rather than with public affairs, and the targets would be those within my range, which meant the society in which I lived, friends, pupils, family, my college, my locality. This did not mean that I was simply retreating into private life. My model was not the Roman Emperor Diocletian – who declared after abdicating that he was happier planting cabbages in Dalmatia than pursuing power – but the hero in Voltaire's *Candide*. I realise that his famous last words '*Il faut cultiver notre jardin*' are open to many different interpretations, but I am persuaded that the message of this brilliant and, in my view, profound story is not a counsel of inaction, of withdrawal from all efforts to better the lot of mankind: it is that there are problems which an individual cannot affect. He can only express outrage. So he should take practical initiatives within his power rather than just registering impotent sorrow. He can enhance the quality of life by working with a little group. Their community can create a quiet haven of contentment and keep out boredom. They should not have moralistic goals, but only aim to let a little light into a dark world.

Admitting the limits of one's influence on the world at large does not commit one to a belief in the relativism of moral values. In my view there are some absolute values which one should seek to further, instead of accepting the justification of certain practices, like for instance female circumcision, on the ground that they are legitimised by the 'culture' of that society.

I could never cease to be interested, indeed obsessively interested, in politics in the widest sense – the state of the world and the activities of our governments. I thought, and still think, that citizens in a democracy have a duty to be political animals, to follow public events, to evaluate official policies, to contribute financially to good causes, but I saw that it was necessary to be less ambitious and to focus on issues where I might possibly have even the smallest effect. In reaching this conclusion, I was also influenced by the non-altruistic desire to cut down on the depression inevitably generated by worrying about distressing events, such as murders, which I am powerless to prevent. There are of course simplistic assumptions behind this aim. One is that it is always possible to classify events into two groups: those which one can and those which one cannot influence, and another that an individual, if sufficiently determined, can control his thoughts in order to shut out worrying topics. But nevertheless this goal, the germ of which was planted in my mind on reading Bertrand Russell's book *The Conquest of Happiness*, seems to me to be a good one.

It is not easy to rank in importance the issues on which I aimed to concentrate, the values I have tried to uphold, but I have no doubt that on the intellectual plane I would put clarity of thought top of the list. The capacity to think clearly may not be a sufficient but it is a necessary condition for progress on both great and small matters. To be 'too clear' about something, as one of my colleagues once reproached me for being, is in my view impossible. It is especially important when abstract concepts are involved, for it will lead to close analysis of what is meant by the terms used. J.L. Austin put the case with his customary dexterity when he said: 'It is not enough to show how clever we are by showing how obscure everything is. Clarity, I know, has been said to be enough; but perhaps it will be time to go into that when we are within measurable distance of achieving clarity on some matter.'[43] If I had studied philosophy and had some training in logic, I would have been better equipped to exemplify my ideal of clarity and to inculcate it in others; but as a tutor I took some comfort in knowing that the Oxford system of requiring undergraduates to write an essay at least once a week would help them, as nothing else would, to clarify their minds. The old adage 'How do I know what I think until I see what I say?' should be altered to 'How do I know what I think until I see what I write?'. In my experience, especially as a tutor, religious people tend to be less clear-headed than the non-religious, for their acceptance of religious doctrines encourages fogginess on other issues, 'rots the mind', as H.A.L. Fisher so succinctly put it after reading the work of candidates for New College when he was the Warden. Religious beliefs of all kinds seem to me to undermine respect for evidence, and generally to foster the

[43] *A Plea for Excuses*, Philosophical Papers, 1961, p. 137.

toleration of unintelligible and meaningless statements. It is for this reason that I would like to see the BBC give less time to religious broadcasting or at least provide more opportunities for humanists, agnostics and atheists to expound their philosophies.

Another but related issue about which I cared was the importance of thinking for oneself and not just accepting the current conventions governing social and moral matters for which one sees no good reason. John Stuart Mill no doubt overstates the case against what he calls 'the despotism of custom' when he says it is 'everywhere the standing hindrance to human advancement',[44] but I find his general attitude deeply sympathetic. I am not suggesting that one should *try* to be eccentric, but that a society in which eccentricity is a reproach is a sad one, and I do not say this only because I myself am often considered eccentric. For the habit of conforming to custom prevents people from thinking out their own values, not just about how they should behave and require others to behave, but also on wider issues, for it strengthens a conservative approach to public affairs. Political institutions and constitutional practices are defended on the ground that they are traditional, have existed continuously for a long time. A prominent conservative politician and lawyer, Quintin Hogg, the later Lord Hailsham, in his book *The Case for Conservatism* (1947), advocates preserving 'the mystique of a traditional authority' – advice which, if followed, would stifle thought about the status quo. Blind veneration would replace the asking of questions.

If I were able to live my life again, I would not wish to alter its general course, asking the Fates to deal with me differently, for, as I said at the beginning, and illustrated in telling my story, I have in many respects been fortunate. But there are things within my own control, at least in theory, which I would hope to handle differently. The most important of these is my behaviour towards my mother. I would try to be nicer to her and cause her less pain. I would also be less harsh in my judgements on other people or at least restrain the sharpness of my tongue, but I must admit my main motive here would be self-interest, for I would do this not so much for their sakes as in the hope of having more friends and a fuller social life. I realise that I am perhaps unusually dependent on the company of

[44] *On Liberty*, ed. David Spitz, 1975, p. 66.

other people. If I were landed on a desert island and knew I would never meet another human being, I would give up everything: reading, thinking, even listening to music, and commit suicide. However though I am often criticised for my indiscretions, I would not be more discreet, for a society where the conversation is restrained by the fear of being too open rapidly becomes boring and bland. This is not to advocate insensitivity in a face to face relationship, but it is to suggest that one should avoid meaningless small talk during social exchanges and not be afraid of dissecting the characters and activities of friends and acquaintances. Other people's idiosyncrasies then become a source of harmless amusement. Nor is this positively to recommend malice, though for much of my life I had belonged to a society in which malice was not incompatible with friendship, and I well understood Ivy Compton Burnett's complaint, when asked if she was finding life difficult during the war, that it was not the black-out and the bombs which she minded, but the absence of malice.

None of the works on the art of autobiography which I consulted before starting this book gave me advice on how to finish. Nor have I got much assistance from looking at how some authors finished theirs. They often talk about what they propose to do in the future. Thus John Stuart Mill hinted at writing further books, but then ended rather abruptly saying, 'Here therefore, for the present, this memoir may close.' Anthony Trollope, after proudly listing his numerous publications and the substantial sums he received for them, trusted for his happiness chiefly to his work, reading and writing more books. Gibbon on the other hand, 'after the completion of an arduous and successful work', looked forward to 15 years of 'autumnal felicity', his natural disposition being, he said, 'to repose rather than to activity'. If I were to set down my plans for the future, the result would be a bathetic anti-climax, for I have not got further than an intention to clear up the Augean stable of my home so as not to leave this massive task to my poor children. The fact that they have at times benefited from my inveterate inability to throw anything away, which I defended on the ground that the object in question might one day come in useful, would not be adequate compensation for their burden. I would like to be remembered for my other characteristics, or at least for some of them.

Appendix

Extracts from the speeches delivered at the memorial ceremony for Herbert Hart on 6 February 1993 by:

Sir Isaiah Berlin
Lord Jay
Professor Ronald Dworkin
Professor Joseph Raz
Dr Bernard Richards
Professor Alan Ryan

SIR ISAIAH BERLIN

I have known Herbert Hart for more than sixty years. He became part of my life early in our acquaintance, and remained so until the end of his life, and indeed beyond it. Others, far better qualified than I, will no doubt speak about his academic career and achievements. I propose to say something of a more personal nature, subjective as this must inevitably be.

I first met him, in I think 1929, at a meeting of the Jowett Society, an Oxford undergraduate philosophical society. During all the long years of our friendship, his appearance, manner, way of life, seemed to me to have altered very little. The same rumpled clothes, the same disregard of domestic surroundings, the same simple, engaging manner, the same quiet, uninterrupted intellectual vitality and humour, eager interest in whatever came up in conversation or in the world – one never had to translate one's views into the idiom he preferred – he understood one at once, however imperfect one's language: and this made talking with him particularly easy, agreeable and fruitful. There never was a touch of pomposity, self-importance, self-righteousness, vanity; he was self-conscious at times, and occasionally withdrawn; but other than natural, never.

At the philosophical meetings I very soon realised that I had met a man of very high intellectual calibre. I was deeply impressed by the remarkable clarity and penetration with which he spoke, his full understanding of the views which he discussed or criticised, and above all, by the sheer power of his mind, and, something rare in a man of such gifts, his complete honesty, his readiness to withdraw or modify his assertions in the face of what seemed to him valid objections. He never tried to defend the indefensible out of *amour propre*, or stubbornness, or desire to win. Our philosophical views were, at that time, somewhat similar; we were both what was then called Oxford realists: we read Cook Wilson – now forgotten – G.E. Moore, Russell, Price. After he left the University to go to the Bar, we used to meet in London and Oxford, and went on talking about philosophy. Philosophy was the first and last love of his life – more so, I should say, than even the law. In the early days his interest lay in logic and the theory of knowledge, more than moral or social issues, which he thought and wrote about in his later years. He was a very frequent visitor to All Souls College during my years there before the war; I was not his only host – Douglas Jay, Richard Wilberforce, John Sparrow, Ian Bowen, used to invite him. This was, perhaps, one of the reasons why my colleague Penderel Moon once remarked that every time he came back from India, the Fellows seemed different, but the guests were always the same.

As the years went on, Herbert became increasingly critical of my views, and I therefore learnt a great deal from him. He was always just, understanding, and generous; nevertheless, I always knew at once when I was embarking on some false or dubious path. He told me that what first turned him toward philosophy was a very stimulating master at Bradford Grammar School (called I think Goddard), who talked about Spengler and the patterns of history, and discussed vast metaphysical systems, and thereby greatly widened the horizons of his pupils. Herbert remained devoted to him.

I saw him often during his years at the Bar, and in those days he described himself as a Liberal; it was only later that he felt drawn to the policies of the Labour Party, probably as a result of a growing moral revulsion, which I shared, caused by the social and political policies of the Conservative governments of the thirties. I saw him rather less during the war, when I was in Washington and he worked for the Intelligence Service in England. Conversations with Gilbert Ryle and Stuart Hampshire, who worked in the same field, helped to convert him from his earlier philosophical realism to a much more radical position: never to anything like full-blown logical positivism, but towards a careful form of what afterwards became called linguistic analysis, or indeed, 'Oxford philosophy'. His old tutor at New College, by this time Warden, A.H. Smith, wrote me – to Washington – about luring Herbert to the college. He explained that he would be all the more valuable since the new trend towards radical empiricism, of which Smith held a low opinion, needed to be resisted, and Herbert would prove to be a very formidable opponent of it, 'a real bulwark' as Smith put it. Alas for Smith, the bulwark turned out to face in the opposite direction; like Balaam, instead of stopping the rot, the new Fellow became a strong ally of the new philosophy.

After the war, the principal intellectual impact on him was, I think, that of J.L. Austin, who changed his approach to jurisprudence, and also to some degree that of Friedrich Waismann, who expounded a modified version of the doctrines of the so-called 'Vienna Circle' of philosophers.

To the end of his life, Herbert Hart tended to feel an unflagging almost boyish enthusiasm for new experience: ideas, methods, thinkers, music, literature, natural beauty, indeed anything that awoke a response in him – anything that he found interesting, important, beautiful, moving, attractive. He reacted strongly to people – their character, their appearance, their foibles. He talked easily with all kinds and conditions of people. He spoke with enthusiasm, or interest, or amusement, or irony – or a mixture of these – about colleagues, friends, and occasionally pupils, many of whom he would stimulate into a natural flow of their own thoughts, and feelings, and views of the world. He tended to describe his intellectual or artistic discoveries with fervour, clarity, and remarkable insight into the flavour and quality of ideas, works of art, authors, whether he thought well of them or not; and this made his conversation illuminating, as well as delightful. He combined a very powerful mind, precision of thought and an unshakeable sanity, with a humane and generous nature – and, more than that, pure goodness, sometimes verging on saintliness, which could not but make a lasting impression upon those who met him for any length of time. I need not add that his moral integrity and unswerving pursuit of truth and justice became universally recognised.

He responded to social and political events, and indeed, to the life around him in every shape and form.

He particularly admired J.S. Mill, and his beloved Bentham (who both impressed and amused him), because, like him, they believed in the value and power of reason. He liked their impatience with nonsense, and forgave the psychological crudity and narrowness of vision, which he recognised, for the sake of the soundness of their general approach – their dedication to human welfare. Like them, he opposed customs and institutions if they seemed to him socially or morally deleterious, all the more if they were ancient, traditional and widely accepted. He was a man of the Enlightenment, *wholly* so. Condorcet would have found him most congenial, so, I think, would Adam Smith. Fallacies, stupidities, cruelties, injustices, were for him all the more threatening if supported by appeals to intuition, faith, metaphysics with no empirical basis.

He was very well read. He particularly liked biographies, memoirs, novels – Victorian and a good deal of modern literature absorbed him: Jane Austen, George Eliot, Dickens, Thackeray, Henry James, the great Russian novelists, Aldous Huxley (he once told me that he had liberated him from various adolescent inhibitions) – these and Nadine Gordimer – almost everything that he came across, or was suggested to him, was grist to that marvellous intellectual and emotional mill. He particularly loved poetry: Dante, Shakespeare, Leopardi, Baudelaire, Tennyson, Verlaine, Yeats, and he quoted freely from them. He loved music too; his friendship with William Glock opened a good many windows for him, in modern as well as classical music. He loved travel, he loved the beauties of nature, he was a tremendous walker, and remarkably eloquent in describing anything that caught his imagination.

He liked countries as such, particularly Italy. I remember his telling me that once, in an Italian train, in an open carriage, he suddenly realised that he had lost his wallet, probably at the booking-office of the railway station. He leapt to his feet and in Italian cried '*ho perduto tutto, tutto, tutto*! – I have lost everything, my passport, my money, my ticket – everything, everything!' Whereupon someone immediately offered him some money, someone else said that at the next station he would telephone the last station, and if he waited there perhaps his wallet would be found and arrive by the next train. And so it turned out. I suspect that his passion for Italy and Italians rose to a new height after this wonderful experience; moreover, he noted, perhaps somewhat uncharacteristically, that Italian policewomen were often quite good looking. It is rather more characteristic of him that he should have broken out so spontaneously – the notion that this quiet, learned, immensely thoughtful, serious, critical man could not, on occasion, be carried away by feeling – fascination, astonishment, excited admiration, curiosity, contempt, indignation – that would be false. There was something perpetually youthful about him: he never lost his eager hope of finding some illuminating new idea, some new manifestation of human genius, whether in thought or art, something which, whenever he thought he had found it – not always correctly – he acclaimed and wanted to share, explain, examine, trace its implications for life, not only for some universe of rational discourse.

He tended to be too critical of himself and his work; he thought better of the ability of others than of his own. No matter how much respect and praise he received, especially in the USA, where he was vastly admired, he remained prey to doubts about the lasting value of his writings. Of course, admiration pleased him, not least from critics of his work, but it was never sufficient to still his self-distrust, his wondering about the validity of his arguments or conclusions. It was a result of this that there were endless corrections, re-corrections, corrections of re-corrections, leading to those heaps of scrawled-over notes, fragments, bundles of papers held together by clips and used envelopes which cluttered his tables and his rooms. This self-doubt and modesty, together with his great charm, was one of his most moving characteristics.

On public issues he was hardly ever dogmatic – always moderate, just, understanding, sane. He always hoped, if he did not always believe, that decency and reason would triumph – in British life, in Israel, in Oxford, in all the societies he cared about.

If I may return to the point from which I began: Herbert Hart was a man of firm, clear and critical mind – he rejected contemptuously everything he thought crude, confused, muddled, intellectually shoddy; he was a man who could not tolerate obscurantism, oppression, injustice, all that he regarded as reactionary and an obstacle to human welfare. Set on this with his whole being, it is remarkable that such a man should at the same time have had so sensitive and complex an inner life, that he was not merely a model of virtue and integrity, but that with all this uncompromising rigour he had so much goodness, pure human goodness and generosity of temper. Surely this is rare. He was truly a major moral as well as intellectual asset to the civilisation for which he worked. Someone once said that no one was irreplaceable. That is not true. Herbert Hart was not replaceable. Like all those to whom, in one way or another, his existence made such a difference, I shall mourn his passing for whatever remains of the rest of my life.

LORD JAY

Herbert Hart was, for me, not primarily a philosopher or lawyer, but a colleague and lifelong friend. We first met in our first week at Oxford returning from our first lecture, which was appropriately on political philosophy by A.D. Lindsay, then Master of Balliol. Before we got back to New College, I was struck first by Herbert's Yorkshire accent, and secondly by how much better he had understood the lecture than I.

In undergraduate years, he was exceptionally generous in his help to weaker vessels. And it was not only the sharpness and force of his mind which impressed his contemporaries, but the example he set of willingness to listen, patience and tolerance in argument, and humour, all so evident in his later life. Some of his undergraduate colleagues gained more intellectually from Herbert than from most of their tutors; and, I suspect, got better classes in the schools than they otherwise would have.

Oxford was, I think his natural home. He never seemed to me wholly happy in Lincoln's Inn during the 1930s, and used to tell me he hoped his whole lifework would not consist in advising very rich men how legally to minimise their tax liabilities. Herbert was of course very far from being a party-politician, or applying labels to himself. But I would say he was throughout his life broadly a social-democrat, in the sense that he assigned equal value to liberty and social justice, and believed that more often than not, each re-inforced, rather than weakened, the other. He certainly did not oscillate with intellectual or political fashion or fade into a mere don't know in later years.

In wartime the Intelligence Services were very fortunate to recruit him. Living in the same house with him and others for much of the war, I greatly admired the scrupulous care with which no hint of a wartime official secret ever passed his lips, and none of those of us unauthorised knew what work he was doing or where. It was very many years after the war that I learnt he had contributed to the D-day disinformation exercise, without which the Normandy landing might not have succeeded.

What stands out as one looks right back to those undergraduate days, is Herbert's unchanging dependability, straightforwardness and integrity. After 66 years one should be a fair judge. And I can only say that outside my own family, he was the closest, most constant and most valued friend I ever had or that one could have wished to have. That is how I shall always remember him.

PROFESSOR RONALD DWORKIN

Nobody ever writes about Herbert's career without pointing to the transforming impact he had on legal and political philosophy. When he became Professor of Jurisprudence in Oxford, in 1952, those subjects were, to put it kindly, deadly. When he left, in 1968, they were exciting growth industries. In the case of political philosophy that was in good part his doing; in the case of legal philosophy he did it nearly alone. Herbert showed how philosophy could be tutor to law, how lawyers' questions about punishment and cause and definition have philosophical dimensions that it is irresponsible to ignore. He also showed how law can be tutor to philosophy, how legal problems, discriminations and attitudes can help philosophers in formulating and attacking those same ancient philosophical puzzles.

These are familiar facts, but it is less often noticed how thoroughly Herbert's character and style and spirit contributed to his impact. I don't mean just that he was a more effective teacher because he was so generous, or a more convincing advocate because he wrote so well, or more of a hero to his admirers because his integrity was so automatic and so comprehensive, though all that is true. I mean that these qualities of style and character entered into the substance of his work as well, that he was so effective because what he said grew so naturally and thoroughly out of who he was, so that the great love people had for him inspired not merely admiration but understanding. We can put a word to this unity of style and personality and substance: Herbert was, in all these ways, a *liberal*, and those who knew or heard or read him understood the liberal imagination better.

He was a liberal of temperament not doctrine. He despaired of finding any great truth about human nature or natural rights or economic psychology that could generate concrete theories of law and justice. He built his liberalism on virtues not abstract principles, on the virtues of sympathy, attention and decency, on tolerance and a good lawyer's passion for fair procedure. He believed in reason, and exemplified it, but more in the way of Hume than of Kant, as an engine not of transcendental thought but of practical accommodation. He thought the best we could do in politics was to turn away from abstract systems or theologies, which draw on subterranean and divisive emotions, and take up instead familiar, day-to-day methods of reasoning, particularly reasoning about matters of fact within agreed procedures for good argument. These methods are much more likely to produce liberal tolerance, he thought, not just by marginalizing ideology, but also because day-to-day, procedure-grounded, cooperative reasoning itself brings people together if anything can.

That combination of tolerance and ordinary reason fused Herbert's personal style and his ideas. It gave a substantive, even moral, point to his prose, which is elegant, very often arresting, but also transparent, comprehensively honest, full of plain fact but no numbing rhetoric. His argumentative style was parallel: courteous, quietly logical, always bent on understanding not triumph. He never became, as so many other philosophers have, a janitor or press flak for his own theories, patching up leaks and working tirelessly for more dominion. He seemed almost embarrassed when he had *not* been persuaded to change his mind, and it gave him great pleasure when he had been.

His legendary absent-mindedness was not the familiar self-absorption of other academics – it never, in my memory at least, took the form of indifference or inattention toward others – but was another aspect of concentration on problems, not himself as problem-solver.

Now look more closely at the substance of Herbert's thought. His famous response to Lord Devlin's argument that homosexuality might be a form of treason, way back in the fifties, was a model of the way in which philosophy can serve government: patient, disentangling, grounded in fact, appealing to no prior conviction beyond a commitment to ordinary, shared standards of good argument, a beautifully liberal argument for a straightforwardly liberal conclusion. Many of his more technical arguments, about punishment and responsibility, were like that too; his influential account of why the criminal law does not punish involuntary acts drew on no metaphysics of free will but on concrete, familiar, widely shared ideas about fair play, for example.

Herbert's greatest professional achievement, of course, was the legal theory set out in *The Concept of Law*, which is still, over three decades on, the best-known work of legal philosophy of our day. You will forgive me for a crude, skeletal summary of his complex and subtle theory. Characteristically, he defined his jurisprudence as a midcourse between two extreme ideas, each with its attractions, but each too doctrinaire, too far removed from common sense. He denied the sceptical view that law is nothing but power, that judges must make up rules as they go along, answerable to nothing but their own passions and interests. He disdained what he took to be the opposite view: that law is not nothing but everything, that there is a right answer to all legal questions judges must try to discover if only they can. He found a middle way in legal positivism, which insists that the actual law of a community is at bottom a question of fact accessible, without deep controversy, to everyone trained in how to look. In Hart's distinctive version, however, what is law depends most fundamentally not on political facts about powerful princes or officials, but on social facts about the shared understandings of the community at large – the shared understanding in Britain, for example, that Parliament makes law even when we disagree with its wisdom – the kind of understanding, again, that unites rather than divides a morally pluralistic community. On that view law is something, a matter of fact, but it is not everything because no formula generated from a shared understanding can decide every case in advance, so that in special, hard cases judges do have a law-making responsibility.

Understood in that way, Hart thought, as a matter of social fact, law has the best chance to form a buffer zone between government and the divisions and intolerance he feared. Of course, as he insisted, law can be wicked as well as wise. But he cherished law mainly for what it can do for the decent but divided state, not for the wholly bad one, and in that way, *The Concept of Law* is an optimistic book. Herbert himself was, I think, more of a pessimist than was often realized, and he felt oddly foreign in his native Britain. He once told me that there had been very few English holders of his chair, and he had not counted himself, I discovered, because he was Jewish. But optimism shines through his writing because it is all lit with the flame of his liberal soul.

We have so much to miss. We cannot reproduce his immense, humane delight in new ideas, his unfailing, amazingly fresh, amazingly young, humor and attention, or his wholly natural, unstudied courtesy. No one can be replaced, but Herbert can scarcely even be imitated. He did, however, leave us, and his vast, worldwide constituency, something to prize in addition to his enduring work. He left a way to live for us to admire: the life he led, an instinctively decent, political, clearheaded, liberal, above all intelligent, life of the mind.

PROFESSOR JOSEPH RAZ

I first met Herbert early in 1964 when he came to Jerusalem, where I was a student, to deliver the prestigious Lionel Cohen lectures. It was a magnificent occasion. Many of the legal luminaries of Israel, judges, barristers and academics, were there to be impressed, indeed bowled over, by the intellectual vigour and the polemical force of Herbert's lectures which, in demolishing Lady Wootton's proposals for the reform of the criminal law, displayed his unique ability to bring the most rigorous philosophical analysis to bear practical fruits for legal reform.

If I was inclined to view the impact of the lectures as a typical reaction of a remote province to the message from an international academic centre, my arrival in Oxford a few months later taught me better. Herbert's prominence in Oxford philosophical life was possibly then at its height. It was three years after the publication of *The Concept of Law*, and a year after the publication of *Law, Liberty and Morality*, the major statements of his jurisprudential and of his liberal positions. Other than Hobbes' *Leviathan* and Bentham's *Of Laws in General* (finally given its true stature in Herbert's edition), no other works in English had made such a contribution to the philosophy of law. And at the time of its publication *Law, Liberty and Morality* was the most cogent statement and defence of the liberal position on the relation between law and morality. In 1964 Oxford and the world were still absorbing the doctrines and arguments of these books. Almost wherever you turned, to political theory seminars conducted by Berlin, Plamenatz and others, to jurisprudential lectures by Brian Simpson, to university societies and informal student discussions, the doctrines and arguments of these books were a major, sometimes the dominating, subject of discussion.

By that time Herbert himself, his creative urge undiminished, had turned to other topics. For several years running he packed North School as I have never seen it since with students, colleagues and visitors eager to hear his lectures on Rights and Duties. Tall, handsome and animated, his imposing figure and agitated immersion in his topics were captivating. Watching him continuously shuffling from distance to reading glasses, wiping them each time with a long white handkerchief, mislaying them and rediscovering their whereabouts, matched in fascination the long and complex arguments, elegantly presented, and greatly taxing the ability of the audience to follow their drift. In the lectures he examined and criticised all the current accounts of rights and duties, and developed his own views. We all expected a major publication to emerge in their wake, but even though some of his thoughts found their way into his *Essays on Bentham*, much of what he taught us then has never been published. Herbert was masterful in his analysis of legal rights, but he encountered difficulties in his attempts to generalise his account to moral and other rights, and was never satisfied with his results.

The other subject that preoccupied him during the mid-60s was the philosophy of punishment. This work yielded the masterly essays in *Punishment and Responsibility*, still the best work on this subject. For those in Oxford at the time this aspect of Herbert's work was displayed in the fascinating seminars which he, Rupert Cross and Nigel Walker held jointly in All Souls. The not too large Hovenden room was overflowing with excitement as the brave competed for seats at the round table and the timid sought obscurity in the corners. It was for me, and I expect for many others, a model of what a university seminar should be like, to emulate which I have often tried and never succeeded. Every week one of them would introduce a topic on which we were given a detailed and annotated reading list in advance. The handout also contained a list of questions for discussion, and the seminar proceeded in that order with Herbert, when it was his turn, raising one question after another, taking views from the audience, presenting some of his own ideas, debating them with his colleagues and with the audience. He was a most incisive polemicist, and the robust common sense of Rupert Cross, and the wealth of empirical information mastered by Nigel Walker were no match for Herbert's orderly mind and quicksilver intelligence. We enjoyed the contest like all fans, eager for our hero to triumph over all comers, as we knew he would, yet agog with excitement to see it happen, and retiring after it was all over to the pubs to celebrate his victory in its retelling.

Not surprisingly, being Herbert's student was, outside the four walls of his room, a matter of pride and envy. But inside the famous room in Kybald House it was a matter of pure awe. There was also some fear: the fear that Herbert would misplace and lose the essay one was meant to discuss with him. No one who knew the room in those days and saw him reaching for this or that would believe that he actually never lost any of the essays. But this precarious good luck never reduced the fear in those days before computers and easy photocopying.

I do not think that Herbert really knew in what awe he was held by his students. If I survived his tutorials intact, it was because of his natural kindness and – most of all – his modesty. By the time we met he knew my essay much better than I did, having read it twice and sprinkled it with two layers of calligraphic comments. Needless to say he also knew the problems I was fumbling to understand infinitely better than I did. It was preposterous to try and defend one's corner. That I nevertheless always tried was only because neither by word nor in his manner did he ever assert his superiority. Though no ambiguity, evasiveness, or non sequitur could ever escape him, he was always inquiring for explanation, generous with his time and patient to hear all one's faltering attempts to salvage a thought from a confusion. You really believed that he was always expecting to learn something new. This fresh, insatiable, almost naive curiosity was to me one of his most endearing qualities when I got to know him personally in later years.

Herbert was forever respectful of his students' autonomy and privacy. Upset by their inclination to turn him into a father figure, he remained distant and reserved. It was both his nature and his intention, as it left plenty of scope for the students to develop their own ideas their own way. His influence became so pervasive in the '60s that it is not surprising that no factional Hart school of jurisprudence arose, but the very thought of followers in that sense would have been anathema to him. Inescapably his soaring intellect sought to conquer and dominate, while personally he was most comfortable retaining his privacy and simplicity, abhorring accolades and acolytes.

It was impossible not to be touched by his modesty and simplicity, his unaffected manner, and his purity. It was impossible not to admire the breadth of his human and cultural sympathies, and not to be awed by the power of his intellect.

Far away in the real world he had become a leading champion of the new liberal spirit: writing against the death penalty, for a right to abortion, for the decriminalisation of victimless conduct, and for putting an end to the persecution of people because of their sexual preferences. Within the more esoteric groves of academe he rejuvenated legal philosophy. The accident which turned his attention to jurisprudence rescued the subject from a long decline. For the first time since the emergence during the nineteenth century of separate faculties of English Law in England which entrusted the subject to the care of gentlemen-lawyers happy to indulge in amateur speculations, a first class philosophical mind was brought to bear on it. In going back to Bentham, Herbert re-established the historical connection between jurisprudence and the main traditions of philosophy. In offering a jurisprudence which is philosophically sophisticated he laid the foundation for the flowering of the subject we are witnessing today.

DR BERNARD RICHARDS

Herbert Hart became Principal of Brasenose in 1973, and he retired in 1978. His reign was brief, but he made a deep impression on the college. I am not sure whether one could say it was a lasting impression, since Brasenose has a degree of impermeability about it, and it tends to go its own sweet way no matter who is at the helm, but certainly while Herbert was there he shook us up a bit – Fellows and undergraduates alike. When he arrived and took stock of the Fellowship he described them, memorably, as a mixture of 'Old Turks and Young Fogeys'. He was an intellectual giant – that at least is how he was described in the States when being introduced at a gathering of intellectuals. He told them, 'I don't feel like an intellectual giant', but in comparison to his predecessor, Sir Noel Hall, he did have high-profile intellectual status. He was wary of the college at first, and concerned that when he was an undergraduate at New College he never regarded Brasenose as a college at all, thinking of it, in his words as 'more of a sporting institution'. His favourite Brasenose story was of a former Principal of the college who had been sorely tempted to admit a brilliant sportsman, but confessed that 'even Brasenose could not take someone who spelt Jesus with a small g'. Herbert was not really interested in sports, and when he attended Bump Suppers he had to overdraw on the bank account of ambiguous words much utilised by Henry James – words such as memorable, wonderful and remarkable – to describe and celebrate the feats. There was a Tennis Bump Supper, and he said that contriving the speech called for as much ingenuity as those French Revolutionary luminaries who had put together the Tennis Court Oath. Herbert was a strange mixture of progressive and traditionalist. He wanted the undergraduates to have as much independence as possible and do their own thing, but he did not hesitate in trying to better their lives intellectually. He instituted Sunday Evening lectures, inviting distinguished speakers. These were organised, under his direct guidance, by an Events Committee, and a sign of the decline of the times, I suppose, is that the Events Committee nowadays spends all its time organising sweaty bops. In theory Herbert approved of freedom for the young, but he did not necessarily like manifestations of youth culture. I remember him saying that the Student Union, which was the burning protest issue of the day, would be, if set up, 'like an M1 cafe with a permanent rock band'.

There was a slightly puritanical side to Herbert. One of his schoolfriends at Bradford Grammar had been the Brasenose chaplain Leslie Styler, who had had a sylph-like form in his youth, but by late middle age had long lost what Herbert called 'the primitive outline' of the original man. Brasenose dinners had done it, and Herbert said on his arrival that when he saw what the college cuisine had done to Leslie he faced the future with some trepidation. He used to accuse us of having Lucullan feasts. Once when he came to one of these blow-outs a colleague, Vernon Bogdanor in fact, said he expected him to arrive in a hair shirt. Herbert said, 'How do you know I am not wearing one now: traditionally it was only discovered that saints had been wearing them when they were dead.' It was not only the Fellows who enjoyed a good time, Herbert used to go to the staff parties at Christmas, and once when he came back from one he said that 'only the pencil of Breughel could do justice to it.' In his time as Principal Stow Wood was sold, and the Fellows no longer got free Christmas trees. Herbert said, 'the feudal age *had* to come to an end sometime.' His radical views often emerged. A little posse of us were appointed to draft a college prospectus, because even then the age was dawning when Oxford colleges could no longer assume that they would automatically attract pupils. I wrote a long historical section, including a lovingly penned few paragraphs on the college shield – a pleasingly rare and arcane example of tierced arms. Herbert put a blue pencil through the whole lot at proof stage, and said that it would not attract a boy from a northern grammar school, and it would have to go. 'Heraldry is a frightfully nobby hobby' he told me.

Herbert often came out with witty and well-turned phrases. It was a natural and effortless expression of his ebullient intelligence. The taste for the *mot juste* could even overcome pain and disaster. Once at one of Herbert's parties for undergraduates in the lodgings there was a young woman who made a violent movement with her arm during a conversation and knocked a stone ornament off the mantelpiece. 'An expansive and expensive gesture', said Herbert. He was never a merciless stickler for absolutely proper behaviour – how could he be when he admitted to having illegally kept Ronny Dworkin's finals papers as a souvenir, because they were so good. Certainly he never stood on his dignity, and I well remember a speech he gave in Hall to old members. Inevitably when two or three old members of Brasenose gather together there is a lawyer in their midst, and this occasion was manifestly no exception, but it did not stop Herbert from reading a long quotation from Robert Burton's *Anatomy of Melancholy* (Burton was an old Brasenose man) on how the prevalence of lawyers in any society suggests that there is something seriously wrong with it. He could be very wry about his job. He once said, when all kinds of elaborate discussion were under way about the undergraduates having a cafeteria-style dinner instead of the nightly Lucullan feast, 'I have been many things, a barrister, a college tutor and a professor, and now look what I am reduced to – a hotel keeper.' One of his wittiest remarks, I recall, was at the expense of the architects Powell and Moya, who in the early sixties erected a startling new building at Brasenose, which had trouble, after the fashion of many a modern construction, with leaking roofs. They were asking advice on getting a motto for the firm, and I remember Herbert saying, 'What about *après moi le déluge*.'

I am aware that I do not seem to have done justice to Herbert, but I hope I have enabled you to catch a glimpse or two of him. I shall never forget the elegant and attentive way he stood as he listened to what you were saying, and the amusing and intelligent responses that would come forth. I treasure the memory of his taste for artistic embroidery – as he would describe, for instance, how in his undergraduate time at New College a complete army of glaziers would descend on the college on Monday mornings to replace virtually every pane of glass, *every* window having been shattered by the orgies of the weekend. I think it is important on occasions such as these to attempt a little of that particularised portraiture. It has always struck me as unfortunate that Arthur Hallam was famed for his wit and his sharp conversation, yet none of it shows up in Tennyson's *In Memoriam* – it may be a grieving tribute to the dead man, but we do not get a lively and particularised picture of him. One last glimpse. Herbert attended the traditional Shrove Tuesday dinner in Hall. He got to his feet, ready to say how his feelings were mixed on this final occasion of listening to the Ale Verses, but before he could launch into a speech, the undergraduates drowned it out with 'For he's a jolly good Fellow.' Indeed he was.

PROFESSOR ALAN RYAN

Anyone remembering Herbert Hart will want to remember the non-academic and more private sides of his life. In doing so, I think particularly of his fifty years of marriage to Jenifer, and his gift to the world of his interesting, lively, radical, and engaging children. Most of the serious things we ought to say this afternoon have been said – and some delightfully frivolous things – and I shall strike a domestic note. My first encounter with Herbert took place some thirty-two years ago, in the kitchen of his house in Manor Place; it was ten minutes to midnight, and in those far off days, curfew for the undergraduates was midnight. An agitated Herbert put his head round the door and said, 'You shouldn't be here, you shouldn't be here.' 'Oh dear,' I said, 'why not?' 'What would they think if they found an undergraduate in my house after midnight?' I left, hurriedly. The second meeting was less alarming; it also took place in the kitchen, but earlier in the evening. We joined forces to stick the sole on Herbert's dress shoe. Herbert possessed a dress shoe – he actually had two, though the second took some finding – but the shoe itself didn't reliably possess a sole. We disagreed mildly on technique. Herbert inclined to drawing pins; I was all for raiding Adam's room and borrowing some rubber cement. Drawing pins prevailed, and Herbert left, clicking gently.

Even to an ignorant and disorganised undergraduate like myself, it was instantly clear that Herbert was both a great and a good man. The greatness depended heavily on the goodness. Reviving the moribund discipline of analytical jurisprudence was not only a matter of logic, imagination, and an acuteness about the point and nature of law that few others have matched. Sleeping Beauty in the fairy tale had to be woken with a kiss, and Herbert surely brought passion to his subject matter. For all his enthusiasm for Bentham, he was not a utilitarian in moral philosophy – he was a natural pluralist, who thought a variety of values had their legitimate claim on us; but he had a tremendous respect for ordinary happiness, and thought that when law was worthy of respect it was for its role in helping people to achieve that happiness. Even more importantly, he had a deep hatred of cruelty, and thought, for instance, that the then existing laws against homosexuality were simply cruel. Once you knew Herbert well, you could see how this hatred of cruelty permeated his work, and it is something we have all been aware of this afternoon.

What I got from Herbert was an education I would not have had from anyone in more formal circumstances. It mostly took place in the kitchen, now the anxiety had died down and we could discuss philosophy over the scrambled eggs. I would usually arrive in a state of blind fury with my Balliol tutors; I would denounce philosophy and philosophers, announce that there was nothing to be learned from either, and one way and another would utter a tremendous quantity of high-pitched and incoherent rubbish. Over an hour or two, the fury was calmed, and my mind was put back in something like order. I would have been unable to say then, and cannot say now, just what I learned on these occasions; but it felt much like the passage from passion to reason described in Spinoza's *Ethics*. I began the evening in prey to irritable emotion, with my thoughts in chaos, and ended it with my intelligence at least somewhat in control. In innumerable conferences, lectures and seminars since then, dozens of Herbert's pupils have spoken of similar experiences.

All the same, most of us did not really wish to emulate Herbert. In the first place, that was out of reach. But the way he drove himself deterred us too. He had a rather low opinion of his own abilities as a philosopher, and often said so. This was not false modesty. It was real modesty – wholly unreasonable but wholly genuine. His notion of how to tackle a philosophical problem was simple. You had to think about it very carefully and for a very long time. You had to read other people's views and think very hard about how much they helped. If, after seven hours of this sort of patient effort, you had half a paragraph of a paper you were writing, you had to keep going. Most of us knew we hadn't the stamina, the patience, the self-control, or the fastidiousness that this presupposed. On Herbert himself, I think in retrospect, it imposed an excessive anxiety and a sort of constraint on his professional activities. I remember him saying that he did not like going to conferences because he could not help wanting his own views to be right. This was surely carrying fastidiousness too far.

To me, a standard issue English schoolboy and an average undergraduate, many aspects of Herbert's character were wonderfully surprising. His Jewishness, for instance, came out in his personal warmth, and a wonderful sense of humour – he told me jokes I have been trading on for thirty years, even at dinner parties in New York. He had a curious distance from England, though he loved it devotedly – he was passionate about the countryside, and passionate about the country. His devotion to his tasks in MI5 during the war was absolute; and so was his contempt for the activities of Philby and Blunt when it finally emerged what they had been doing. It was not a lack of patriotism but a feeling that the real interests of the country were being sacrificed to mere pride that led him to oppose the Falklands campaign. Yet at the same time there was a certain arm's length quality about his attachment. To some extent, it was an aspect of his passion for Greece and Italy, countries whose luminousness attracted him as they have attracted so many Northerners. To some extent, he felt that the Jewish view of the world was rich, earthy and unsnobbish, and that the academic, English view of the world was too often none of these things.

Among the things nobody has mentioned this afternoon that it would be a pity to overlook, and one which has a domestic side to it, is Herbert's work for the Home Farm Trust. The last thirty years of Herbert's life were made more anxious by the need to provide for Jacob, and it was typical of Herbert that he did not think to provide for Jacob alone. When the Home Farm Trust began to organise in the area, Herbert threw himself into its fund-raising. He used his connections in the wider world to lay on the most wonderful concerts at Ditchley, Broughton Castle and other grand and beautiful houses in north Oxfordshire. They were perfect occasions, when one truly did very well by doing good, and many people have reason to be grateful to Herbert for his efforts.

Herbert's liberalism was lifelong; it was kept up by Jenifer and by successive waves of radical assault from the children. He wasn't frightened by the young; like most of us, as he got older, he found them harder to understand, but during an acrimonious period the Hart Report did much to bring junior members peacefully into the governance of Oxford and enable them to contribute usefully to the place, while the disciplinary procedures he persuaded the University to put in place headed off much trouble. If only by attrition they wore out the insurrectionists, and if only by attrition reconciled his conservative colleagues to the new order by showing them that Oxford was not about to go the way of Berkeley or Vincennes. He joined in the campaign to refuse Mrs Thatcher an honorary degree, unbothered by people who said it would cost the University a lot of money, and equally unbothered by those who thought distinguished elderly people ought never to side with the radical young.

Jenifer expressed some anxiety to me that people would represent Herbert as altogether perfect. I therefore thought it was only proper that I should end by playing the role of a secular *advocatus diaboli*. I searched my memory for Herbert's vices, faults, errors, and assorted wickednesses; after a good deal of scouring, I found some. When I was twenty, I thought he took an altogether too light-hearted attitude towards the workings of his motor car. He seemed uninterested in when he might change out of second gear into third; he wasn't always absolutely committed to driving on the left hand side of the road, and his parking was a somewhat aleatoric exercise. At the age of twenty, I thought this was really terribly light minded in a serious thinker. Looking further, I find nothing. He was both great and good. He was a moral and intellectual beacon, as well as a standing example of how to combine sweetness of character with toughness of intellect. We shall greatly miss his friendship as well as the light he shone on so many aspects of life.

Index

INDEX